Fifth Edition

NorthStar 2

Reading & Writing

Authors:	Natasha Haugnes
	Beth Maher
Series Editors:	Frances Boyd
	Carol Numrich

Dedication

For John, Tom, Charlie, Emmet, Oliver, Niko, Toby, and Theo.
—Beth Maher and Natasha Haugnes

NorthStar: Reading & Writing Level 2, Fifth Edition

Copyright © 2020, 2015, 2009, 2004 by Pearson Education, Inc.
All rights reserved.

Pearson Education, 221 River St, Hoboken, NJ 07030

Staff credits: The people who made up the *NorthStar: Reading & Writing Level 2, Fifth Edition* team, representing content creation, design, marketing, manufacturing, multimedia, project management, publishing, rights management, and testing, are Pietro Alongi, Stephanie Callahan, Gina DiLillo, Tracey Cataldo, Dave Dickey, Warren Fishbach, Sarah Hand, Lucy Hart, Gosia Jaros-White, Stefan Machura, Linda Moser, Dana Pinter, Karen Quinn, Katarzyna Starzynska - Kosciuszko, Paula Van Ells, Claire Van Poperin, Joseph Vella, Peter West, Autumn Westphal, Natalia Zaremba, and Marcin Zimny.

Project consultant: Debbie Sistino
Text composition: ElectraGraphics, Inc.
Development editing: Françoise Leffler
Cover design: Studio Montage

Library of Congress Cataloging-in-Publication Data

A Catalog record for the print edition is available from the Library of Congress.

Printed in the United States of America

ISBN-13: 978-0-13-523262-0 (Student Book with Digital Resources)
ISBN-10: 0-13-523262-7 (Student Book with Digital Resources)

6 2021

ISBN-13: 978-0-13-522700-8 (Student Book with MyEnglishLab Online Workbook and Resources)
ISBN-10: 0-13-522700-3 (Student Book with MyEnglishLab Online Workbook and Resources)

6 2021

CONTENTS

WELCOME TO NORTHSTAR

A Letter from the Series Editors

We welcome you to the 5th edition of *NorthStar Reading & Writing Level 2*.

Engaging content, integrated skills, and critical thinking continue to be the touchstones of the series. For more than 20 years *NorthStar* has engaged and motivated students through contemporary, authentic topics. Our online component builds on the last edition by offering new and updated activities.

Since its first edition, *NorthStar* has been rigorous in its approach to critical thinking by systematically engaging students in tasks and activities that prepare them to move into high-level academic courses. The cognitive domains of Bloom's taxonomy provide the foundation for the critical thinking activities. Students develop the skills of analysis and evaluation and the ability to synthesize and summarize information from multiple sources. The capstone of each unit, the final writing or speaking task, supports students in the application of all academic, critical thinking, and language skills that are the focus of unit.

The new edition introduces additional academic skills for 21st century success: note-taking and presentation skills. There is also a focus on learning outcomes based on the Global Scale of English (GSE), an emphasis on the application of skills, and a new visual design. These refinements are our response to research in the field of language learning in addition to feedback from educators who have taught from our previous editions.

NorthStar has pioneered and perfected the blending of academic content and academic skills in an English Language series. Read on for a comprehensive overview of this new edition. As you and your students explore *NorthStar*, we wish you a great journey.

Carol Numrich and Frances Boyd, the editors

New for the FIFTH EDITION

New and Updated Themes

The new edition features one new theme per level (i.e., one new unit per book), with updated content and skills throughout the series. Current and thought-provoking topics presented in a variety of genres promote intellectual stimulation. The real-world-inspired content engages students, links them to language use outside the classroom, and encourages personal expression and critical thinking.

Learning Outcomes and Assessments

All unit skills, vocabulary, and grammar points are connected to GSE objectives to ensure effective progression of learning throughout the series. Learning outcomes are present at the opening and closing of each unit to clearly mark what is covered in the unit and encourage both pre- and post-unit self-reflection. A variety of assessment tools, including online diagnostic, formative, and summative assessments and a flexible gradebook aligned with clearly identified unit learning outcomes, allow teachers to individualize instruction and track student progress.

Note-Taking as a Skill in Every Unit

Grounded in the foundations of the Cornell Method of note-taking, the new note-taking practice is structured to allow students to reflect on and organize their notes, focusing on the most important points. Students are instructed, throughout the unit, on the most effective way to apply their notes to a classroom task, as well as encouraged to analyze and reflect on their growing note-taking skills.

Explicit Skill Instruction and Fully-Integrated Practice

Concise presentations and targeted practice in print and online prepare students for academic success. Language skills are highlighted in each unit, providing students with multiple, systematic exposures to language forms and structures in a variety of contexts. Academic and language skills in each unit are applied clearly and deliberately in the culminating writing or presentation task.

Scaffolded Critical Thinking

Activities within the unit are structured to follow the stages of Bloom's taxonomy from *remember* to *create*. The use of **APPLY** throughout the unit highlights culminating activities that allow students to use the skills being practiced in a free and authentic manner. Sections that are focused on developing critical thinking are marked with 🔍 to highlight their critical focus.

Explicit Focus on the Academic Word List

AWL words are highlighted at the end of the unit and in a master list at the end of the book.

The Pearson Practice English App

The **Pearson Practice English App** allows students on the go to complete vocabulary and grammar activities, listen to audio, and watch video.

ExamView

ExamView Test Generator allows teachers to customize assessments by reordering or editing existing questions, selecting test items from a bank, or writing new questions.

MyEnglishLab

New and revised online supplementary practice maps to the updates in the student book for this edition.

THE NORTHSTAR UNIT

1 FOCUS ON THE TOPIC

Each unit begins with an eye-catching unit opener spread that draws students into the topic. The learning outcomes are written in simple, student-friendly language to allow for self-assessment. Focus on the Topic questions connect to the unit theme and get students to think critically by making inferences and predicting the content of the unit.

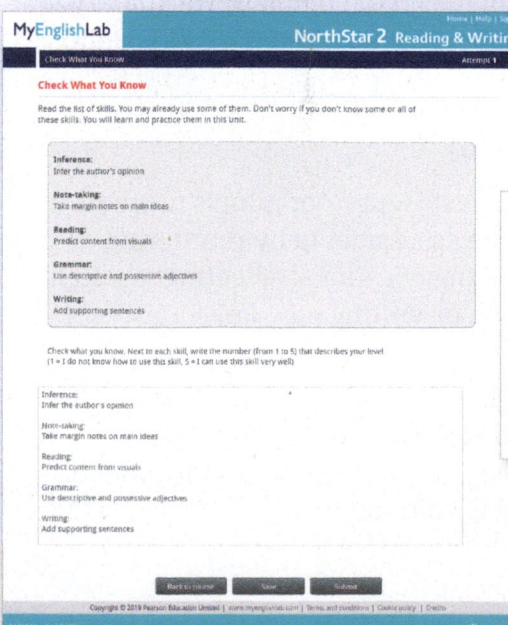

MyEnglishLab

The "Check What You Know" pre-unit diagnostic checklist provides a short self-assessment based on each unit's GSE-aligned learning outcomes to support the students in building an awareness of their own skill levels and to enable teachers to target instruction to their students' specific needs.

2 FOCUS ON READING

A vocabulary exercise introduces words that appear in the readings, encourages students to guess the meanings of the words from context, and connects to the theme presented in the final writing task.

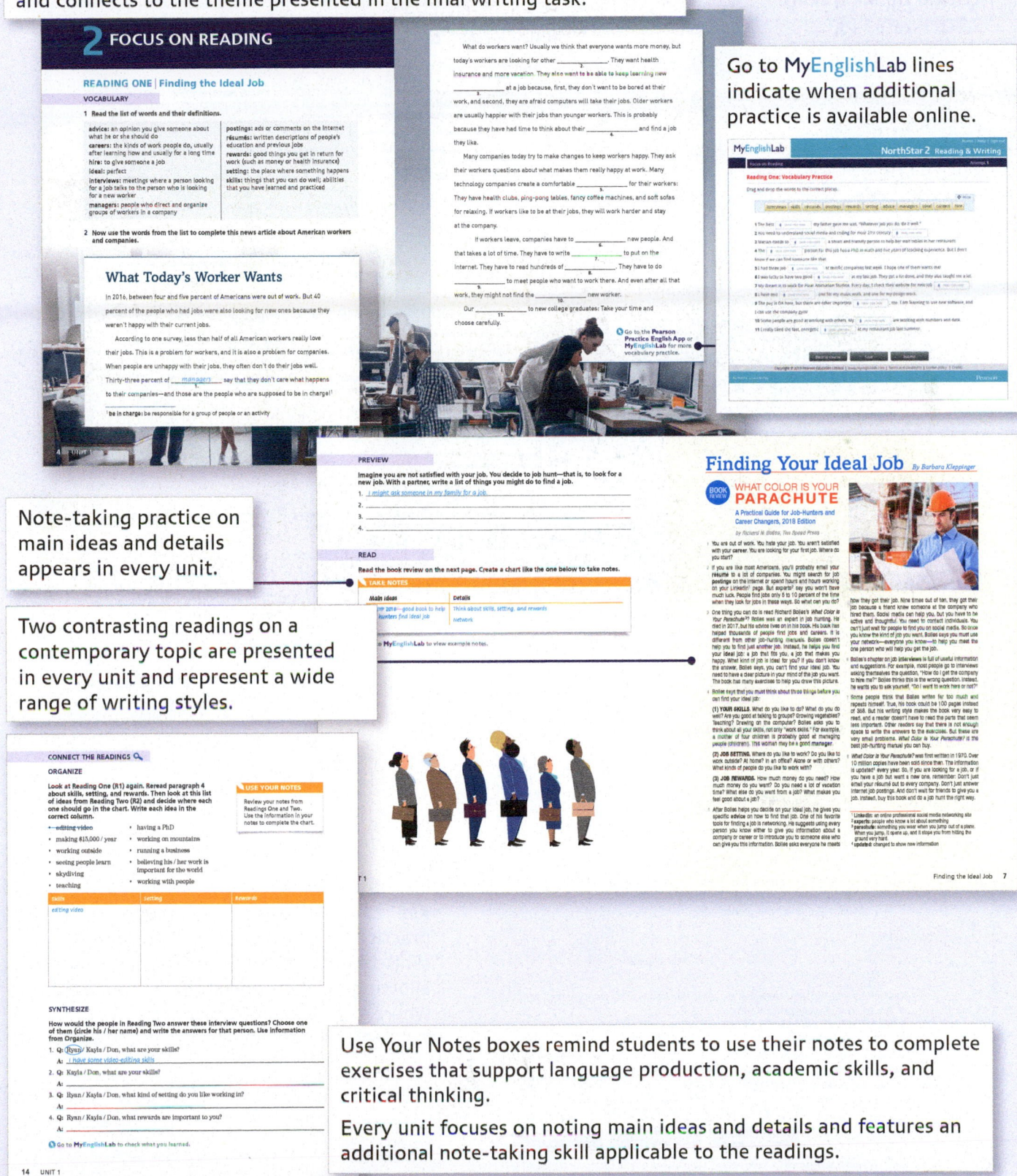

Go to MyEnglishLab lines indicate when additional practice is available online.

Note-taking practice on main ideas and details appears in every unit.

Two contrasting readings on a contemporary topic are presented in every unit and represent a wide range of writing styles.

Use Your Notes boxes remind students to use their notes to complete exercises that support language production, academic skills, and critical thinking.

Every unit focuses on noting main ideas and details and features an additional note-taking skill applicable to the readings.

EXPLICIT SKILL INSTRUCTION AND PRACTICE

Step-by-step instructions and practice guide students to move beyond the literal meaning of the text. 🔍 highlights activities that help build critical thinking skills.

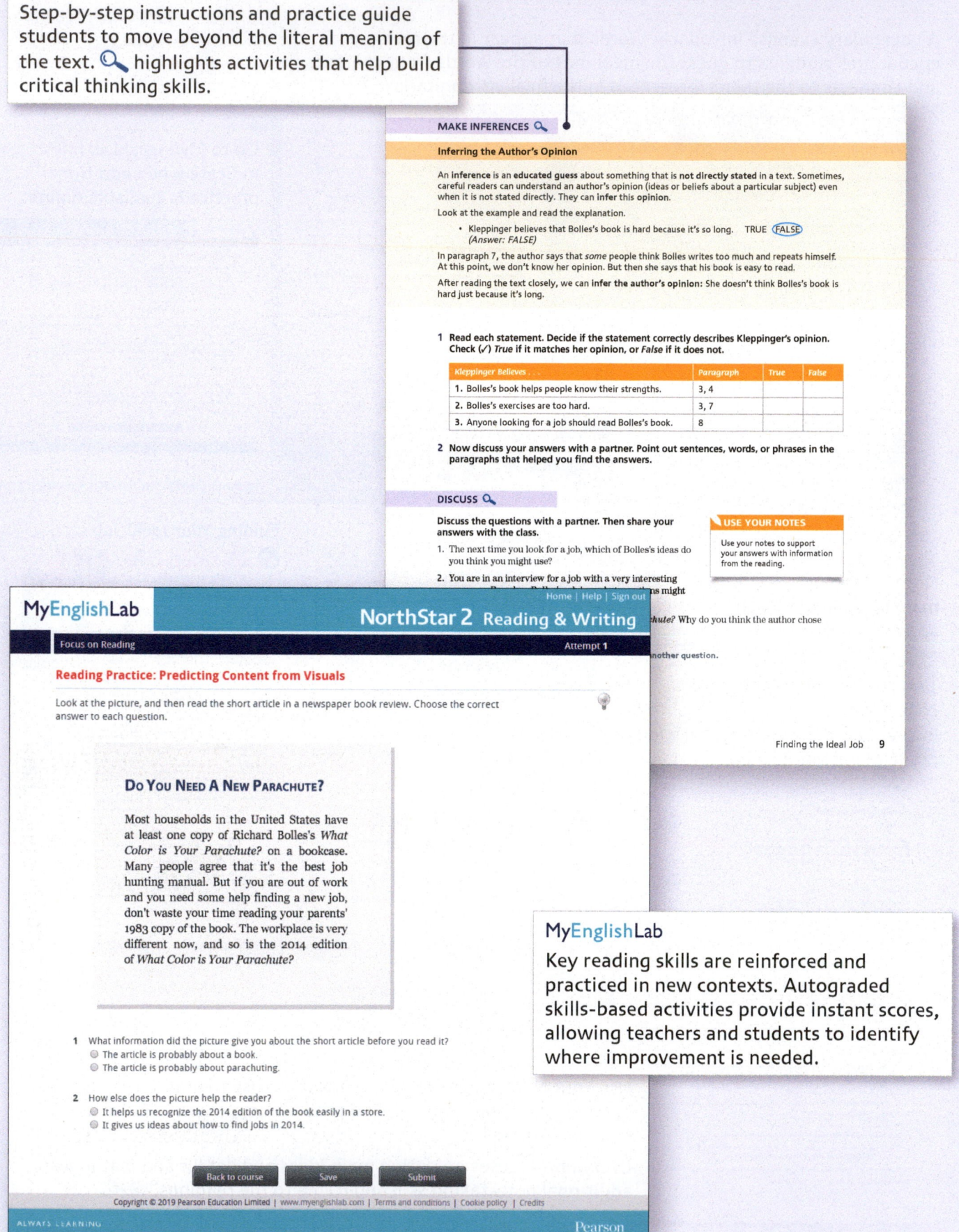

MAKE INFERENCES 🔍

Inferring the Author's Opinion

An **inference** is an **educated guess** about something that is **not directly stated** in a text. Sometimes, careful readers can understand an author's opinion (ideas or beliefs about a particular subject) even when it is not stated directly. They can **infer** this **opinion**.

Look at the example and read the explanation.

- Kleppinger believes that Bolles's book is hard because it's so long.   TRUE (FALSE)
  (Answer: FALSE)

In paragraph 7, the author says that *some* people think Bolles writes too much and repeats himself. At this point, we don't know her opinion. But then she says that his book is easy to read.

After reading the text closely, we can **infer the author's opinion**: She doesn't think Bolles's book is hard just because it's long.

1 Read each statement. Decide if the statement correctly describes Kleppinger's opinion. Check (✓) *True* if it matches her opinion, or *False* if it does not.

Kleppinger Believes . . .	Paragraph	True	False
1. Bolles's book helps people know their strengths.	3, 4		
2. Bolles's exercises are too hard.	3, 7		
3. Anyone looking for a job should read Bolles's book.	8		

2 Now discuss your answers with a partner. Point out sentences, words, or phrases in the paragraphs that helped you find the answers.

DISCUSS 🔍

Discuss the questions with a partner. Then share your answers with the class.

1. The next time you look for a job, which of Bolles's ideas do you think you might use?

2. You are in an interview for a job with a very interesting ... Bolles ... ...ns might

...chute? Why do you think the author chose

...nother question.

Finding the Ideal Job **9**

MyEnglishLab

Home | Help | Sign out

NorthStar 2 Reading & Writing

Focus on Reading   Attempt **1**

Reading Practice: Predicting Content from Visuals

Look at the picture, and then read the short article in a newspaper book review. Choose the correct answer to each question.

Do You Need A New Parachute?

Most households in the United States have at least one copy of Richard Bolles's *What Color is Your Parachute?* on a bookcase. Many people agree that it's the best job hunting manual. But if you are out of work and you need some help finding a new job, don't waste your time reading your parents' 1983 copy of the book. The workplace is very different now, and so is the 2014 edition of *What Color is Your Parachute?*

1 What information did the picture give you about the short article before you read it?
  ○ The article is probably about a book.
  ○ The article is probably about parachuting.

2 How else does the picture help the reader?
  ○ It helps us recognize the 2014 edition of the book easily in a store.
  ○ It gives us ideas about how to find jobs in 2014.

Back to course   Save   Submit

MyEnglishLab
Key reading skills are reinforced and practiced in new contexts. Autograded skills-based activities provide instant scores, allowing teachers and students to identify where improvement is needed.

3 FOCUS ON WRITING

Productive vocabulary targeted in the unit is reviewed, expanded upon, and used creatively.

Grammar presentations focus on skills that are used in the readings and applied in the final writing task. A concise grammar skills box serves as a reference point for students throughout the unit and beyond.

MyEnglishLab

Auto-graded vocabulary and grammar practice activities reinforce meaning, form, and function. Meaningful and instant feedback guides students to self-correct and provides students and teachers with essential information to monitor progress.

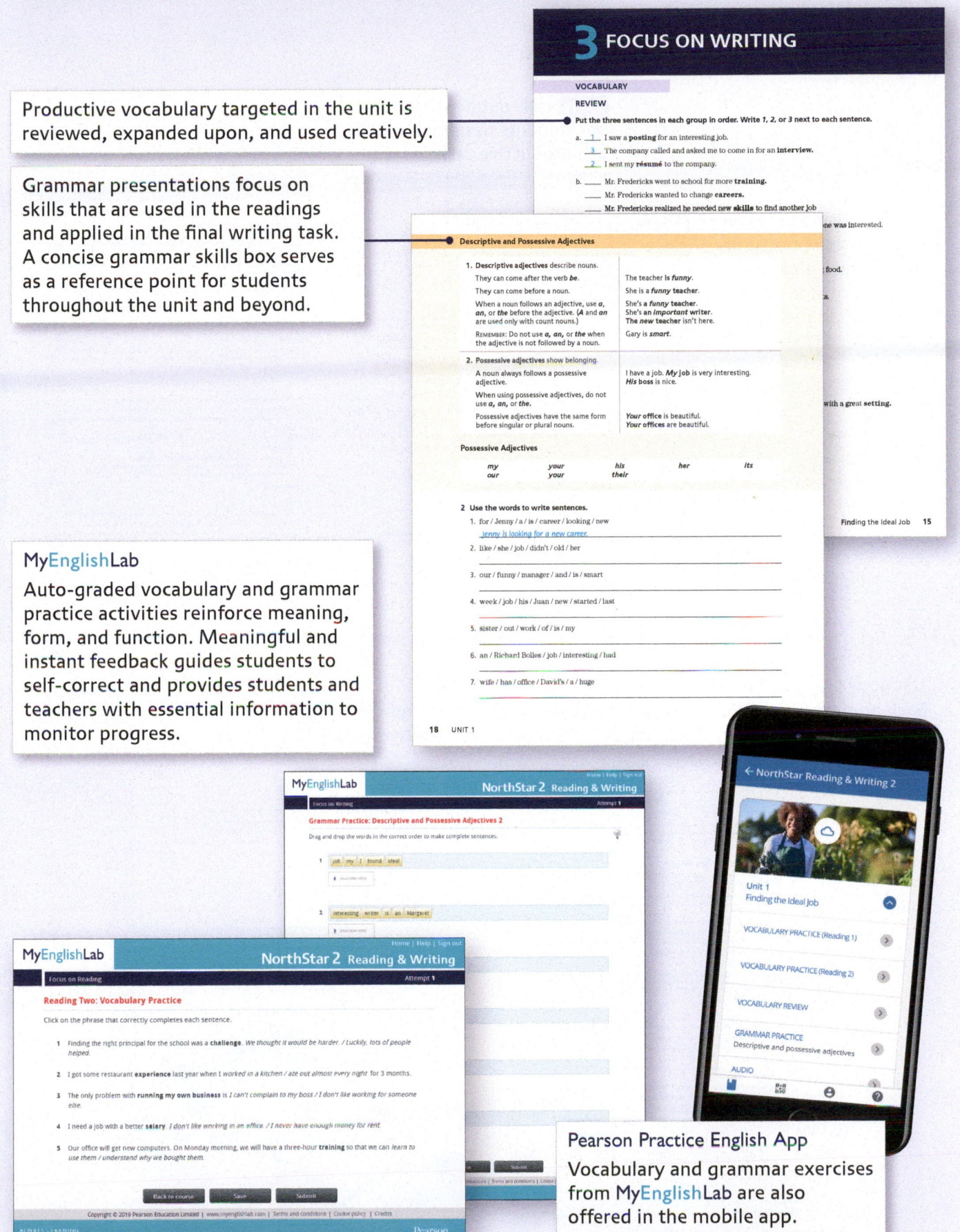

Pearson Practice English App

Vocabulary and grammar exercises from MyEnglishLab are also offered in the mobile app.

A TASK-BASED APPROACH TO PROCESS WRITING

APPLY calls out activities that get students to use new skills in a productive task.

A final writing task gives students an opportunity to integrate ideas, vocabulary, and grammar presented in the unit.

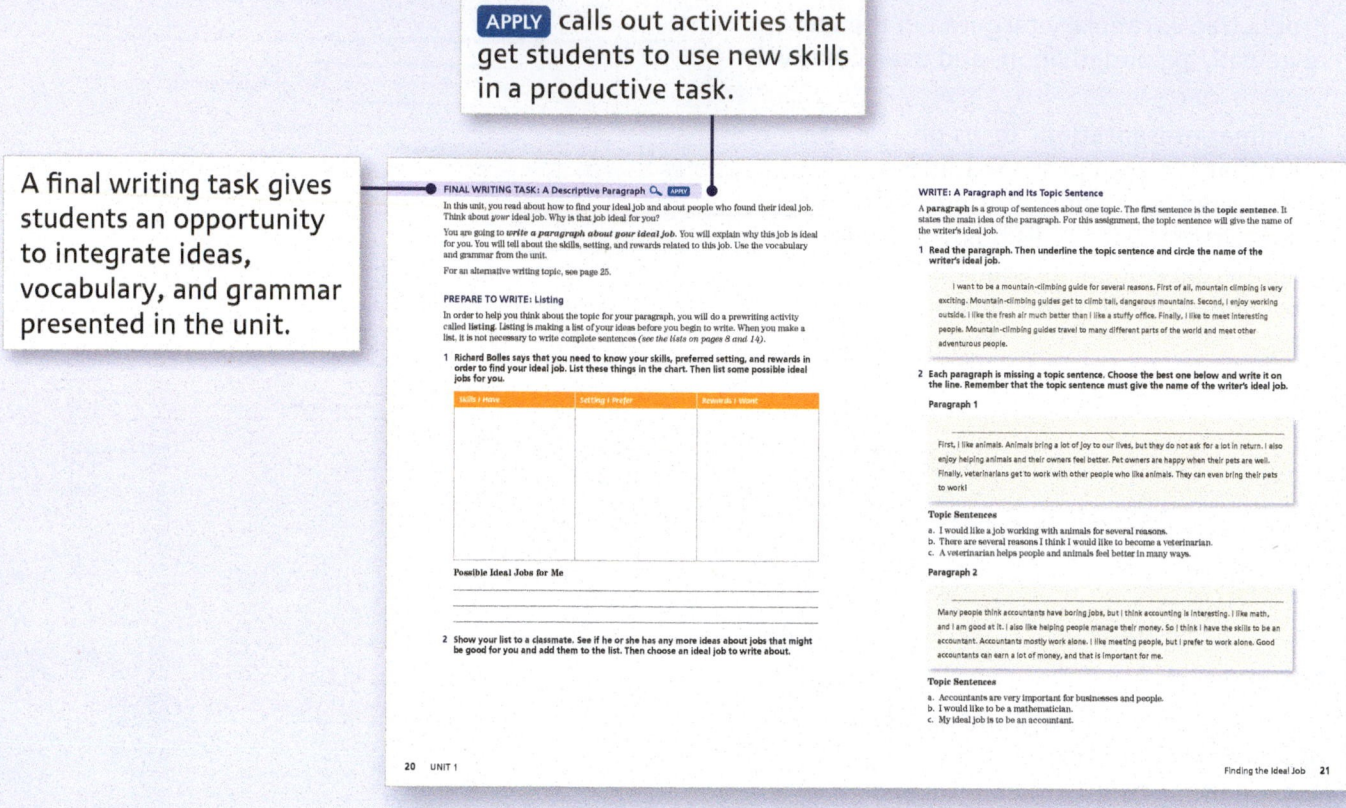

Each unit presents different stages of the writing process and encourages the structured development of writing skills both practical and academic.

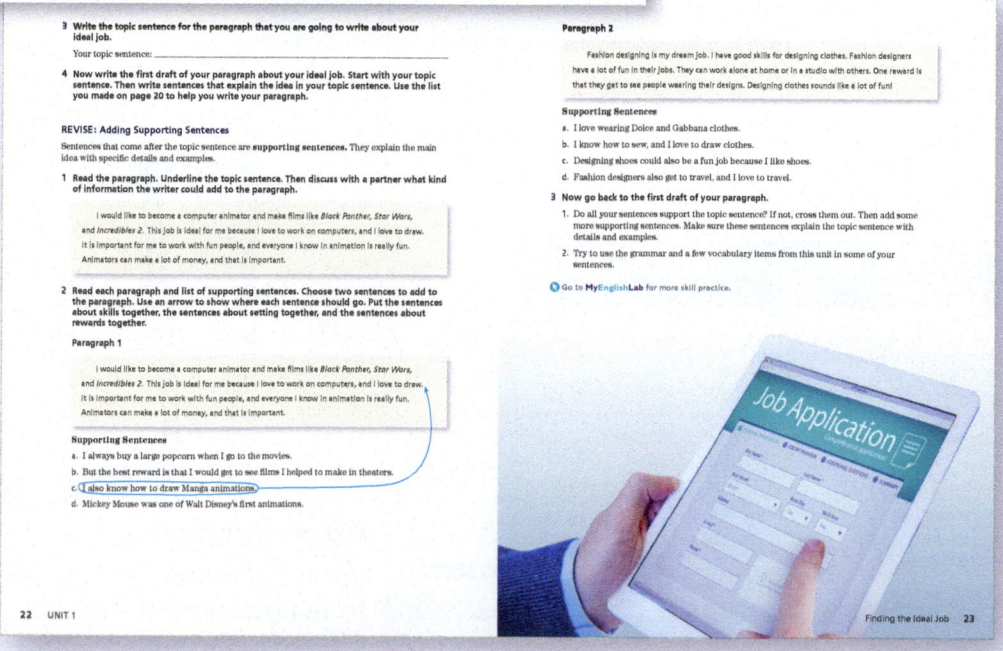

Students continue through the writing process to learn revision techniques that help them move toward coherence and unity in their writing. Finally, students edit their work with the aid of a checklist that focuses on essential outcomes.

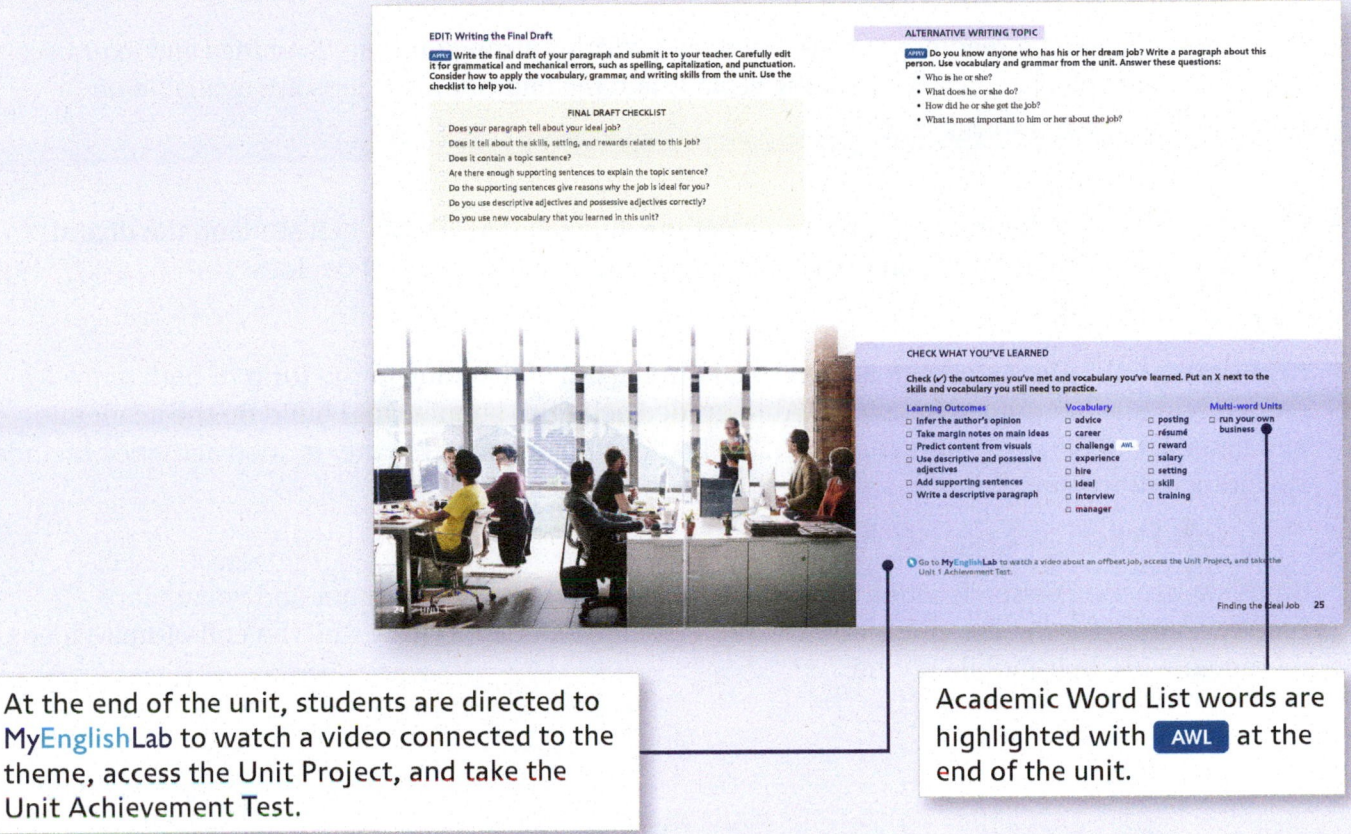

At the end of the unit, students are directed to MyEnglishLab to watch a video connected to the theme, access the Unit Project, and take the Unit Achievement Test.

Academic Word List words are highlighted with **AWL** at the end of the unit.

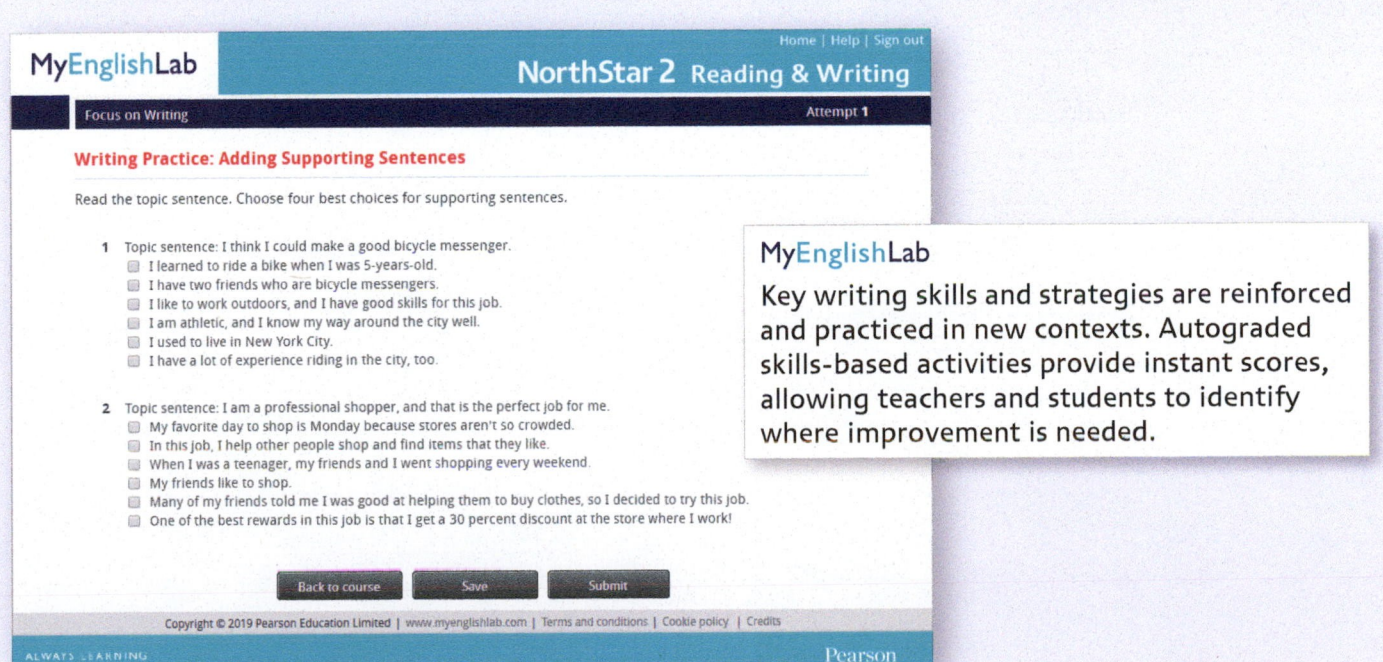

MyEnglishLab
Key writing skills and strategies are reinforced and practiced in new contexts. Autograded skills-based activities provide instant scores, allowing teachers and students to identify where improvement is needed.

COMPONENTS

Students can access the following resources on the Pearson English Portal.

- **Classroom Audio and Videos**

  Classroom audio (the readings for the Reading & Writing strand and the listenings and exercises with audio for the Listening & Speaking strand) and the end-of-unit videos are available on the portal.

- **Etext**

  Offering maximum flexibility in order to meet the individual needs of each student, the digital version of the student book can be used across multiple platforms and devices.

- **MyEnglishLab**

  MyEnglishLab offers students access to additional practice online in the form of both auto-graded and teacher-graded activities. Auto-graded activities support and build on the academic and language skills presented and practiced in the student book. Teacher-graded activities include speaking and writing.

- **Pearson Practice English App**

  Students use the Pearson Practice English App to access additional grammar and vocabulary practice, audio for the listenings and readings from the student books, and the end-of-unit videos on the go with their mobile phone.

INNOVATIVE TEACHING TOOLS

With instant access to a wide range of online content and diagnostic tools, teachers can customize learning environments to meet the needs of every student. Digital resources, all available on the Pearson English Portal, include **MyEnglishLab** and ExamView.

Using MyEnglishLab, *NorthStar* teachers can

Deliver rich online content to engage and motivate students, including

- student audio to support listening and speaking skills, in addition to audio versions of all readings.
- engaging, authentic video clips tied to the unit themes.
- opportunities for written and recorded reactions to be submitted by students.

Use diagnostic reports to

- view student scores by unit, skill, and activity.
- monitor student progress on any activity or test as often as needed.
- analyze class data to determine steps for remediation and support.

Access Teacher Resources, including

- unit teaching notes and answer keys.
- downloadable diagnostic, achievement and placement tests, as well as unit checkpoints.
- printable resources including lesson planners, videoscripts, and video activities.
- classroom audio.

Using ExamView, teachers can customize Achievement Tests by

- reordering test questions.
- editing questions.
- selecting questions from a bank.
- writing their own questions.

SCOPE AND SEQUENCE

	1 Finding the Ideal Job Pages: 2–25 Reading 1: Finding the Ideal Job Reading 2: The Ideal Job	2 Creative Thinking Pages: 26–51 Reading 1: Can we Teach Creative Thinking Reading 2: Tips for Success in College: How to be Creative
Inference	Inferring the author's opinion	Inferring connections between statements and examples
Note-Taking	Taking margin notes on main ideas	Listing details in notes
Reading	Predicting content from visuals	Recognizing the meaning of *we*, *us*, and *our*
Grammar	Descriptive and possessive adjectives	Simple past
Revise	Adding supporting sentences	Using visuals to support writing
Final Writing Task	A descriptive paragraph	A complete paragraph
Video	An offbeat job	Creativity
Assessments	Pre-Unit Diagnostic: Check What You Know Checkpoint 1 Checkpoint 2 Unit Achievement Test	Pre-Unit Diagnostic: Check What You Know Checkpoint 1 Checkpoint 2 Unit Achievement Test
Unit Project	Conduct an interview and write a paragraph about it	Create a tourism guide for unusual activities in students' town or a town they know

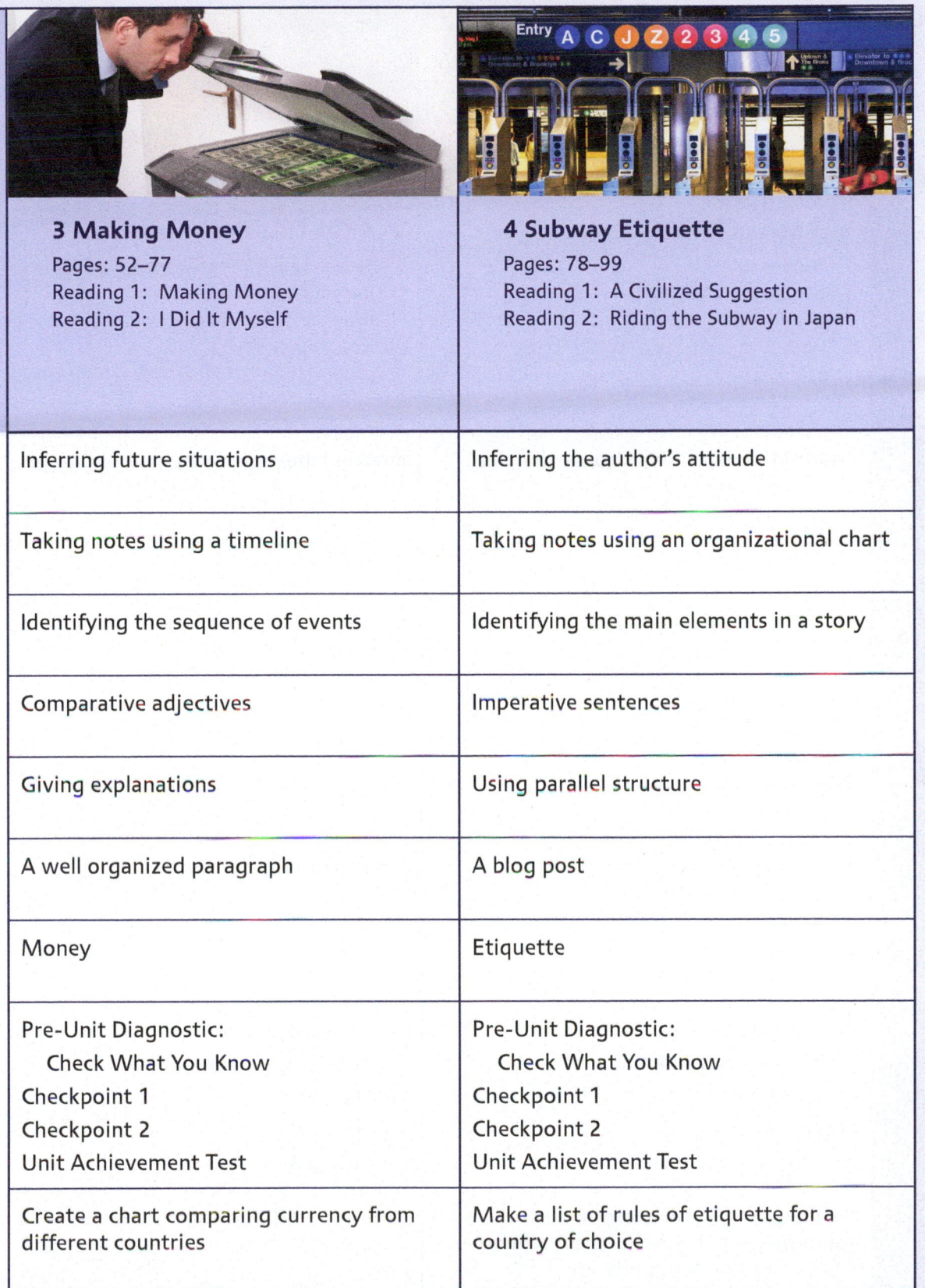

3 Making Money	4 Subway Etiquette
Pages: 52–77 Reading 1: Making Money Reading 2: I Did It Myself	Pages: 78–99 Reading 1: A Civilized Suggestion Reading 2: Riding the Subway in Japan
Inferring future situations	Inferring the author's attitude
Taking notes using a timeline	Taking notes using an organizational chart
Identifying the sequence of events	Identifying the main elements in a story
Comparative adjectives	Imperative sentences
Giving explanations	Using parallel structure
A well organized paragraph	A blog post
Money	Etiquette

Pre-Unit Diagnostic:
    Check What You Know
Checkpoint 1
Checkpoint 2
Unit Achievement Test
	Pre-Unit Diagnostic:
	    Check What You Know
	Checkpoint 1
	Checkpoint 2
	Unit Achievement Test

Create a chart comparing currency from different countries	Make a list of rules of etiquette for a country of choice

SCOPE AND SEQUENCE

	5 Sensory Perception Pages: 100–125 Reading 1: Is Blue Always Blue? Reading 2: The Dress that Almost Broke the Internet	6 The Heart of a Hero Pages: 126–151 Reading 1: What is a Hero? Reading 2: Book Review: Harry Potter and the Sorcerer's Stone
Inference	Inferring abstract ideas from examples	Inferring meaning from metaphors
Note-Taking	Taking notes using abbreviations and symbols	Creating an outline to take notes
Reading	Scanning for information	Recognizing the use of present tense in a story about the past
Grammar	Linking verbs	Time clauses in the present tense
Revise	Using descriptive adjectives	Adding explanations and examples
Final Writing Task	A personal experience paragraph	A one paragraph story
Video	Color Psychology	Heroes

Assessments	Pre-Unit Diagnostic:
	  Check What You Know
	Checkpoint 1
	Checkpoint 2
	Unit Achievement Test
		Pre-Unit Diagnostic:
		  Check What You Know
		Checkpoint 1
		Checkpoint 2
		Unit Achievement Test

Unit Project	Write a comparison paragraph about how your sensory perception on something differs from a classmate's	Write a paragraph about a real life hero

7 What's Your Medicine

Pages: 152–177
Reading 1: Leeches
Reading 2: Gross Medicine

8 Endangered Cultures

Pages: 178–207
Reading 1: Will Indigenous Cultures Survive?
Reading 2: Touring Penan Country

Inferring judgements	Inferring the author's attitude
Taking double entry notes	Taking notes using a mind map
Visualizing while reading	Identifying the purpose of quoted speech
Adverbs of manner	*Will* and *be going to*
Time order words in a narrative	Concluding sentences
A narrative paragraph	A prediction paragraph
Health problems	Endangered cultures

Pre-Unit Diagnostic:
  Check What You Know
Checkpoint 1
Checkpoint 2
Unit Achievement Test
	Pre-Unit Diagnostic:
	  Check What You Know
	Checkpoint 1
	Checkpoint 2
	Unit Achievement Test

Write a summary paragraph about a traditional method of curing an illness	Follow a format to write a status report about an endangered culture or people

ACKNOWLEDGMENTS

With gratitude to our mentors: Dr. Pat Porter, and the MATESOL program at San Francisco State University, our generous, inspiring colleagues: Kate Griffeath and others at Laney College, the Academy of Art University and California College of the Arts, our writing team: Carol Numrich, Peter West, Françoise Leffler and numerous others on the *NorthStar* team, and our students, who continue to be the best teachers of all.

—Beth Maher and Natasha Haugnes

REVIEWERS

Chris Antonellis, Boston University – CELOP; Gail August, Hostos; Aegina Barnes, York College; Kim Bayer, Hunter College; Mine Bellikli, Atilim University; Allison Blechman, Embassy CES; Paul Blomquist, Kaplan; Helena Botros, FLS; James Branchick, FLS; Chris Bruffee, Embassy CES; Joyce Cain University of California at Fullerton; Nese Cakli, Duzce University; Molly Cheny, University of Washington; María Cordani Tourinho Dantas, Colégio Rainha De Paz; Jason Davis, ASC English; Lindsay Donigan, Fullerton College; Mila Dragushanskaya, ASA College; Bina Dugan, BCCC; Sibel Ece Izmir, Atilim University; Érica Ferrer, Universidad del Norte; María Irma Gallegos Peláez, Universidad del Valle de México; Vera Figueira, UC Irvine; Rachel Fernandez, UC Irvine; Jeff Gano, ASA College; Emily Ellis, UC Irvine; María Genovev a Chávez Bazán, Universidad del Valle de México; Juan Garcia, FLS; Heidi Gramlich, The New England School of English; Phillip Grayson, Kaplan; Rebecca Gross, The New England School of English; Rick Guadiana, FLS; Sebnem Guzel, Tobb University; Esra Hatipoglu, Ufuk University; Brian Henry, FLS; Josephine Horna, BCCC; Judy Hu, UC Irvine; Arthur Hui, Fullerton College; Zoe Isaacson, Hunter College; Kathy Johnson, Fullerton College; Marcelo Juica, Urban College of Boston; Tom Justice, North Shore Community College; Lisa Karakas, Berkeley College; Eva Kopernacki, Embassy CES; Drew Larimore, Kaplan; Heidi Lieb, BCCC; Patricia Martins, Ibeu; Cecilia Mora Espejo, Universidad del Valle de México; Oscar Navarro University of California at Fullerton; Eva Nemtson, ASA College; Kate Nyhan, The New England School of English; Julie Oni, FLS; Willard Osman, The New England School of English; Olga Pagieva, ASA College; Manish Patel, FLS; Paige Poole, Universidad del Norte; Claudia Rebello, Ibeu; Amy Renehan, University of Washington; Lourdes Rey, Universidad del Norte; Michelle Reynolds, FLS International Boston Commons; Mary Ritter, NYU; Ellen Rosen University of California at Fullerton; Dana Saito-Stehiberger, UC Irvine; Dariusz Saczuk, ASA College; Miryam Salimov, ASA College; Minerva Santos, Hostos; Sezer Sarioz, Saint Benoit PLS; Gail Schwartz, UC Irvine; Ebru Sinar, Tobb University; Beth Soll, NYU (Columbia); Christopher Stobart, Universidad del Norte; Guliz Uludag, Ufuk University; Debra Un, NYU; Hilal Unlusu, Saint Benoit PLS; María del Carmen Viruega Trejo, Universidad del Valle de México; Reda Vural, Atilim University; Douglas Waters, Universidad del Norte; Emily Wong, UC Irvine; Leyla Yucklik, Duzce University; Jorge Zepeda Porras, Universidad del Valle de México

LEARNING OUTCOMES

> Infer the author's opinion
> Take margin notes on main ideas
> Predict content from visuals

> Use descriptive and possessive adjectives
> Add supporting sentences
> Write a descriptive paragraph

🔵 Go to **MyEnglishLab** to check what you know.

Finding the Ideal Job

1 FOCUS ON THE TOPIC

1. What job or profession does this person have?

2. Is this a popular job? What kinds of jobs are popular today?

3. What is the ideal job for you? Explain your answer.

2 FOCUS ON READING

READING ONE | Finding the Ideal Job

1 Read the list of words and their definitions.

advice: an opinion you give someone about what he or she should do

careers: the kinds of work people do, usually after learning how and usually for a long time

hire: to give someone a job

ideal: perfect

interviews: meetings where a person looking for a job talks to the person who is looking for a new worker

managers: people who direct and organize groups of workers in a company

postings: ads or comments on the Internet

résumés: written descriptions of people's education and previous jobs

rewards: good things you get in return for work (such as money or health insurance)

setting: the place where something happens

skills: things that you can do well; abilities that you have learned and practiced

2 Now use the words from the list to complete this news article about American workers and companies.

What Today's Worker Wants

In 2016, between four and five percent of Americans were out of work. But 40 percent of the people who had jobs were also looking for new ones because they weren't happy with their current jobs.

According to one survey, less than half of all American workers really love their jobs. This is a problem for workers, and it is also a problem for companies. When people are unhappy with their jobs, they often don't do their jobs well. Thirty-three percent of ____managers____ say that they don't care what happens
                                                  1.
to their companies—and those are the people who are supposed to be in charge![1]

_____

[1] **be in charge:** be responsible for a group of people or an activity

What do workers want? Usually we think that everyone wants more money, but today's workers are looking for other _rewards_. They want health insurance and more vacation. They also want to be able to keep learning new _skills_ at a job because, first, they don't want to be bored at their work, and second, they are afraid computers will take their jobs. Older workers are usually happier with their jobs than younger workers. This is probably because they have had time to think about their _careers_ and find a job they like.

Many companies today try to make changes to keep workers happy. They ask their workers questions about what makes them really happy at work. Many technology companies create a comfortable _setting_ for their workers: They have health clubs, ping-pong tables, fancy coffee machines, and soft sofas for relaxing. If workers like to be at their jobs, they will work harder and stay at the company.

If workers leave, companies have to _hire_ new people. And that takes a lot of time. They have to write _postings_ to put on the Internet. They have to read hundreds of _resumes_. They have to do _interviews_ to meet people who want to work there. And even after all that work, they might not find the _ideal_ new worker.

Our _advice_ to new college graduates: Take your time and choose carefully.

► Go to the **Pearson Practice English App** or **MyEnglishLab** for more vocabulary practice.

Imagine you are not satisfied with your job. You decide to job hunt—that is, to look for a new job. With a partner, write a list of things you might do to find a job.

1. _I might ask someone in my family for a job._
2. _____
3. _____
4. _____

Read the book review on the next page. Create a chart like the one below to take notes.

TAKE NOTES	
Main Ideas	**Details**
WCIYP 2018—good book to help job hunters find ideal job	Think about skills, setting, and rewards
	Network

▶ Go to **MyEnglishLab** to view example notes.

Finding Your Ideal Job
By Barbara Kleppinger

WHAT COLOR IS YOUR PARACHUTE

A Practical Guide for Job-Hunters and Career Changers, 2018 Edition

by Richard N. Bolles, Ten Speed Press

1 You are out of work. You hate your job. You aren't satisfied with your **career**. You are looking for your first job. Where do you start?

2 If you are like most Americans, you'll probably email your **résumé** to a lot of companies. You might search for job **postings** on the Internet or spend hours and hours working on your LinkedIn[1] page. But experts[2] say you won't have much luck. People find jobs only 5 to 10 percent of the time when they look for jobs in these ways. So what can you do?

3 One thing you can do is read Richard Bolles's *What Color Is Your Parachute*[3]? Bolles was an expert in job hunting. He died in 2017, but his advice lives on in his book. His book has helped thousands of people find jobs and careers. It is different from other job-hunting manuals. Bolles doesn't help you to find just another job. Instead, he helps you find your **ideal** job: a job that fits you, a job that makes you happy. What kind of job is ideal for you? If you don't know the answer, Bolles says, you can't find your ideal job. You need to have a clear picture in your mind of the job you want. The book has many exercises to help you draw this picture.

4 Bolles says that you must think about three things before you can find your ideal job:

(1) YOUR SKILLS. What do you like to do? What do you do well? Are you good at talking to groups? Growing vegetables? Teaching? Drawing on the computer? Bolles asks you to think about all your skills, not only "work skills." For example, a mother of four children is probably good at managing people (children!). This woman may be a good **manager**.

(2) JOB SETTING. Where do you like to work? Do you like to work outside? At home? In an office? Alone or with others? What kinds of people do you like to work with?

(3) JOB REWARDS. How much money do you need? How much money do you want? Do you need a lot of vacation time? What else do you want from a job? What makes you feel good about a job?

5 After Bolles helps you decide on your ideal job, he gives you specific **advice** on how to find that job. One of his favorite tools for finding a job is networking. He suggests using every person you know either to give you information about a company or career or to introduce you to someone else who can give you this information. Bolles asks everyone he meets how they got their job. Nine times out of ten, they got their job because a friend knew someone at the company who hired them. Social media can help you, but you have to be active and thoughtful. You need to contact individuals. You can't just wait for people to find you on social media. So once you know the kind of job you want, Bolles says you must use your network—everyone you know—to help you meet the one person who will help you get the job.

6 Bolles's chapter on job **interviews** is full of useful information and suggestions. For example, most people go to interviews asking themselves the question, "How do I get the company to **hire** me?" Bolles thinks this is the wrong question. Instead, he wants you to ask yourself, "Do I want to work here or not?"

7 Some people think that Bolles writes far too much and repeats himself. True, his book could be 100 pages instead of 368. But his writing style makes the book very easy to read, and a reader doesn't have to read the parts that seem less important. Other readers say that there is not enough space to write the answers to the exercises. But these are very small problems. *What Color Is Your Parachute?* is the best job-hunting manual you can buy.

8 *What Color Is Your Parachute?* was first written in 1970. Over 10 million copies have been sold since then. The information is updated[4] every year. So, if you are looking for a job, or if you have a job but want a new one, remember: Don't just email your résumé out to every company. Don't just answer Internet job postings. And don't wait for friends to give you a job. Instead, buy this book and do a job hunt the right way.

---

1 **LinkedIn:** an online professional social media networking site
2 **experts:** people who know a lot about something
3 **parachute:** something you wear when you jump out of a plane. When you jump, it opens up, and it stops you from hitting the ground very hard.
4 **updated:** changed to show new information

Read each statement. Decide if it is true or false. Write *T* (true) or *F* (false) next to it. Use your notes to help you.

__F__ 1. *What Color Is Your Parachute?* is similar to other job-hunting manuals.

__T__ 2. People who read *What Color Is Your Parachute?* find jobs on the Internet more quickly.

__T__ 3. According to *What Color Is Your Parachute?*, job hunters should think about their skills, the job setting, and the job rewards they want.

__T__ 4. *What Color Is Your Parachute?* includes specific advice on finding jobs.

__F__ 5. The reviews of Bolles's book are all positive.

DETAILS

1 Look at the list of job-hunting methods. Decide where each one should go in the chart. Write each method in the correct column. Use your notes to help you.

✓ decide what kind of job is ideal

✓ decide what kind of place you want to work in

✓ do exercises in *What Color Is Your Parachute?*

• ~~look on the Internet~~

✓ update your LinkedIn page

• send out lots of résumés

• think about job rewards

• think about your skills

• network with people

FIND A JOB	
What Many People Do	**What Bolles Says Will Help You**
look on the Internet Update your LinkedIn Page Send out lots of résumés. Network with People.	Decide what kind of job is ideal. Decide what kind of Place you want to work in Do exercises in What Color is Your Parachute? Think about job rewards. Think about your skills.

2 Look at your notes and at your answers in the Preview section. Were any of your ideas the same as Bolles's ideas? Put a check (✓) next to your ideas that were similar to Bolles's. How did they help you understand the book review?

Inferring the Author's Opinion

An **inference** is an **educated guess** about something that is **not directly stated** in a text. Sometimes, careful readers can understand an author's opinion (ideas or beliefs about a particular subject) even when it is not stated directly. They can **infer** this **opinion**.

Look at the example and read the explanation.

- Kleppinger believes that Bolles's book is hard because it's so long.   TRUE (FALSE)
  (Answer: FALSE)

In paragraph 7, the author says that *some* people think Bolles writes too much and repeats himself. At this point, we don't know her opinion. But then she says that his book is easy to read.

After reading the text closely, we can **infer the author's opinion:** She doesn't think Bolles's book is hard just because it's long.

1 **Read each statement. Decide if the statement correctly describes Kleppinger's opinion. Check (✓) *True* if it matches her opinion, or *False* if it does not.**

Kleppinger Believes . . .	Paragraph	True	False
1. Bolles's book helps people know their strengths.	3, 4	✓	
2. Bolles's exercises are too hard.	3, 7		✓
3. Anyone looking for a job should read Bolles's book.	8	✓	

2 **Now discuss your answers with a partner. Point out sentences, words, or phrases in the paragraphs that helped you find the answers.**

DISCUSS 🔍

Discuss the questions with a partner. Then share your answers with the class.

1. The next time you look for a job, which of Bolles's ideas do you think you might use?

2. You are in an interview for a job with a very interesting company. Based on Bolles's advice, what questions might you ask the interviewer about this company?

3. The title of the book is *What Color Is Your Parachute?* Why do you think the author chose this title?

▶ Go to **MyEnglishLab** to give your opinion about another question.

> **USE YOUR NOTES**
>
> Use your notes to support your answers with information from the reading.

READING TWO | The Ideal Job

1 Look at the bold quotes in the reading and at the photos. What do you think each person's job is?

Ryan's Job: _____

Kayla's Job: _____

Don's Job: _____

2 Look at the boldfaced words in the reading. Which words do you know the meaning of?

READ

1 ALLJOBS is a blog that posts about interesting and unusual jobs. Read this blog about some people who have found their ideal job in some very unexpected places. As you read, guess the meanings of the words that are new to you. Remember to take notes on main ideas and details.

ALLJOBS

ARTICLES | VIDEO | PHOTOGRAPHY | ABOUT

THE IDEAL JOB
By Alex Frost

1 Believe it or not, some people get paid for doing the things that make them really happy. Read about a few people who have the jobs of their dreams.

"I get paid to make videos!"—Ryan

2 When I was 14, my uncle gave me his old video camera, and I started making videos. I didn't do very well in school, but I loved getting to know people and making videos about them. I taught myself to edit the videos on a simple computer program of my dad's. One day a friend of my mom's asked me to make a video of her family. She wanted to send it to her mother who lived in China. It was a lot of fun, and she paid me $150. Soon her friends asked me to make videos for them, and suddenly I had a business. That was 10 years ago. Things change a lot in this work, so I'm always taking classes. But I have to say I love **running my own business**.

"I study volcanoes for a living."—Kayla

3 When I was a young girl, I loved science fiction—like "Star Trek" and "Star Wars." When I grew up, I wanted to make science fiction movies. I went to college to study film. One day during my first year, I saw a job announcement that said: "Get paid to melt[1] rocks. No **experience** necessary." Interesting, right? I got the job and started working with rocks. I soon realized I didn't want to make movies about science. Instead, I wanted to be a scientist. Six years later, I had a PhD and my dream job—I was a volcanologist. I study volcanoes for a living. I try to predict when the volcanoes will erupt. I think my work is important and exciting. One volcano I study is Mt. Erebus in Antarctica. I think it's one of the most beautiful, strange, and interesting places in the world.

"I have a job with an incredible view."—Don

4 Teaching skydiving[2] is exciting. I get to be outside, and I love seeing students on their first jump. They are nervous and excited. For them, that first step out of the plane is the biggest **challenge**. After they take that step, it's all good. When they get to the ground, they can't wait to call everyone they know and tell them they just jumped out of an airplane. Later, when they learn to turn and move, they realize that they're not just falling stones. They realize that they're like birds—they can fly!

5 It wasn't easy to get this job. I had to have about 1,000 jumps and about two years of **training**. And the **salary** was only $15,000 for the first year. But I don't do it for the money. In fact, I don't need to get paid at all. I love it that much!

[1] **melt:** to heat something until it becomes liquid
[2] **skydiving:** the sport of jumping out of airplanes with a parachute

2 **Compare your notes on main ideas and details with a partner's. How can you improve your notes next time?**

🔍 Go to the **Pearson Practice English App** or **MyEnglishLab** for more vocabulary practice.

Taking Margin Notes on Main Ideas

Writing **notes in the margins** can help you **identify main ideas.** Later, you can look back at these margin notes to help you remember the main ideas in texts.

As you read, find the main idea of each paragraph and write it in the margin. Sometimes, you can use key words from the text, and sometimes you need to use your own words. Do not make complete sentences. Do not worry about perfect grammar. Write **short phrases or words.**

Look at this example from Reading One *(paragraph 2)*:

sending résumés, searching Internet—5–10% find jobs	2	If you are like most Americans, you'll probably email your **résumé** to a lot of companies. You might search for job **postings** on the Internet or spend hours and hours working on your LinkedIn page. But experts say you won't have much luck. People find jobs only 5 to 10 percent of the time when they look for jobs in these ways. So what can you do?

Don't just write the first idea. Be sure it's the most important idea. And don't write whole sentences in your margin notes.

~~Most Americans send résumés to a lot of companies when they look for jobs.~~	2	If you are like most Americans, you'll probably email your **résumé** to a lot of companies. You might search for job **postings** on the Internet or spend hours and hours working on your LinkedIn page. But experts say you won't have much luck. People find jobs only 5 to 10 percent of the time when they look for jobs in these ways. So what can you do?

1 Reread two paragraphs from Reading One, and choose the best margin note for each one.

Paragraph 3

a. Bolles—expert in job hunting *b. book helps find ideal job* *c. What Color Is Your Parachute? is a book by Bolles that has exercises to help you find your ideal job.*	3	One thing you can do is read Richard Bolles's *What Color Is Your Parachute?* Bolles was an expert in job hunting. He died in 2017, but his advice lives on in his book. His book has helped thousands of people find jobs and careers. It is different from other job-hunting manuals. Bolles doesn't help you to find just another job. Instead, he helps you find your **ideal** job: a job that fits you, a job that makes you happy. What kind of job is ideal for you? If you don't know the answer, Bolles says, you can't find your ideal job. You need to have a clear picture in your mind of the job you want. The book has many exercises to help you draw this picture.

Paragraph 5

a. specific advice—how to find job *b. networking—best way to find job* *c. Social media helps.*	5	After Bolles helps you decide on your ideal job, he gives you specific **advice** on how to find that job. One of his favorite tools for finding a job is networking. He suggests using every person you know either to give you information about a company or career or to introduce you to someone else who can give you this information. Bolles asks everyone he meets how they got their job. Nine times out of ten, they got their job because a friend knew someone at the company who hired them. Social media can help you, but you have to be active and thoughtful. You need to contact individuals. You can't just wait for people to find you on social media. So once you know the kind of job you want, Bolles says you must use your network—everyone you know—to help you meet the one person who will help you get the job.

2 **Look at Reading Two again. Make a margin note about the main idea of paragraph 2 and paragraph 3.**

🖰 Go to **MyEnglishLab** for more note-taking practice.

COMPREHENSION

Complete the sentences with the correct name from Reading Two. Use your notes from Reading Two to help you.

1. _____*Don*_____ made $15,000 his first year.
2. _____ studies rocks.
3. _____ didn't do well in school as a child.
4. _____ has a PhD.
5. _____ is studying to get better skills.
6. _____ loves teaching.
7. _____ studied and practiced for his job for two years.
8. _____ is in charge of a video business.

READING SKILL

1 **Look at the photos in Reading Two. Do the photos help you understand the reading?**

Predicting Content from Visuals

Before reading any text, strong readers look at all the **visuals** (pictures, photos, graphs, etc.) on the page. This gets them to think about what they already know about the topic and allows them to **predict the content** of the text.

Example

In the photo for paragraph 2, I see a man behind a video camera.
The paragraph must be about a man whose ideal job is to make videos.

2 **Work with a partner. Discuss the questions about the photographs in Reading Two.**

1. Look closely at the photo for paragraph 3.

   What do you see in the photo that helped you better understand paragraph 3?

2. Look closely at the photo for paragraphs 4 and 5.

   What do you see in the photo that helped you better understand paragraphs 4 and 5?

🖰 Go to **MyEnglishLab** for more skill practice.

ORGANIZE

Look at Reading One (R1) again. Reread paragraph 4 about skills, setting, and rewards. Then look at this list of ideas from Reading Two (R2) and decide where each one should go in the chart. Write each idea in the correct column.

- editing video
- making $15,000 / year
- working outside
- seeing people learn
- skydiving
- teaching
- having a PhD
- working on mountains
- running a business
- believing his / her work is important for the world
- working with people

Skills	Setting	Rewards
editing video		

SYNTHESIZE

How would the people in Reading Two answer these interview questions? Choose one of them (circle his / her name) and write the answers for that person. Use information from Organize.

1. **Q:** (Ryan) / Kayla / Don, what are your skills?

   A: _I have some video-editing skills_ _____

2. **Q:** Kayla / Don, what are your skills?

   A: _____

3. **Q:** Ryan / Kayla / Don, what kind of setting do you like working in?

   A: _____

4. **Q:** Ryan / Kayla / Don, what rewards are important to you?

   A: _____

🔵 Go to **MyEnglishLab** to check what you learned.

3 FOCUS ON WRITING

REVIEW

Put the three sentences in each group in order. Write *1*, *2*, or *3* next to each sentence.

a. __1__ I saw a **posting** for an interesting job.

__3__ The company called and asked me to come in for an **interview.**

__2__ I sent my **résumé** to the company.

b. ____ Mr. Fredericks went to school for more **training.**

____ Mr. Fredericks wanted to change **careers.**

____ Mr. Fredericks realized he needed new **skills** to find another job

c. ____ Myron realized that he needed to pay a higher **salary** because no one was interested.

____ Myron put **postings** on the Internet for a new manager.

____ Myron's best **manager** quit.

d. ____ John was looking for someone with strong **skills** in photographing food.

____ John **hired** Karen.

____ John met Karen, who is **ideal** because she made ads for restaurants.

e. ____ Kelly quit because she wanted a job with different **rewards.**

____ Kelly started **running her own business.**

____ Kelly had a big **salary,** but she did not like her job.

f. ____ Theo had 20 years of **experience** as a cook.

____ Theo decided to find a new **career.**

____ Cooking was no longer a **challenge** for Theo.

g. ____ Time in nature is important to Rose, so Mark told her to find a job with a great **setting.**

____ They discussed the **rewards** Rose might want from a job.

____ Rose asked her brother, Mark, for **advice** on job hunting.

EXPAND

Each word or phrase in parentheses changes the meaning of the sentence. Cross out the word or phrase that does not make sense.

1. Kate's salary is (huge / pretty good / ~~expensive~~).

2. The rewards at my last job were (happy / great / not very good).

3. You will get some (teaching / technical / lazy) skills at this job.

4. Vladimir is a very (organized / long / unfriendly) manager.

5. Julie's friend gave her (useful / bad / used) advice.

6. I want to move up in my job, so I'm signing up for (setting / advanced / special) training.

7. Sam works in a(n) (outdoor / delicious / beautiful) setting.

8. I want to work with (manager / smart / friendly) people.

9. For this job, you must have plenty of (experience / advice / skills).

10. Some workers really enjoy working (alone / on teams / in settings).

CREATE

APPLY **Complete the email this college student is writing to his parents about his job search. Use the words from the box for items 1–3. For items 4–6, use your own words. Consider using words you've learned in this unit.**

advice	résumé	skills

Dear Mom and Dad,

    Stop worrying. I've got this job thing all worked out. I have a degree in Computer Science.

Any company will see that my computer _____ are excellent. My professor at
                           1.

school has given me a lot of good _____ about how to get a job next year. First,
                           2.

she says I should make sure my _____ is on my LinkedIn page. Second, she wants
                           3.

me to _____ . Third, she thinks I should _____ . Fourth, she wants me
    4.   **5.**

to _____ .
   6.

    So don't worry. You see I have it all under control.

Love,
Nick

🔵 Go to the **Pearson Practice English App** or **MyEnglishLab** for more vocabulary practice.

GRAMMAR FOR WRITING

1 Read the email. Notice the boldfaced words. There are two kinds of adjectives: descriptive adjectives and possessive adjectives.

Subject: Old Job :(

From: Cristina_Bond@NetMakers.com

To: JRIOS@springboard.com

Hey Jenny,

Bad week for me. WebCool bought NetMakers. Lost **my new** job. NetMakers is a **small** company, so I knew this might happen. But I didn't expect it so soon! It was such a **great** job for me because I could use **my** skills. And the job was **fun**. I guess I'll have to start job hunting again. How about **your** job hunt? How is it going? The **last** time we talked, you were going on an interview. Did you get the job? Hope you were **successful**. Don't email me at this address anymore. Just call me on **my** cell phone.

Cristina

List each adjective in the email on one of the lines.

1. Descriptive adjectives *bad,* ________________
2. Possessive adjectives *my,* ________________

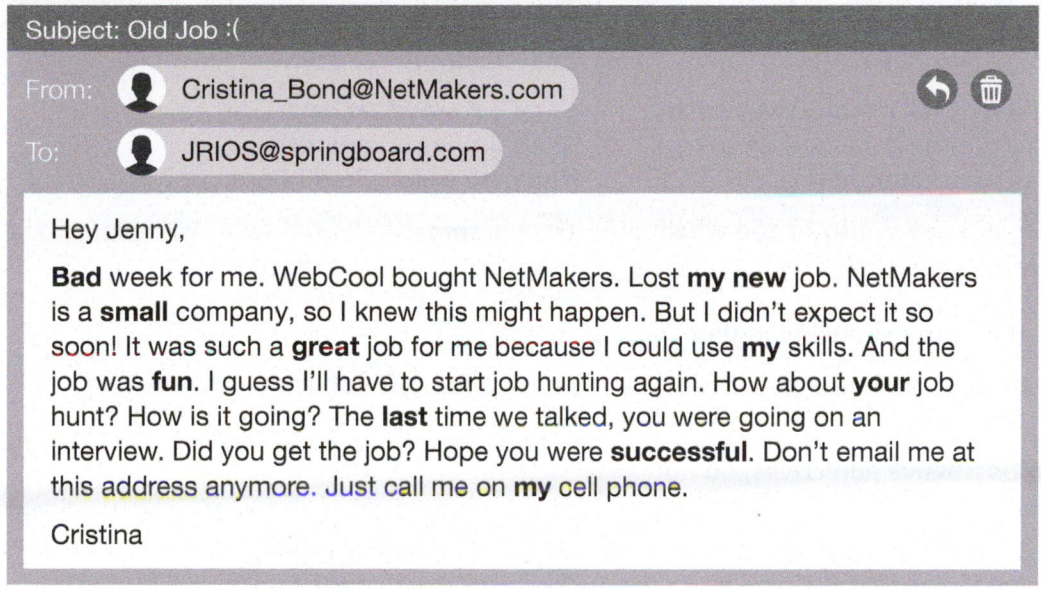

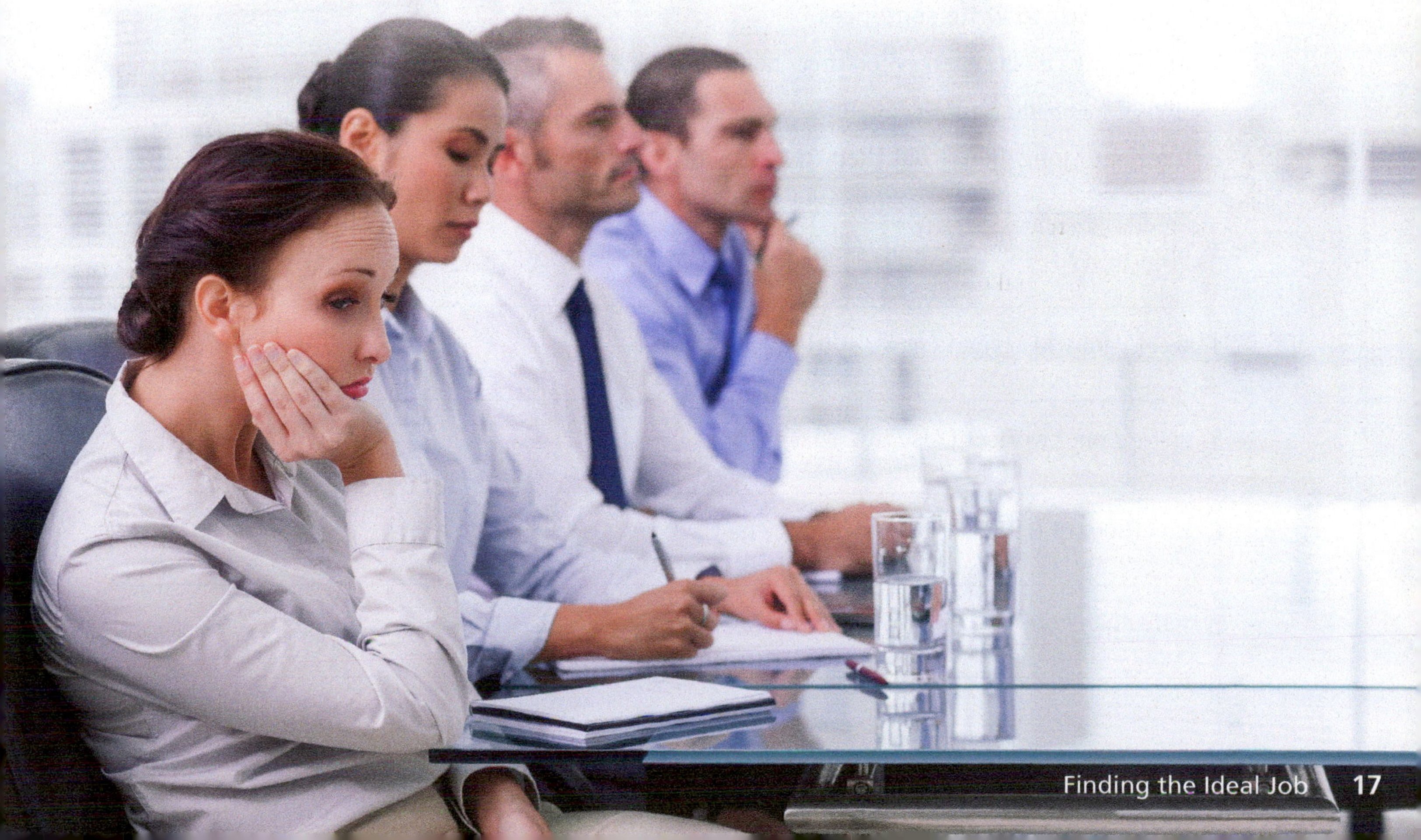

1. **Descriptive adjectives** describe nouns.

   They can come after the verb *be*.

   The teacher **is** *funny*.

   They can come before a noun.

   She is a *funny* teacher.

   When a noun follows an adjective, use *a*, *an*, or *the* before the adjective. (*A* and *an* are used only with count nouns.)

   She's **a** *funny* teacher.
   She's **an** *important* writer.
   The *new* teacher isn't here.

   REMEMBER: Do not use *a, an,* or *the* when the adjective is not followed by a noun.

   Gary is *smart*.

2. **Possessive adjectives** show belonging.

   A noun always follows a possessive adjective.

   I have a job. **My job** is very interesting.
   His boss is nice.

   When using possessive adjectives, do not use *a, an,* or *the.*

   Possessive adjectives have the same form before singular or plural nouns.

   Your office is beautiful.
   Your offices are beautiful.

Possessive Adjectives

my	your	his	her	its
our	your	their		

2 **Use the words to write sentences.**

1. for / Jenny / a / is / career / looking / new

   Jenny is looking for a new career.

2. like / she / job / didn't / old / her

   _____

3. our / funny / manager / and / is / smart

   _____

4. week / job / his / Juan / new / started / last

   _____

5. sister / out / work / of / is / my

   _____

6. an / Richard Bolles / job / interesting / had

   _____

7. wife / has / office / David's / a / huge

   _____

8. Tom / Andrea / business / and / their / sold

_____

9. pays / that / well / company / workers / very / its

_____

10. résumé / has / a / Dee / great

_____

3 APPLY **Describe the pictures. For each picture, write at least three sentences. Use at least one possessive adjective, one descriptive adjective before a noun, and one descriptive adjective after *be*. You can use the descriptive adjectives from the box.**

big	dirty	hungry	messy	sad	sleepy	young
curly	happy	long	old	short	straight	

1. The man:

   The man is young. He has short hair. He is hungry.

   He drives an old truck.

   The truck:

   His truck is old. The old truck is dirty.

2. The woman:

   _____

   _____

   The desk:

   _____

   _____

3. The doctor:

   _____

   _____

   The patient:

   _____

   _____

Go to the **Pearson Practice English App** or **MyEnglishLab** for more grammar practice.
Check what you learned in **MyEnglishLab**.

In this unit, you read about how to find your ideal job and about people who found their ideal job. Think about *your* ideal job. Why is that job ideal for you?

You are going to **write a paragraph about your ideal job.** You will explain why this job is ideal for you. You will tell about the skills, setting, and rewards related to this job. Use the vocabulary and grammar from the unit.

For an alternative writing topic, see page 25.

PREPARE TO WRITE: Listing

In order to help you think about the topic for your paragraph, you will do a prewriting activity called **listing**. Listing is making a list of your ideas before you begin to write. When you make a list, it is not necessary to write complete sentences *(see the lists on pages 8 and 14).*

1 **Richard Bolles says that you need to know your skills, preferred setting, and rewards in order to find your ideal job. List these things in the chart. Then list some possible ideal jobs for you.**

Skills I Have	Setting I Prefer	Rewards I Want

Possible Ideal Jobs for Me

_____

_____

_____

2 **Show your list to a classmate. See if he or she has any more ideas about jobs that might be good for you and add them to the list. Then choose an ideal job to write about.**

WRITE: A Paragraph and Its Topic Sentence

A **paragraph** is a group of sentences about one topic. The first sentence is the **topic sentence**. It states the main idea of the paragraph. For this assignment, the topic sentence will give the name of the writer's ideal job.

1 **Read the paragraph. Then underline the topic sentence and circle the name of the writer's ideal job.**

> I want to be a mountain-climbing guide for several reasons. First of all, mountain climbing is very exciting. Mountain-climbing guides get to climb tall, dangerous mountains. Second, I enjoy working outside. I like the fresh air much better than I like a stuffy office. Finally, I like to meet interesting people. Mountain-climbing guides travel to many different parts of the world and meet other adventurous people.

2 **Each paragraph is missing a topic sentence. Choose the best one below and write it on the line. Remember that the topic sentence must give the name of the writer's ideal job.**

Paragraph 1

> _____
>
> First, I like animals. Animals bring a lot of joy to our lives, but they do not ask for a lot in return. I also enjoy helping animals and their owners feel better. Pet owners are happy when their pets are well. Finally, veterinarians get to work with other people who like animals. They can even bring their pets to work!

Topic Sentences

a. I would like a job working with animals for several reasons.
b. There are several reasons I think I would like to become a veterinarian.
c. A veterinarian helps people and animals feel better in many ways.

Paragraph 2

> _____
>
> Many people think accountants have boring jobs, but I think accounting is interesting. I like math, and I am good at it. I also like helping people manage their money. So I think I have the skills to be an accountant. Accountants mostly work alone. I like meeting people, but I prefer to work alone. Good accountants can earn a lot of money, and that is important for me.

Topic Sentences

a. Accountants are very important for businesses and people.
b. I would like to be a mathematician.
c. My ideal job is to be an accountant.

3 Write the topic sentence for the paragraph that you are going to write about your ideal job.

Your topic sentence: _____

4 Now write the first draft of your paragraph about your ideal job. Start with your topic sentence. Then write sentences that explain the idea in your topic sentence. Use the list you made on page 20 to help you write your paragraph.

REVISE: Adding Supporting Sentences

Sentences that come after the topic sentence are **supporting sentences.** They explain the main idea with specific details and examples.

1 Read the paragraph. Underline the topic sentence. Then discuss with a partner what kind of information the writer could add to the paragraph.

> I would like to become a computer animator and make films like *Black Panther, Star Wars,* and *Incredibles 2.* This job is ideal for me because I love to work on computers, and I love to draw. It is important for me to work with fun people, and everyone I know in animation is really fun. Animators can make a lot of money, and that is important.

2 Read each paragraph and list of supporting sentences. Choose two sentences to add to the paragraph. Use an arrow to show where each sentence should go. Put the sentences about skills together, the sentences about setting together, and the sentences about rewards together.

Paragraph 1

> I would like to become a computer animator and make films like *Black Panther, Star Wars,* and *Incredibles 2.* This job is ideal for me because I love to work on computers, and I love to draw. It is important for me to work with fun people, and everyone I know in animation is really fun. Animators can make a lot of money, and that is important.

Supporting Sentences

a. I always buy a large popcorn when I go to the movies.

b. But the best reward is that I would get to see films I helped to make in theaters.

c. I also know how to draw Manga animations.

d. Mickey Mouse was one of Walt Disney's first animations.

Paragraph 2

Fashion designing is my dream job. I have good skills for designing clothes. Fashion designers have a lot of fun in their jobs. They can work alone at home or in a studio with others. One reward is that they get to see people wearing their designs. Designing clothes sounds like a lot of fun!

Supporting Sentences

a. I love wearing Dolce and Gabbana clothes.

b. I know how to sew, and I love to draw clothes.

c. Designing shoes could also be a fun job because I like shoes.

d. Fashion designers also get to travel, and I love to travel.

3 Now go back to the first draft of your paragraph.

1. Do all your sentences support the topic sentence? If not, cross them out. Then add some more supporting sentences. Make sure these sentences explain the topic sentence with details and examples.

2. Try to use the grammar and a few vocabulary items from this unit in some of your sentences.

Go to **MyEnglishLab** for more skill practice.

EDIT: Writing the Final Draft

APPLY Write the final draft of your paragraph and submit it to your teacher. Carefully edit it for grammatical and mechanical errors, such as spelling, capitalization, and punctuation. Consider how to apply the vocabulary, grammar, and writing skills from the unit. Use the checklist to help you.

FINAL DRAFT CHECKLIST

☐ Does your paragraph tell about your ideal job?

☐ Does it tell about the skills, setting, and rewards related to this job?

☐ Does it contain a topic sentence?

☐ Are there enough supporting sentences to explain the topic sentence?

☐ Do the supporting sentences give reasons why the job is ideal for you?

☐ Do you use descriptive adjectives and possessive adjectives correctly?

☐ Do you use new vocabulary that you learned in this unit?

ALTERNATIVE WRITING TOPIC

APPLY Do you know anyone who has his or her dream job? Write a paragraph about this person. Use vocabulary and grammar from the unit. Answer these questions:

- Who is he or she?
- What does he or she do?
- How did he or she get the job?
- What is most important to him or her about the job?

CHECK WHAT YOU'VE LEARNED

Check (✔) the outcomes you've met and vocabulary you've learned. Put an X next to the skills and vocabulary you still need to practice.

Learning Outcomes	Vocabulary		Multi-word Units
☐ Infer the author's opinion	☐ advice	☐ posting	☐ run your own business
☐ Take margin notes on main ideas	☐ career	☐ résumé	
☐ Predict content from visuals	☐ challenge **AWL**	☐ reward	
☐ Use descriptive and possessive adjectives	☐ experience	☐ salary	
☐ Add supporting sentences	☐ hire	☐ setting	
☐ Write a descriptive paragraph	☐ ideal	☐ skill	
	☐ interview	☐ training	
	☐ manager		

🔵 Go to **MyEnglishLab** to watch a video about an offbeat job, access the Unit Project, and take the Unit 1 Achievement Test.

LEARNING OUTCOMES

> Infer connections between statements and examples
> List details in notes
> Recognize the meaning of *we*, *us*, and *our*

> Use the simple past
> Use visuals to support writing
> Write a complete paragraph

🔊 Go to **MyEnglishLab** to check what you know.

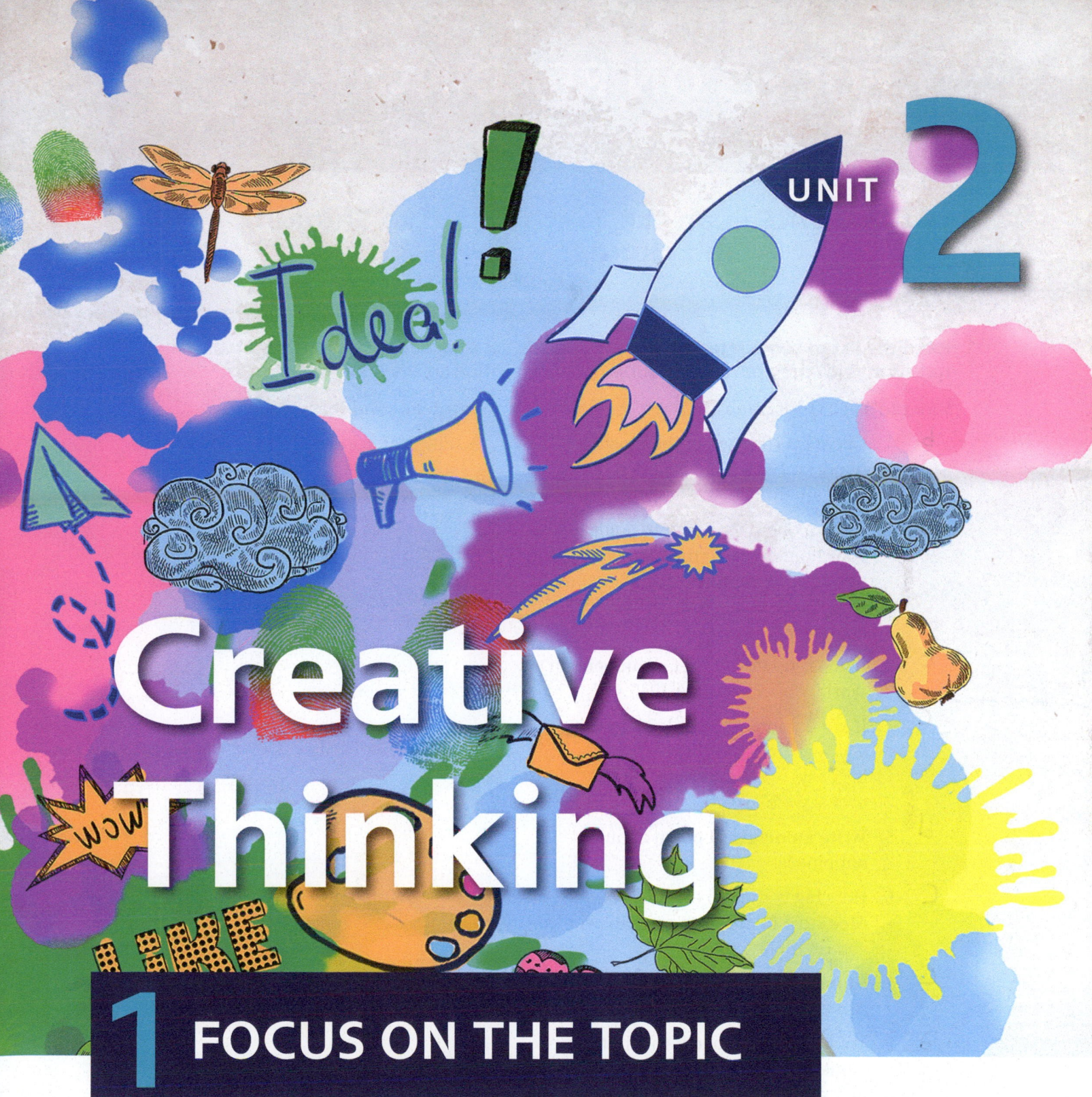

UNIT **2**

Creative Thinking

1. How does this photo show the idea of creative thinking? Which side of the picture looks more creative?

2. Can schools teach creative thinking? Why or why not?

READING ONE | Can We Teach Creative Thinking in Schools?

VOCABULARY

1 Read the list of sample test questions and the list of academic subjects. Match each question with the appropriate subject. Pay attention to the boldfaced words.

Sample Test Questions

___b___ 1. **Create** a timeline of the most important events in England between 1500 and today.

___d___ 2. Write a one-page essay to compare your hometown to the town you live in now. **Focus on** one topic, for example, scenery, food, nature, fashion, or community.

___b___ 3. Is the following a **fact** or an opinion? World War II ended in 1945.

___c___ 4. If x = 7 and y = z, it is **logical** to say:
   a. 7 + y = z + 7
   b. x = y
   c. x + y = z

___d___ 5. Write an **original** poem about happiness.

___c___ 6. How big is the top of your desk? **Measure** it, and give your answer in square inches.

___c___ 7. **Solve** the following problem for x:
   5 (− 3x − 2) − (x − 3) = − 4 (4x + 5) + 13

___a___ 8. Your soccer team lost the first three games. What can you say to yourself and your team to **encourage** them to play better?

___c___ 9. **Prove** that two sides of the triangle below are equal:

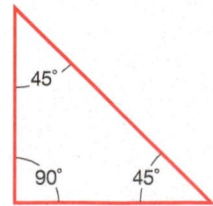

Academic Subjects

a. Physical Education (sports)

b. History

c. Math or Geometry

d. English

2 Match the boldfaced words on the left with the definitions on the right.

<u>b</u> 1. **create** (something)   a. making sense
<u>f</u> 2. **focus on** (something)   ~~b. to make something~~
<u>g</u> 3. **fact**   c. not copied; one of a kind
<u>a</u> 4. **logical**   d. to find the answer to something
<u>c</u> 5. **original**   e. to show that something is true
<u>h</u> 6. **measure** (something)   f. to pay very close attention to something)
<u>d</u> 7. **solve** (something)   g. a statement that is true
<u>i</u> 8. **encourage** (someone)   h. to find out the size of something
<u>e</u> 9. **prove** (something)   i. to say and do things to help someone do well

▶ Go to the **Pearson Practice English App** or **MyEnglishLab** for more vocabulary practice.

PREVIEW

The following magazine article is about creative thinking. Look at the title of the article and think about the question it asks. From your experience, do schools teach creative thinking? In which classes are students most likely to learn creative thinking skills? Check (✓) the appropriate classes.

☐ Math class

☑ Art class

☐ History class

☑ Science class

☑ English class

READ

Read the article on the next page. Create a chart like the one below to take notes.

TAKE NOTES	
Main Ideas	**Details**
Creative thinking— important skill	Helps: —make new things (iPhone, hit songs) —solve everyday problems (dinner, fix car)

▶ Go to **MyEnglishLab** to view example notes.

Can We Teach CREATIVE Thinking in Schools?

by Martha Maddux

Steve Jobs created the iPhone. Lady Gaga writes hit songs. Mom made a delicious dinner with the food she found in the refrigerator. Uncle Fred fixed our broken car with a can opener.

1 These creative people all did important things. Some people are famous and changed the way we live and think; others were not well known and only helped one family for a day.

2 None of the people on the list finished college. Many of the world's most creative thinkers learned their creative skills outside of school.

3 Creative thinking is a very important skill. It helps us make new things. It also helps us **solve** everyday problems that don't have one easy answer. Yet traditional schools often don't **encourage** creative thinking. Many teachers don't know how to teach it or **measure** it.

4 Schools like to **prove** that students are learning. So they usually **focus on** teaching **logical** thinking and **facts,** which are easy to measure.

5 In contrast, creative thinking results in **original** answers— new answers that others don't usually think of. 2 + 2 = 4 if you are counting houses or apples. But if a student is counting 2 hungry foxes[1] + 2 fat chickens, then 2 + 2 = 2 happy foxes.

6 Most people think creative thinking is difficult to understand. They think it is hard to teach. They think they can't measure or grade it. But actually, it is not so complicated. Creative thinking is putting different ideas together in new ways.

7 Some skilled teachers teach creative thinking all the time in addition to teaching facts. They might teach students to measure the size of a room and also have them describe the size of a room ("It's the size of a racquetball court," or "It's big enough for a salsa band to practice"). They might teach facts about history and also have students discuss possible meanings of a painting from that time ("The red colors seem angry, and that is how people were feeling during that war."). They might even tell students to create stories about when 2 + 2 does not equal 4!

8 Measuring creative thinking is not easy, but it is possible. There is no one right or wrong answer to a creative thinking question. How can a teacher (or a computer!) know if "2 + 2 = 2" is a creative answer about foxes and chickens, or if it is simply a wrong answer? Teachers need to see students' reasons for their answers in order to measure creative thinking. The student with the creative answer to 2 + 2 is putting math together with her knowledge from English class. She just read a novel about farming and learned that foxes are often a big problem for small farms with chickens. Another student might say, "2 + 2 = 2 because I like the number two!" That is not creative thinking because that student is only saying what she likes.

2 + 2 = _____	Mahatma Gandhi . . .
○ 0	○ was an English politician.
○ 2	● led India to independence.
● 4	○ is the current president of India.
○ 8	

Yesterday, Youssef _____ his first year at university.	
● began	○ have begun
○ begin	○ begun

Examples of traditional test questions that have right and wrong answers.

9 Can schools teach creative thinking? Absolutely! And they must! Teaching logical thinking and facts is still important. We need math skills to make sure we don't spend more money than we have, for example. But many other questions in life do not have clear right and wrong answers. For example, how do you feed a family healthy food with only a small amount of money? Our schools need to prepare students for those tasks as well. Teaching creative thinking to our students helps them to solve more problems, and that helps the rest of us. The world needs creative thinkers to create the next iPhone. But we also need them to make dinner.

[1] **fox:** a wild animal, similar to a dog

Check (✓) the statement that best describes the main idea of the article. Use your notes to help you.

_____ a. You need to leave school to learn creative thinking skills.

_____ b. Math teachers need to teach more creative thinking because sometimes math has many interesting answers.

_____ c. Schools can and must teach creative skills because the world needs creative thinkers.

_____ d. Creative people should become teachers so that we can have more creative teaching in our schools.

DETAILS

1 Cross out the incorrect ending to each statement. Use your notes to help you.

1. Creative skills are important because _____ .

   a. they help us make new things

   b. they help us solve everyday problems

   c. they help us learn math better

2. Schools often don't teach creative thinking because _____ .

   a. students don't want to learn creative thinking

   b. teachers don't know how to teach it

   c. creative thinking is difficult to measure

3. Creative thinking __a__ .

   a. is impossible to understand

   b. is putting ideas together in new ways

   c. results in original answers

4. Creative thinking questions __a__ .

   a. usually have one correct answer

   b. have many possible answers

   c. ask you to put information together in new ways

2 Look at your notes and at your answers in the Preview section. Were any of your experiences in class similar to the classes that Martha Maddux described? Put a check (✓) next to your ideas that were similar to Maddux's. How did they help you understand the article?

Inferring Connections Between Statements and Examples

An **inference** is an educated guess about something that is not directly stated in the text. Writers often use examples to help readers understand a general statement. Sometimes readers need to **infer** the **connection between a general statement** (or definition) **and an example** in a text.

Look at the general statement and example and read the explanation.

- **General statement:** Creative thinking is putting different ideas together in new ways. *(paragraph 6)*

- **Example:** It's [the room is] the size of a racquetball court. *(paragraph 7)*

In this example of creative thinking, the student puts different ideas together in new ways: He describes the size of a room by putting together his knowledge of math and sports.

After reading the example closely, we can **infer its connection with the general statement,** and we get a better understanding of what creative thinking is.

1 Look at each example of creative thinking from the text and answer the question. Choose subjects from the box.

| Art | Business | English | Health | History | Math | Music | Science |

Example Of Creative Thinking	What Subject Knowledge Does The Student Put Together?
1. It's [the room is] big enough for a salsa band to practice. *(paragraph 7)*	
2. The red colors seem angry, and that is how people were feeling during that war. *(paragraph 7)*	
3. [Trying to] feed a family healthy food with only a small amount of money. *(paragraph 9)*	

2 Now discuss your answers with a partner. Point out sentences, words, or phrases in the paragraphs that helped you find the answers.

Discuss the questions with a partner. Then share your answers with the class.

1. Explain the creative answer to the fox and chicken question. Can you think of other possible answers to that question?

2. List the author's main idea and reasons for her opinion. Which of the author's reasons do you agree or disagree with? What other reasons do you have for your opinion?

▶ Go to **MyEnglishLab** to give your opinion about another question.

USE YOUR NOTES

Use your notes to support your answers with information from the reading.

READING TWO | Tips for Success in College: How to Be Creative

PREVIEW

1 **Look at the title of the reading on the next page. Read the first paragraph. Rewrite the title in your own words.**

_____

_____

2 **Look at the boldfaced words in the reading. Which words do you know the meaning of?**

1 "Skills for success in college" is a website with lots of advice for undergraduate students. Read the tips for how to be creative. As you read, guess the meanings of the words that are new to you. Remember to take notes on main ideas and details.

Tips for Success in College: How to Be Creative

1　As you begin college, you will receive lots of advice about how to be a good student; for example, always attend your classes, be organized, and get to know your teachers. This is all great advice, and it will certainly help you to succeed in your classes. But there is another kind of advice that is less common: advice to help you *use* what you learn in your classes to make something new and original!

2　The following tips may be the most important ones that you get: Tips on how to be creative.

Be curious

3　This is the most important tip, and there are so many ways to do it: If you walk the same way to school every day, take another path. List three classes that you don't know anything about at your school. Then take one. When your roommate invites you to a cricket match, say "YES!" Even if you don't know anything about cricket, go and learn about it. Being **curious** helps us learn new things. The more things we know about, the more possibilities we have for combining information in original ways. One common definition of creative thinking is **combining** information in new ways.

A cricket match

Take risks

4　Many of us are afraid of **taking risks** because we are afraid of making mistakes. This fear may come from parents or others who say, for example: "You are not very good at singing—you should keep quiet" or "I'm afraid you'll do it wrong." Stop listening to those people. Never fear making mistakes. Try out your Spanish with a native speaker! Write a song, even if you are not sure how to do it. Learn a new sport. Thomas Edison's first light bulbs didn't work. They were mistakes, but each one gave him the information he needed to create a light bulb that worked. Creative people take risks, but you won't take risks if you are afraid of making mistakes.

A ceramics class

Whatever you create, make a lot of it

5　Write lots of stories. Draw lots of pictures. Build lots of models. A **study** compared work from two college ceramics classes. One teacher told students, "make as many **pieces** as you can." The other teacher told students, "make the best piece you can." You can guess where the best work was—in the class where students made lots of pieces.

2 Compare your notes on main ideas and details with a partner's. How can you improve your notes next time?

🔎 Go to the **Pearson Practice English App** or **MyEnglishLab** for more vocabulary practice.

Listing Details in Notes

Listing can help you **group ideas into logical categories** as you read. Lists can help you remember groups of related ideas and examples in a text.

As you read, find ideas that fit into each list. Do not make complete sentences. Do not worry about perfect grammar. Write short phrases or words.

Look at this example from Reading One *(paragraphs 3 and 6)*:

3 Creative thinking is a very important skill. It helps us make new things. It also helps us **solve** everyday problems that don't have one easy answer. Yet traditional schools often don't **encourage** creative thinking. Many teachers don't know how to teach it or **measure** it.

6 Most people think creative thinking is difficult to understand. They think it is hard to teach. They think they can't measure or grade it. But actually, it is not so complicated. Creative thinking is putting different ideas together in new ways.

Reasons traditional schools don't teach creative thinking:
—teachers don't know how
—difficult to understand creative thinking
—hard to teach
—hard to measure

Don't just copy all of the sentences from whole paragraphs. Make sure each idea is short, is not repeated, and fits the list.

3 Creative thinking is a very important skill. It helps us make new things. It also helps us **solve** everyday problems that don't have one easy answer. Yet traditional schools often don't **encourage** creative thinking. Many teachers don't know how to teach it or **measure** it.

6 Most people think creative thinking is difficult to understand. They think it is hard to teach. They think they can't measure or grade it. But actually, it is not so complicated. Creative thinking is putting different ideas together in new ways.

Reasons traditional schools don't teach creative thinking:
—~~Many teachers think it is hard to teach or to measure.~~ (full sentence)
—~~hard to teach~~ (repeated idea)
—~~not so complicated~~ (doesn't fit list)

1 Reread paragraphs 7 and 8 from Reading One, and list the important information for each one.

Paragraph 7

7 Some skilled teachers teach creative thinking all the time in addition to teaching facts. They might teach students to measure the size of a room and also have them describe the size of a room ("It's the size of a racquetball court", or "It's big enough for a salsa band to practice"). They might teach facts about history and also have students discuss possible meanings of a painting from that time ("The red colors seem angry, and that is how people were feeling during that war"). They might even tell students to create stories about when 2 + 2 does not equal 4!

Ways to teach creativity & facts:
— Measure the size of a room or describe
— Discuss of a painting.
— Create stories about when 2+2 ≠ 4.

Paragraph 8

8 Measuring creative thinking is not easy, but it is possible. There is no one right or wrong answer to a creative thinking question. How can a teacher (or a computer!) know if "2 + 2 = 2" is a creative answer about foxes and chickens, or if it is simply a wrong answer? Teachers need to see students' reasons for their answers in order to measure creative thinking. The student with the creative answer to 2 + 2 is putting math together with her knowledge from English class. She just read a novel about farming and learned that foxes are often a big problem for small farms with chickens. Another student might say, "2 + 2 = 2 because I like the number two!" That is not creative thinking because that student is only saying what she likes.

How to tell if answer is creative:
— With student's reasons for their answer.
— Combining math with english.
— There is no right or wrong answer.

2 Look at Reading Two again. Make a list of examples from one of the tips.

🖱 Go to **MyEnglishLab** for more note-taking practice.

COMPREHENSION

Complete the sentence by checking (✓) all possible endings. Use your notes from Reading Two to help you.

In order to be creative, you should

_____ a. follow the tips on the website.

_____ b. stop going to your regular classes.

__✓__ c. learn about many different subjects.

__✓__ d. learn from mistakes.

_____ e. be very careful in everything you do.

_____ f. focus on one long project at a time.

1 Look at the final paragraph of Reading One again. Notice that the author uses *we, us,* and *our* several times in that paragraph. Underline all of the uses of *we, us,* and *our*.

Recognizing the Meaning of *We, Us,* and *Our*

Authors sometimes use **we, us,** and **our** to refer to "me, the author, and you, the reader," instead of saying "people (in general)." Using *we, us,* and *our* suggests that the **author and reader are similar,** or they are **part of the same community.** It tells the reader: "This is about you and me, not just other people."

we, us, or our Statement	What It Means
We need math skills to make sure we don't spend more money than we have, for example.	The author and the reader are similar. Both need to be careful of money.
Our schools need to prepare . . . Teaching creative thinking to our students . . . that helps the rest of us.	The author and the reader are both in communities where schools need to teach creativity.
But we also need them to make dinner.	The author and the reader both benefit from everyday creativity.

2 Work with a partner. Read two versions of the same text from paragraph 3 of Reading Two. Underline all of the uses of *we, us,* and *our* in Version 1. In Version 2, circle the words that are used instead of *we, us,* and *our*. How does Version 2 feel different from Version 1?

Version 1

Being curious helps us learn new things. The more things we know about, the more possibilities we have for combining information in original ways. One common definition of creative thinking is combining information in new ways.

Version 2

Being curious helps people learn new things. The more things they know about, the more possibilities they have for combining information in original ways. One common definition of creative thinking is combining information in new ways.

3 Fill in the blanks with *1* or *2* to create true statements about your reaction.

1. Version __1__ makes me feel like the author is talking to me.

2. Version __2__ feels like it is about other people, not me.

3. Version __1__ makes me feel like I have more in common with the author.

▶ Go to **MyEnglishLab** for more skill practice.

ORGANIZE

Look at Reading One (R1) and Reading Two (R2) again. Choose phrases from the list to complete the chart. The example answer is the only one that uses a phrase twice.

- take risks
- whatever you create, make a lot of it
- logical thinking and facts
- helps us make new things [and] solve everyday problems that don't have one easy answer
- college students
- be curious
- schools
- ~~teach creative thinking~~
- ~~combining ideas in new ways~~
- help you use what you learn in your classes to make something new and original

USE YOUR NOTES

Review your notes from Readings One and Two. Use the information in your notes to complete the chart.

	Reading One (R1)	Reading Two (R2)
1. Definition of creative thinking	combining ideas in new ways	combining ideas in new ways
2. Opposite of creative thinking	Logical thinking and facts.	✕
3. Why is creative thinking important?	helPs us make new things...	helP you use what ...
4. Who or what needs to change?	Schools	College students
5. What should they do?	teach creative thinking	a. be Curious b. Take risks. c. Whatever you create, make a lot.

SYNTHESIZE

Complete the conversation between Kristin and Joshua, two engineering students. Use ideas from Organize, as well as your own ideas.

JOSHUA: My design class is making me crazy. I think I'm going to drop it.

KRISTIN: But you are an engineering major! You have to take design.

JOSHUA: I know. But I don't understand what Professor Sousa wants me to do. I'm getting lots of Cs.

KRISTIN: Professor Sousa's class was also hard for me at first. He teaches some _logical thinking and facts_, but he also wants you to learn creative thinking.

JOSHUA: But I am not an artist!

KRISTIN: Creative thinking is important in *all* subjects, not just art. We need to learn creative thinking because _helps us make new things [and] solve everyday problems ..._.

JOSHUA: But I don't have time to learn creative thinking! We have to make 25 drawings every day!

KRISTIN: That is a perfect example of one "how to be creative" tip! To become more creative, you should: _Take risks._.

Professor Sousa doesn't give you bad grades for *bad* drawings. He gives you bad grades for *not enough* drawings.

JOSHUA: Really? So if I just make lots drawings, I can become more creative and get better grades?

KRISTIN: Exactly. Another tip for becoming more creative is: _be curious._.
For example, _help you use what you learn in your classes to make ..._.

JOSHUA: I see. This is helpful. What else did you learn?

KRISTIN: The last tip is: _Whatever you create, make a lot of it._.
For example, _Combining ideas in new ways._.

JOSHUA: I think I am beginning to understand. Thank you, Kris.

🔵 Go to **MyEnglishLab** to check what you learned.

3 FOCUS ON WRITING

VOCABULARY

REVIEW

Complete the sentences with the correct words or phrases from the box.

combining ✓	encourage ✓	logical ✓	pieces ✓	study ✓
create ✓	fact	measure ✓	prove ✓	take a risk ✓
curious ✓	focus on ✓	original ✓	solve ✓	

1. My favorite class is History and Literature of the American Revolution. ___Combining___ English and history in one class is a great idea!

2. Tell me more about your life. I am ___Curious___.

3. I know you think you are a terrible dancer. ___Take a risk___ and sign up for the class anyway!

4. Being bored can help you be more creative. That is what a recent ___study___ at the University of Central Lancashire found.

5. Each art student painted six ___Pieces___ for the final.

6. If you want to be an engineer, you need to be able to think in a ___logical___ way.

7. You may not like online education, but it is a ___Prove___ that more students are taking classes online every year.

8. Steve just wrote 14 ___original___ songs. He is a great songwriter!

9. My roommate is not doing well in his classes. We need to ___encourage___ him to do better.

10. For Creative Writing class, I have to ___Create___ a blog. I will put my writing there, and other students can comment on it.

11. My advisor tells me I have to ___focus on___ one major. But I can't decide. I love studying all different things!

12. I have to ___measure___ my paintings to see how many can fit on the wall.

13. I need to take the English entrance test tomorrow. If I ___Fact___ I can write an essay, I don't have to take English 1A.

14. Ben, can you help me ___Solve___ this problem? I can't get the computer to work with the projector.

EXPAND

1 Read the sentences on the left, paying attention to the boldfaced expressions. Then match the sentences on the left with the sentences that have similar meanings on the right.

_c_ 1. I **solved the problem.**

_d_ 2. I **had an idea.**

_a_ 3. I **realized** Pam was an artist.

_b_ 4. I **remembered** Pam was an artist.

_e_ 5. That film **made me think of** Pam.

a. This was always true, but I only just understood it.

b. I knew this, but I forgot until now.

c. First, it was difficult, but then I found an answer that worked.

d. I thought of something new.

e. I saw it and I thought of her.

2 Now complete each sentence with the appropriate boldfaced expression from the sentences above.

1. I saw the beautiful weather yesterday morning. Then I ___had an idea___. I called some friends, and we had a picnic at the beach.

2. I didn't understand what that woman said to me at first. Then I ___realized___ she was speaking Dutch, not English.

3. I thought there was nothing in the house for lunch. Then I ___remembered___ I had bought a frozen pizza last week.

4. I heard a new band called Japandroids today. They ___made me think of___ you. I think you will like them.

5. We lost our electricity on Christmas Day last year. At first, it was terrible! But we ___solved the problem___. We cooked dinner on the barbecue, and we used candles for light.

CREATE

APPLY Use the vocabulary and expressions in parentheses to complete the conversations between freshman students in the Student Lounge Discussion Area. For the last question, use new vocabulary from the unit. Your partner will try to answer your question.

STUDENT LOUNGE DISCUSSION AREA

Use this discussion area to get to know each other and to ask each other for advice about your classes.

Valencia Scott 4:45 P.M. March 24, 2019

Hey everyone! Help! I am having trouble in ENG 145. We have to write research papers. I went to a high school for the arts. We wrote lots of poetry and stories, but this seems completely different. Any advice?

Sebastian Duran _____ (your name) 7:32 P.M. March 24, 2019

(logical thinking / facts / studies)

Hi Valencia! Yes, ENG 145 essays are not very creative. I learned to write research papers in high school, though, so I understand them.

Try to use _logical thinking_ . Facts and Studies will help you supporting the research Papers.

Shakeam Clements 2:31 A.M. March 25, 2019

Is anyone having the same problem as me? I want to study art, but my counselor tells me I have to also study math and history. I am in college now, and I want to do what I want! Why do I need to take all these other classes that are not about art?

Sebastian Duran _____ (your name) 11:05 A.M. March 25, 2019

(focus on / curious / realize / combine)

Hey Shakeam: I used to ask the same question. Math and history are super important for artists, too!

Try to _focus on them_ . It is curious how learning about the history would help you think different, I realize it is a good idea to study a little bit of all to combine at the end with your creativity.

Sebastian Duran _____ (your name) 11:25 A.M. March 25, 2019

Can anyone help me solve this problem? _I broke my book code, so that delays me, however, I'm still doing homework but it takes too much time. Is there something I can do to get a new code?_

🔺 **Go to the Pearson Practice English App** or **MyEnglishLab** for more vocabulary practice.

1 **Read the paragraph. Underline the verbs that tell about the past. Then answer the questions.**

> My mother helped me learn to keep working on problems. She always told me, "There are no mistakes, only lessons." In my first year of college, I failed math. I wanted to quit college. When she talked to me, I remembered all of the reasons for going to college. We looked at my math tests and homework together. She helped me see which things were most difficult for me. When I took math again, I went to extra study sessions, and I passed with a B+! I also finished college. That was ten years ago. Today, I don't ask my mom for advice as much. But her lessons are still with me.

1. How is the simple past formed for most verbs (regular verbs)? *adding -ed.*
2. Which past verbs are irregular? What is the base form of each one of these verbs? *Verb with a different pattern.*

Simple Past

1. When we talk about things that **started and finished in the past,** we use the **simple past.**	I **failed** math last year. I **went** to extra study sessions.	
	Base Form	**Simple Past**
2. To form the simple past for **regular** verbs, add **-ed** to the base form of the verb.	help talk	help**ed** talk**ed**
If the verb ends in **-e,** add only **-d.**	live arrive	live**d** arrive**d**
If the verb ends in a consonant **+ y,** change the **y** to **i** and then add **-ed.**	study try	stud**ied** tr**ied**
3. Many verbs have **irregular** past forms. Here are some of these irregular verbs.	be begin come do have get go make meet say take think write	**was / were** **began** **came** **did** **had** **got** **went** **made** **met** **said** **took** **thought** **wrote**
4. In negative statements, use: **didn't** (**did not**) + base form of the verb, except with the verb **be.**	need go be	**didn't** need **didn't** go **wasn't / weren't**

2 **Complete the student's blog about his first week at art school, using the simple past forms of the verbs in parentheses.**

Andreas's Art Adventures

Hello everyone!

I ___*got*___ into art school! I am now a student at the University of Art and Design!
1. (get)

Classes _____ one week ago, and I am so busy!
2. (begin)

Here are a few highlights from my first week:

- I _____ my department head. He _____ at Disney for many years!
  3. (meet)   **4. (work)**

  He _____ that art school is a lot of hard work. (He _____ right.)
  5. (say)   **6. (be)**

- I _____ to my first drawing class and _____ drawing ellipses for
  7. (go)   **8. (practice)**

  one hour! I think I _____ 500! I am getting better, but my teacher says
  9. (make)

  they are still not good enough.

- I _____ figure drawing homework for 15 hours on Sunday!
  10. (do)

- I _____ my favorite artist (Andy Warhol) and _____ a paper about him.
  11. (research)   **12. (write)**

- I _____ of 25 ways to use a paperclip. (I don't know why we
  13. (think)

  _____ this, but I will find out this week.)
  14. (do)

- I _____ a song and _____ it for my English class. (I _____
  15. (write)   **16. (play)**   **17. (not / be)**

  excited about this, but I _____ a risk!!)
  18. (take)

- I _____ the names, dates, and artists of 25 Renaissance paintings.
  19. (learn)

- I _____ much!
  20. (not / sleep)

Thank you all for your emails and messages! I will try to post again soon.

Andreas

ellipses

3 Read a page of Cory's application for college. Complete the sentences in the simple past. Choose the correct verb from the box. One verb will be used twice.

Application p. 1

Name: Cory Hansen   **Date of birth:** January 27, 2000

Schools and dates
Crocker Elementary School   September 2005–June 2011
Jerry Brown Middle School   September 2011–June 2014
Oakland Technical High School   September 2014–June 2018
De Anza Community College   January 2019–present

Last semester's classes and final grades
English   A
Spanish   A–
Biology   B

Clubs
JBMS Skateboarding Club   2012–2014
Oakland Tech Chess Club   2014–2017

Sports
Oakland Tech Varsity Football   2016–2018

| attend | finish | get | go | join | play | start |

1. Cory _____finished_____ high school in June 2018.

2. He (not) _____ to school from June 2018 until January 2019.

3. He _____ taking classes at De Anza Community College in January 2019.

4. He _____ an A in English.

5. He (not) _____ an A in Biology.

6. He _____ the JBMS Skateboarding Club in 2012.

7. He _____ Jerry Brown Middle School from 2011 until 2014.

8. He _____ varsity football for Oakland Tech from 2016 until 2018.

🔊 Go to the **Pearson Practice English App** or **MyEnglishLab** for more grammar practice. Check what you learned in **MyEnglishLab**.

In this unit, you read about the differences between creative thinking and logical thinking. You also read some suggestions for how to be creative.

Now you are going to *write a paragraph about a time you (or someone you know) used creative thinking to solve a problem.* Introduce the story. Describe the problem. Tell how you (or someone else) used creative thinking (being curious, combining ideas, taking risks, making a lot of something) to solve it. Use the vocabulary and grammar from the unit.

For an alternative writing topic see p. 51.

PREPARE TO WRITE: Charting a Writing Prompt

Charting your writing prompt can help you make sure you answer all the parts of a question when you write. The chart below has one row for each part of the question you will answer in your paragraph.

1. Introduce the story	*Being curious helped me solve a big problem for my grandfather.*
2. Describe the problem	*My grandfather can't type emails or texts because he has very shaky hands.*
3. Tell how you (or someone else) used creative thinking (being curious, combining ideas, taking risks, making a lot of something) to solve it.	*I was curious about iPads because so many people love them.* *I found the VoiceText app.* *I gave it to my grandfather.*

Look at the chart and think about a time you or someone else used creative thinking to solve a problem. The problem might be a difficult assignment in school, or it might be an everyday problem. Complete the chart. Then discuss your answers with a partner.

1. Introduce the story	
2. Describe the problem	
3. Tell how you (or someone else) used creative thinking (being curious, combining ideas, taking risks, making a lot of something) to solve it.	

WRITE

Writing a Complete Paragraph

A complete paragraph usually has **three parts:** a topic sentence, supporting sentences, and a conclusion. In this assignment, do the following in each part:

- **Topic sentence:** Introduce the topic and make a general statement. (This may be one or two sentences.)

- **Supporting sentences:** Explain the problem and the creative process you introduced in the topic sentence.

- **Conclusion:** Tell the end of the story, or make a final comment about the story.

1 Read the paragraph. Put brackets [ ] around the three parts of the paragraph.

Emmet is a musician who learned that brainstorming is a good way to find creative ideas. Nobody ever paid attention to Emmet's posters for his band because they were just black and white words. His friend, Jamika, told him he needed a picture on the poster, so he added a photo. But the poster was still not very interesting. She told him to make 25 different posters in one hour. Emmet thought she was crazy, but he followed her advice. He found out that it was fun to make so many posters quickly, and he got many new ideas. In the end, he created a great design that his band still uses.

2 Each paragraph is missing one part. Circle the name of the part that is missing.

Paragraph 1

Being curious helped me solve a big problem for my grandfather. He can't type emails or texts because he has very shaky hands. I was curious about iPads because so many people love them. I borrowed my friend's iPad and looked at all the games and other apps on the screen. I played a few games and learned about a few apps. But the best app was VoiceText. I touched it, I talked, then all of my words came on the screen. It was like someone else was typing my words! It made me think of my grandfather. He can't type, but he can talk!

What is missing?

a. Topic sentence
b. Supporting sentences
c. Conclusion

Paragraph 2

During the first class, she got angry with students because they looked at their phones during class. For the second class, she asked who had Twitter accounts. Half of the class raised their hands. She put us in pairs so that each pair had a phone with a Twitter account. She told us to search for the hashtag #hist232 in Twitter. We did, and we found a history question from her! We discussed the question with our partners, then tweeted the answer with the hashtag #hist232. We looked at all our answers on the big screen at the front of the class. We had interesting conversations with each other on Twitter and in person. This teacher combined her knowledge of history, Twitter, and young students to create that fun exercise. After that day, history was always fun, and the teacher didn't get angry anymore.

What is missing?

a. Topic sentence
b. Supporting sentences
c. Conclusion

(continued on next page)

Paragraph 3

> Last semester in English, I took a big risk and wrote a very creative essay about my grandmother. My teacher loved it and told me it was very creative. After that, I began to take more risks in my writing. Now I am a better writer, and I also enjoy it more.

What is missing?

a. Topic sentence

b. Supporting sentences

c. Conclusion

3 Now write the first draft of your paragraph about a time you (or someone else) used creative thinking to solve a problem. Start with your topic sentence, follow with supporting sentences explaining the problem and the process, and then finish with a conclusion. Use the ideas in your chart on page 46 to help you write your paragraph.

REVISE: Using Visuals to Support Writing

Sometimes words do not communicate the whole message in a piece of writing. **Visuals** like pictures or charts can be useful, too. As you revise, use your creative skills to think of visuals to include that will help you communicate better with your readers.

1 Read the revisions of two paragraphs from the previous section and finish the sentence below each one.

Paragraph 1

> Being curious helped me solve a big problem for my grandfather. He can't type emails or texts because he has very shaky hands. I was curious about iPads because so many people love them. I borrowed my friend's iPad and looked at all the games and other apps on the screen. I played a few games and learned about a few apps. But the best app was VoiceText. I touched it, I talked, then all of my words came on the screen. It was like someone else was typing my words! It made me think of my grandfather. He can't type, but he can talk! My cousins and I bought him an iPad with VoiceText, and now he can text or email us any time!

The picture gives the reader more information about _____ .

Paragraph 2

My history teacher last semester used a very creative way to teach our class. During the first class, she got angry with students because they looked at their phones during class. For the second class, she asked who had Twitter accounts. Half of the class raised their hands. She put us in pairs so that each pair had a phone with a Twitter account. She told us to search for the hashtag #hist232 in Twitter. We did, and we found a history question from her! We discussed the question with our partners, then tweeted the answer with the hashtag #hist232. We looked at all our answers on the big screen at the front of the class. We had interesting conversations with each other on Twitter and in person. This teacher combined her knowledge of history, Twitter, and young students to create that fun exercise. After that day, history was always fun, and the teacher didn't get angry anymore.

Results for #hist232 · March 5

@HistoryBuff · March 5
What helps economies grow? Give examples of specific countries. Use #hist232.

@ShutIn1 · March 5
Oil (Norway, Saudi Arabia) #hist232

@TaniMan · March 5
#hist232 education for girls (India).

@CocoMonroe · March 5
smaller population-China #hist232

The picture gives the reader more information about _____ .

2 Work with a partner. Read the paragraph. Then discuss the two questions.

A man in Denmark used creative thinking to get a job. Getting a job is often a big problem to solve. This man wrote his name and a short résumé in the snow in a parking lot. Then he lay down on the ground next to the résumé. The people in the office building looked out the window and saw him with his résumé. I think he took a big risk! Usually people dress very well for job interviews, and they make their résumés look very professional. I don't know if he got a job, but his idea was very original.

1. What will the reader be curious to know more about?

2. What visuals can the writer add to give the reader more information?

3 Now go back to the first draft of your paragraph.

1. What will your reader be curious to know more about? What visuals can you add to give more information?

2. Revise your paragraph, trying to use the grammar and some of the vocabulary items in this unit.

🔼 Go to **MyEnglishLab** for more skill practice.

EDIT: Writing the Final Draft

APPLY Write the final draft of your paragraph and submit it to your teacher. Carefully edit it for grammatical and mechanical errors, such as spelling, capitalization, and punctuation. Consider how to apply the vocabulary, grammar, and writing skills from the unit. Use the checklist to help you.

FINAL DRAFT CHECKLIST

☐ Does your paragraph tell about a time you or someone else used creative thinking?

☐ Does it have a topic sentence?

☐ Does your paragraph have supporting sentences that tell about the problem and the creative thinking process?

☐ Does it have a conclusion that finishes the story or adds a comment to the story?

☐ Does it have a picture, chart, or other element that helps the reader understand the message better?

☐ Do you use past verbs correctly?

☐ Do you use new vocabulary that you learned in this unit?

ALTERNATIVE WRITING TOPIC

APPLY In Reading Two, you read about the importance of making mistakes in order to be creative. Write a paragraph about a time you made a big mistake. Did you fear mistakes afterwards, or did you learn from your mistake? Use vocabulary and grammar from the unit.

_____

_____

_____

_____

_____

CHECK WHAT YOU'VE LEARNED

Check (✔) the outcomes you've met and vocabulary you've learned. Put an X next to the skills and vocabulary you still need to practice.

Learning Outcomes

☐ Infer connections between statements and examples

☐ List details in notes

☐ Recognize the meaning of *we, us,* and *our*

☐ Use the simple past

☐ Use visuals to support writing

☐ Write a complete paragraph

Vocabulary

☐ combining

☐ create AWL

☐ curious

☐ encourage

☐ fact

☐ logical AWL

☐ measure

☐ original

☐ piece

☐ prove

☐ solve

☐ study

Multi-word Units

☐ focus on AWL

☐ take risks

↖ Go to **MyEnglishLab** to watch a video about study skills, access the Unit Project, and take the Unit 2 Achievement Test.

LEARNING OUTCOMES

> Infer future situations
> Take notes using a time line
> Identify the sequence of events

> Use comparative adjectives
> Give explanations
> Write a well-organized paragraph

Go to **MyEnglishLab** to check what you know.

Making Money

1 FOCUS ON THE TOPIC

1. Copying money becomes easier as copier technology becomes better. What equipment do people need to copy money?

2. What is the best way to stop people from copying money?

3. How can you tell real money from copied (fake) money?

READING ONE | Making Money

VOCABULARY

When you read a story, there may be many words you don't know. Often you can still understand the story, and sometimes you can even understand these new words.

1 Read the story. See if you can understand it even though some words are missing.

One day last year, some New York City sanitation workers were very surprised when they emptied a garbage can. Along with the banana peels and empty Coke cans, they found $18 million in new _____bills_____ .
1.

Who would throw out all that money? The workers felt that something was not right, so they called the United States Bureau of Engraving and Printing, the part of the government that makes paper money. The Bureau employees said that the money looked real but that, in fact, it wasn't. It was _____fake_____—and not legal. The garbage must have belonged
2.
to _____Counterfeiters_____ , people who make money that is not real. They use both old and new
3.
_____equipment_____ , or ways, to make money. For example, some make the money by using
4.
printing presses, big machines similar to those for making books or newspapers; others use _____Scanners_____ and other computer _____technologies_____ . These counterfeiters probably
5.   6.
printed a lot of money and weren't happy with how it looked. Maybe the drawing wasn't good enough. Or maybe the _____ink_____ was not exactly the right color. So they threw it
7.
all out.

The people at the Bureau of Engraving and Printing were mad. Copying money is _____illegal_____ . Counterfeiters who get caught can go to prison for a long time. The
8.
people at the Bureau work very hard to _____prevent_____ people from making fake money.
9.

The Bureau never caught these counterfeiters. Nobody knows if they were able to make another $18 million that looked _____completely_____ real.
10.

Now answer the questions. Then discuss your answers with a classmate.

1. What did the New York City sanitation workers find?

   They found $18 million cash.

2. Who threw out all that money?

   The counterfeiters

2 Read the story again. Work with a partner. Use information in the story to guess the missing words. Write your guesses on the lines.

3 Now read the list of words and their definitions. Then read the story again and use these words to complete it. Write the new vocabulary words above your own guesses.

✓**bills:** pieces of paper money

✓**completely:** 100 percent

✓**counterfeiters:** people who make money that is not real

✓**equipment:** machines and tools used to make other things

✓**fake:** not real

✓**illegal:** not legal; against the law

✓**ink:** a colored liquid in pens and printers, used for writing and printing

✓**prevent:** to stop something from happening before it happens

✓**scanners:** machines that copy pictures from paper onto a computer

✓**technologies:** ways to make things, usually with some kind of machine

▶ Go to the **Pearson Practice English App** or **MyEnglishLab** for more vocabulary practice.

The following magazine article is about how some counterfeiters make fake money. It is also about how the U.S. government tries to stop counterfeiting.

Work in a small group. Make a list of things that you think the government might do to make money harder to copy.

1. _Use special paper._

2. _____

3. _____

4. _____

5. _____

Read the article. Create a chart like the one below to take notes.

▶ TAKE NOTES	
Main Ideas	**Details**
Counterfeiting easier today with new tech machines	scanners
	copiers
	computers
	printers

🔵 Go to **MyEnglishLab** to view example notes.

MAKING MONEY

By Amelia Laidlaw

1 It was so quick and easy. A fourteen-year-old boy in Scottsdale, Arizona, pulled out a $50 **bill** and put it onto his school's new **scanner**. Then he printed ten copies of his $50 bill on a color copier. Within seconds he changed $50 into $550, and he was ready to go shopping.

2 Thirty-five years ago only a few people had the skills or **equipment** to make counterfeit money. Good computers, copiers, scanners, cameras, and printers are cheaper than ever, so today anyone can "make" money. The people using today's **technology** to make **fake** money are called casual **counterfeiters**, and like the fourteen-year-old in Arizona, they can be anywhere.

3 The number of fake bills made by casual counterfeiters on their home or office computer is growing fast. Although there is no way to **completely prevent** counterfeiting, in the 1990s and 2000s, the U.S. government made some changes to U.S. bills that made casual counterfeiting more difficult.

4 One change they made was to put very, very small words, called microprint, in hidden places on the bill. These words are only 6/1,000 inch. No one can read them without a magnifying glass, a special glass that makes things look bigger. And they are too small to come out clearly on a copier. If someone copies a bill that has microprint and you look at the copy through a magnifying glass, you see only black lines instead of microprinted words.

5 Another change the government made to U.S. bills was to use special color-changing **ink**.

6 Money printed with color-changing ink looks green from one direction and yellow from another. Home computers cannot use color-changing ink. So any **illegal** copies of money from a home computer have normal ink that is easy to notice.

7 The third change was to add a special line from the top to the bottom of each new bill. When you hold a $20 bill up to the light for example, you can see the line has the words "USA twenty" in it. The line turns red if you put it under a special UV (ultraviolet) light. Fake bills printed on regular paper do not have this special line. You can tell they are fake by holding them up to the light or by putting them under UV light.

8 All these changes to the U.S. bills help. The United States has less counterfeit money than any other country in the world. Less than .01 percent of U.S. money is counterfeit. However, the Bureau of Engraving and Printing can't slow down now. It needs to always stay a step or two ahead of the counterfeiters. The most recent step they took was adding a 3D image to the U.S. $100 bill. But technology improves every year for both the Bureau and the counterfeiters. Today, home copiers can't print microprinted words or 3D images. But in a few years, who knows?

1 Each statement tells the main idea of a paragraph in the article. Read each statement, then write the correct paragraph number next to it. Use your notes to help you.

Paragraph

a. Casual counterfeiting is becoming a big problem, and the government is fighting the problem. _3_

b. Using color-changing ink is a way to prevent counterfeiting. _6_

c. A child can easily copy paper money. _1_

d. The government must keep changing the bills to prevent counterfeiting. _8_

e. Putting microprint on bills helps prevent counterfeiting. _4_

f. New technology makes casual counterfeiting possible. _2_

g. The special lines on U.S. paper money help prevent counterfeiting. _7_

2 Check (✓) the statement that best describes the main idea of the whole article. Use your notes to help you.

_____ a. It's easier to counterfeit money today than it was thirty-five years ago, especially with the right equipment.

_✓_ b. The government has several ways to try to prevent counterfeiting.

_____ c. Better home computers and printers made counterfeiting easier, so the U.S. government changed the bills to make counterfeiting more difficult.

1 Complete the statements with information from the article. Use your notes to help you.

1. Thirty-five years ago, only a few people had the _skills_ or _equipment_ to make fake money.

2. One way to prevent counterfeiters from making fake money on a _____ or _____ is to use microprinted words.

3. Bills have a _line_ that you can see if you hold them up to the light.

4. A boy in Scottsdale, Arizona, used his school's scanner to make _ten_ copies of a $_50_ bill.

5. Money printed with color-changing ink looks green from one direction and _yellow_ from another.

6. Most other countries in the world have _more_ counterfeit money than the United States.

2 Look at your notes and at your answers in Preview. How did they help you understand the article?

MAKE INFERENCES 🔍

Inferring Future Situations

An **inference** is an educated guess about something that is not directly stated in the text. Readers often use information in a text to **infer what will happen in the future.**

Look at the example and read the explanation.

- In the future, more people will make fake money.

Is this true? Choose the best answer.

a. Probably true, based on what we read in the article.

b. There is not enough information in the article to know if this statement is true.

*(The best answer is **a**.)*

In paragraph 2, we learn that anyone with basic computer equipment can be a counterfeiter.
In paragraph 3, we learn that the number of counterfeit bills is growing fast.
In paragraph 7, we learn that technology improves every year.

So, from all this information, we can **infer** that in the future, the **number of casual counterfeiters will continue to grow** because it's easy, and computers are getting cheaper and better.

---

1 **Read each prediction. Can you tell if it is true or not from the information in the article? Circle the best answer. Refer to the paragraphs in parentheses.**

1. Copiers will not be able to copy color-changing ink. *(paragraphs 5 and 7)*

   (a.) True, based on what we read in the article.

   b. There is not enough information in the article to know if this statement is true.

2. Copiers will be able to copy microprinted words. *(paragraph 7)*

   a. True, based on what we read in the article.

   (b.) There is not enough information in the article to know if this statement is true.

3. The Bureau of Engraving and Printing will try to learn about new home computer technology before people buy it. *(paragraph 7)*

   a. True, based on what we read in the article.

   (b.) There is not enough information in the article to know if this statement is true.

4. The police will be able to catch most counterfeiters. *(paragraph 7)*

   a. True, based on what we read in the article.

   (b.) There is not enough information in the article to know if this statement is true.

2 **Now discuss your answers with a partner. Point out sentences, words, or phrases in the paragraphs that helped you find the answers.**

USE YOUR NOTES

Use your notes to support your answers with information from the reading.

Work in groups of three. Read the questions. Discuss your ideas. Then choose one person in your group to report the ideas to the class.

1. Review the changes the U.S. government made to bills to prevent people from counterfeiting. Which of them seems the most effective to you? Why?

2. What else can the Bureau of Engraving and Printing do to stay a step ahead of casual counterfeiters?

🔵 Go to **MyEnglishLab** to give your opinion about another question.

READING TWO | I Made It Myself

PREVIEW

1 Look at the title of the reading and the picture below. Answer the question.

What do you think "it" refers to in the title?

Bills.

2 Look at the boldfaced words in the reading. Which words do you know the meaning of?

nervous, breaking the law and arrest.

READ

Before computers and copiers, counterfeiting was not easy. You needed the artistic skill to draw a copy of a bill, a large printing press, and the skill to use it. Counterfeiting often took a lot of time, planning, and hard work. And the results were excellent. The counterfeit money looked and felt like the real thing. Today, professional counterfeiters still make fake money the old-fashioned way—on printing presses.

1 Now read this story of one of these professional counterfeiters. As you read, guess the meanings of the words that are new to you. Remember to take notes on main ideas and details.

I Made it Myself

By Michael Landress

1 It took months of planning, of trying to find the perfect paper, of mixing and remixing ink to get the right color, of printing and reprinting to get the right feel, but I did it. I made a perfect copy of a $100 bill.

2 During the days, I did regular print jobs at the shop. Then every evening at five o'clock, I sent my workers home, hoping no one would ask why I stayed late. I pulled out the special paper, ink, and other equipment I hid away the night before and slowly, carefully, worked until the sun came up. I didn't have time to sleep. I was too **nervous** to sleep anyway. As I worked, I worried about the Secret Service[1] agents coming to get me. In the beginning, as I prepared the paper, I said to myself, "I'm just printing little blue and red hairlines on paper. They can't **arrest** me for that. I'm not **breaking the law**." Then as I printed the numbers, I said, "I'm just printing small numbers in four corners of a page. They can't arrest me for *this*. What I'm doing isn't illegal." Finally, as I got closer and closer to printing something they could arrest me for, I began to wonder, "Is this really that bad? Who am I hurting? I'm making myself a few thousand dollars so I can take my son and move to the beach. I'm just trying to do my best for my family. Is that so wrong?"

3 After about three weeks of slow work, I finally printed out a whole sheet of $100 bills. I took out the magnifying glass and studied my work. "No. Oh, Ben, no. Ben, you don't look right," I said aloud to the empty shop. The portrait[2] of Ben Franklin on the front of the bill just didn't look right. To most people, he probably looked like the one on the real bill. However, I could see that it wasn't a perfect copy. I needed it to be perfect. So, slowly, painfully, I started over.

4 A week later, I was printing the last of the bills. I didn't hear them come in because of the noise of the press. I just looked up from studying the now-perfect portraits of Ben Franklin to see a gun at my head and hear the Secret Service agent say, "Just like getting caught with your hand in the cookie jar, huh, Mike?"

---

[1] **Secret Service:** government agency that tries to prevent crime, including counterfeiting

[2] **portrait:** a drawing or painting of someone's head

2 Compare your notes on main ideas and details with a partner's. How can you improve your notes next time?

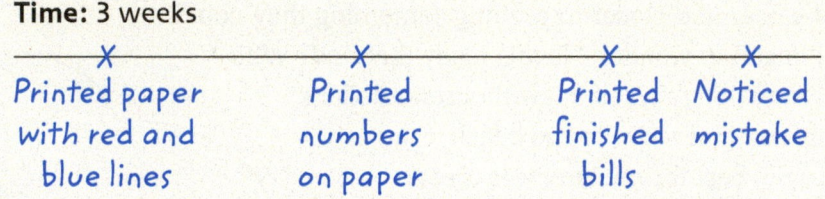 Go to the **Pearson Practice English App** or **MyEnglishLab** for more vocabulary practice.

NOTE-TAKING SKILL

Taking Notes Using a Time Line

Making a **time line** can help you to **understand and remember the events in a story**. Sometimes the story will give you the events in the order they happen. But sometimes the events are discussed out of order. Making a time line can help you understand.

Example

Reread paragraphs 2 and 3. These paragraphs describe the activities Michael Landress did to make the first batch of money.

Now read the time line of the printing of the first batch of money. See how the time line is simply short notes, not full sentences, of the main events of this paragraph.

Time: 3 weeks

| Printed paper with red and blue lines | Printed numbers on paper | Printed finished bills | Noticed mistake |

1 Below is a list of the events from paragraphs 2, 3, and 4, not necessarily in order. Put a check (✓) next to the events you think are important to put on the time line. Choose six events.

☐ Did regular printing jobs   ☐ Noticed a mistake

☐ Was nervous   ☐ Sent workers home

☐ Printed numbers on paper   ☐ Started over

☐ Printed complete $100 bill first time   ☐ Printed second version of complete $100 bills

☐ Pulled out a magnifying glass   ☐ Prepared the paper

2 Now place these events onto the time line below.

Time: 4 weeks

3 Reread paragraph 4. What key event could you add to the above time line?

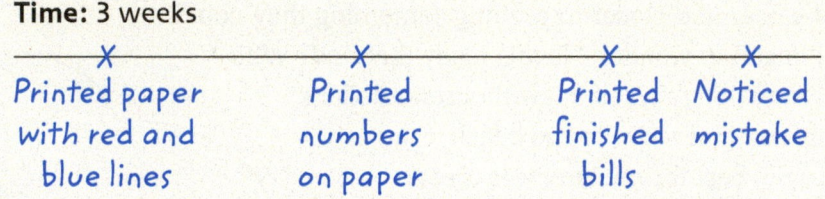 Go to **MyEnglishLab** for more note-taking practice.

Answer the questions. Use your notes from Reading Two to help you. Discuss your answers with a partner.

1. How long did the first batch of bills take to complete before Michael Landress noticed his mistake?

   _____

2. How long did the second batch of bills take to complete before he was caught?

   _____

3. In paragraph 3, Landress says, "No. Oh, Ben, no." Who is Ben? What was wrong? How does Landress feel?

   _____

   _____

4. Why does Landress think it's OK to counterfeit money?

   _____

   _____

5. In paragraph 4, Landress says, "I didn't hear them come in because of the noise of the press." Who does "them" refer to? What were they coming to do? Why?

   _____

   _____

6. The story ends with "Just like getting caught with your hand in the cookie jar, huh, Mike?" What do you think "getting caught with your hand in the cookie jar" means?

   _____

   _____

READING SKILL

1 **Look at Reading Two again, and think about how much time the events in the story took. Underline the phrases in the story that help you know how much time each event took.**

Identifying the Sequence of Events

When telling a story, a writer uses **time phrases** to **show the passage of time** between plot elements. Recognizing these time phrases helps readers understand the story's sequence of events.

Look at the examples and read the explanations:

- **"It took months** of planning. . . ." *(paragraph 1)*

This gives an overall time structure to the story.

- **"During the days**. . . ." *(paragraph 2)*

This shows that the paragraph describes actions that went on over a long period of time.

2 Work with a partner. Identify two additional time phrases and discuss how they move the story along.

1. Time phrase in paragraph 3: _____

   What does it tell us? _____

2. Time phrase in paragraph 4: _____

   What does it tell us? _____

▶ Go to **MyEnglishLab** for more skill practice.

CONNECT THE READINGS 🔍

ORGANIZE

There are two kinds of counterfeiters: casual counterfeiters, like the fourteen-year-old boy in Scottsdale, Arizona, and professional counterfeiters, like Michael Landress.

Based on Reading One (R1) and Reading Two (R2), compare the two kinds of counterfeiters. Look at the list of phrases. Then write each phrase in the correct box in the chart. Some phrases may be used twice.

> **USE YOUR NOTES**
>
> Review your notes from Readings One and Two. Use the information in your notes to complete the chart.

- ~~artistic skills~~
- printing presses
- color-changing ink
- line doesn't change color with UV light
- a print shop
- special paper
- computer printer ink

- know how to run a printing press
- scanners
- microprint looks like black lines
- ink is not color-changing
- home computer skills
- computer printer paper
- no special line

	Casual Counterfeiters (R1)	Professional Counterfeiters (R2)
1. What kind of skills do they need?		*artistic skills*
2. What tools, equipment, and materials do they need?		
3. How can you tell their bills are fake?		

SYNTHESIZE

The U.S. government does a lot to prevent counterfeiting, but it has different ways of catching casual and professional counterfeiters.

Complete the two memos regarding counterfeit prevention. Use information from Organize.

1.

U.S. Bureau of Counterfeit Prevention

To: Shopkeepers in the Washington, D.C. area

Re: Catching casual counterfeiters

We are finding many counterfeit bills in the Washington, D.C. area this month. These bills are made with home computer technology and are easy to recognize. Please help us to catch counterfeiters.

Tips for recognizing counterfeit bills:

1. (paper / feel) _The paper feels different._ _____

2. (special line) _____

3. (microprint) _____

4. (*your idea*) _____

5. (*your idea*) _____

2.

U.S. Bureau of Counterfeit Prevention

To: All U.S. agents

Re: Professional counterfeiter investigation

Professionally-made counterfeit bills are showing up in the New York, Philadelphia, and Boston areas. We cannot rely on shopkeepers to help us find these counterfeiters because the bills are very well done and difficult to recognize as counterfeit.

Very few people have the equipment, materials, and skills to counterfeit this well. It is important that we find those people who have the special counterfeiting equipment and materials.

Here is a list of questions we need to answer in order to begin our investigation:

1. (printing presses) _Who owns printing presses?_ _____

2. (ink) _____

3. (*your idea*) _____

4. (*your idea*) _____

🔵 Go to **MyEnglishLab** to check what you learned.

3 FOCUS ON WRITING

REVIEW

1 The following sentences do not make sense. In each sentence, cross out the boldfaced word or phrase. Above it, write the correct antonym (opposite) from the box so the sentence makes sense.

~~arrested~~	~~completely~~	~~illegal~~	prevent
~~breaking the law~~	~~counterfeiter~~	~~nervous~~	

1. When I got the $100 bill, I noticed that the paper didn't feel right. "Is it possible that a *counterfeiter* ~~government worker~~ made this?" I asked myself.

2. The police officer took the woman by her arms, put her in the police car, and took her to the police station. He ~~set her **free.**~~ *arrested*

3. His legs were shaking. His heart was going very fast. His lips were dry. He felt very **relaxed** *nervous* as he gave the bank the counterfeit money.

4. The fire destroyed everything in the shop. The expensive designer clothing and all the jewelry were ~~**not at all**~~ destroyed. *completely*

5. It's ~~**not a problem**~~ to make photocopies of money. Teachers should use real bills when they *breaking the law* teach students about American money. *illegal* b. the. L

6. Take that dollar bill out of the copier! You are **following the law!**

7. New Zealand, Brazil, and China now use special plastic instead of paper for their bills to ~~**make**~~ counterfeiting **easier.** *Prevent*

2 Complete the sentences with the words from the box.

bill	equipment	fake	ink	scanner	technology

1. Printing presses, copiers, scanners, and magnifying glasses are different kinds of

   _____ used in counterfeiting.

2. Even new printing presses use _____ that is over 500 years old.

3. I want to be able to put this magazine photograph on my computer screen. I need a(n)

   _____ .

4. Don't be fooled by that "Rolex" watch. It's cheap because it's _____ .

5. I need change. Can I have four quarters for a one-dollar _____ ?

6. Professor Porter always corrected my papers with purple _____ since she didn't like red.

EXPAND

1 Money isn't the only counterfeit product. Look at the pictures of other counterfeit products. How can you tell that these products are fake? Discuss with a partner.

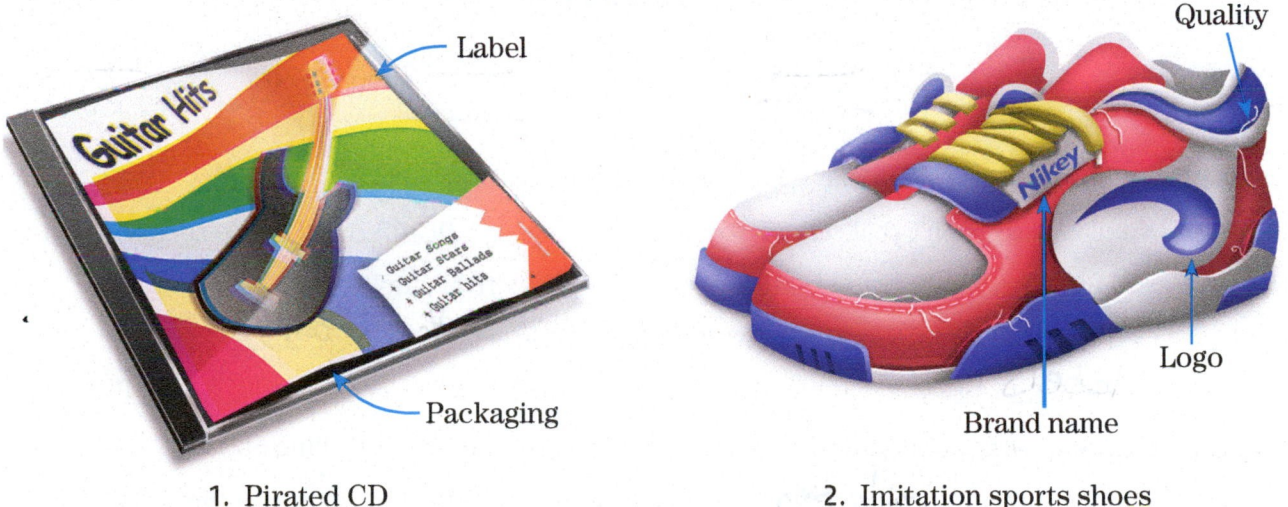

1. Pirated CD

2. Imitation sports shoes

2 Read about Nicola and Jim, and look at the picture.

Nicola and Jim are at the flea market, a market where people sell lots of cheap products. Nicola is surprised that there are so many cheap designer products. Jim knows that these products are all fake.

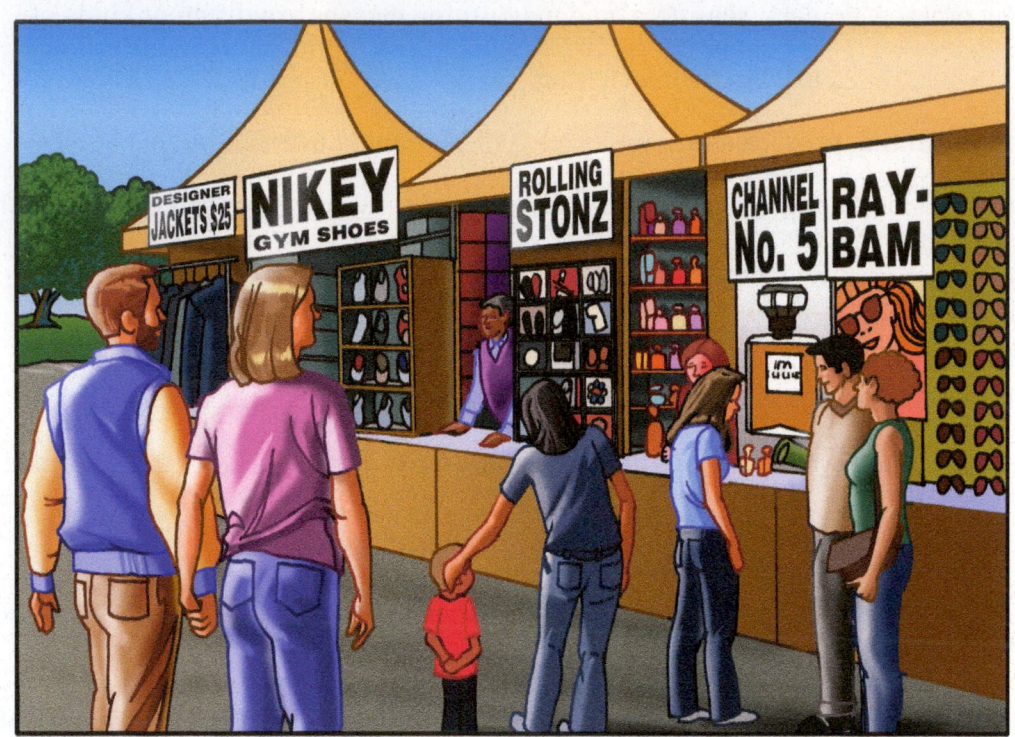

Now complete the conversation with the words from the box.

~~brand name~~	~~labels~~	~~packaging~~	~~quality~~
~~imitation~~	~~logo~~	~~pirated~~	

NICOLA: Jim! Look at this! They have Rayban sunglasses for only $25!

JIM: Nicola, those aren't real. Those are *Raybams*—the ___brand name___ is spelled wrong!
1.

NICOLA: Oh. But what about these bottles of perfume? They're Chanel!

JIM: Can't you tell that those are fake? They have different ___Packaging___ and
2.
___labels___.
3.

NICOLA: Oh, look! Here are some CDs of the Rolling Stones. I love the Rolling Stones!

JIM: These CDs are ___imitation___. Someone just copied the covers on their scanner.
4.

NICOLA: Well what about the shoes? These are Nikes, and they are really cheap!

JIM: You can tell that they are not Nikes because the ___logo___ looks wrong . . .
5.
They are cheaper because the ___quality___ is bad. They will probably fall apart
6.
in one week!

NICOLA: What about those jackets? They look like Hollister.

JIM: For $25? They are ___Pirated___ Hollister. Nicola, *everything* here is fake!
7.

CREATE

APPLY Look at the picture and complete the conversation. Use as many of the words from the box as you can.

arrest	counterfeit	illegal	nervous	real
bills	counterfeiter	imitation	~~packaging~~	quality
brand name	equipment	~~label~~	~~pirated~~	scanner
completely	~~fake~~	logo	prevent	

NICOLA: Well, maybe *you* know that these products are all fake, but that kid over there is buying a lot of stuff. Look! He just bought some software.

JIM: Oh, that is _____*pirated*_____ . You can tell because *the packaging is different.* *Also, look at the label. It looks fake, don't you think?*

NICOLA: And now he's buying _____ . How do you think he got all that money?

JIM: That's not real money. I think _____

NICOLA: Really? _____

JIM: It looks like he used _____

NICOLA: You're right. He also seems _____

JIM: Uh, oh. Look behind you! There are some policemen.

NICOLA: Do you think _____

JIM: I don't know, but I think we should leave before there is trouble!

▶ Go to the **Pearson Practice English App** or **MyEnglishLab** for more vocabulary practice.

1 Read the public service announcement. Underline the words that end in *-er*. Then answer the questions.

WARNING!
Counterfeit drugs can kill you!
Pharmacies are safer than Internet sites!

- Counterfeit drugs are more common today than ten years ago. They are usually <u>cheaper</u> than real drugs, but they are very dangerous!

- These drugs are often for sale on the Internet. Buying things online is <u>easier</u> than going to a real pharmacy, but it can be dangerous.

- Always buy your medicines at pharmacies. If you want to check your drugs to see if they are real, ask your pharmacist to check. They can tell which pills are counterfeit and which are real.

1. What three words did you underline? _Chealer, easier and are._

2. What word follows each of these words? _Than, than, which._

The words you underlined are adjectives in the comparative form.

Comparative Adjectives

1. Use the **comparative** form of adjectives to compare two people, places, or things.	They are usually **cheaper** than real drugs. Buying things online is **easier** than going to the store.
2. If the adjective has one syllable, add *-er* to make the comparative.	fast fast**er** old old**er**
Add only *-r* if the word ends in *-e*.	large large**r**
3. When a one-syllable adjective ends in a consonant + vowel + consonant, double the last consonant and add *-er*.	big big**ger** hot hot**ter**
4. If a two-syllable adjective ends in *-y,* change *y* to *i* and add *-er*.	easy eas**ier** busy bus**ier**
5. Some adjectives have **irregular** comparative forms.	good **better** bad **worse**
6. For most adjectives that have two or more syllables, add *more* or *less* before the adjective to make the comparative.	Counterfeit drugs are **more common** today than ten years ago. Computers are **less expensive** than they used to be.
7. Use *than* after the comparative form and before the second person, place, or thing.	This camera is **cheaper** *than* that one. This bag is **more expensive** *than* that one.
If the second person, place, or thing is understood, do not use *than*.	Bart doesn't like his computer. He wants to buy one that is **faster**.
If the subject and the object are the same, but have changed over time, don't use *than*.	Wow, Timmy is getting **taller**.

2 **Read the following shoppers' blog on counterfeit merchandise. Complete the blog with the comparative form of the adjective in parentheses.**

The Ultimate Shoppers' Blog

You read it in the news every day. Police find millions of dollars in fake

computers, clothing, drugs, and shoes every year. They say their job is getting

___hardest___ because the copies get ___better___ each year.
1. (hard)   2. (good)

The copies are so good, it's difficult for even the police to know if they are real or not.

If the police can't tell, what is a shopper to do?

My advice:

Shop at a store you trust. Online you see some shampoo that is

___Cheaper___ than what you pay at your salon. You could save $10 per
3. (cheap)

bottle. Who do you trust? Do you feel ___more Comfortable___ trusting the online
4. (comfortable)

company you don't know or the salon you visit every six weeks?

Know the price. Everyone wants to pay less. But you know a D&G bag

costs $1,500. When you see it for $100, don't buy it. Yes, the real thing is

___more expensive___, but it's real, not fake. Remember, it's ___easier___
5. (expensive)   6. (easy)

to tell the fakes from the real thing if you know the price.

Be smart. Counterfeiters want you to believe them. But you have to be

___Smarter___ than them. Look at the label carefully. Pay attention to the
7. (smart)

language. Look for mistakes in the label and in the tags.

3 APPLY **Read the descriptions of two anti-counterfeit machines. Then write sentences comparing the two machines. Use the adjectives from the box.**

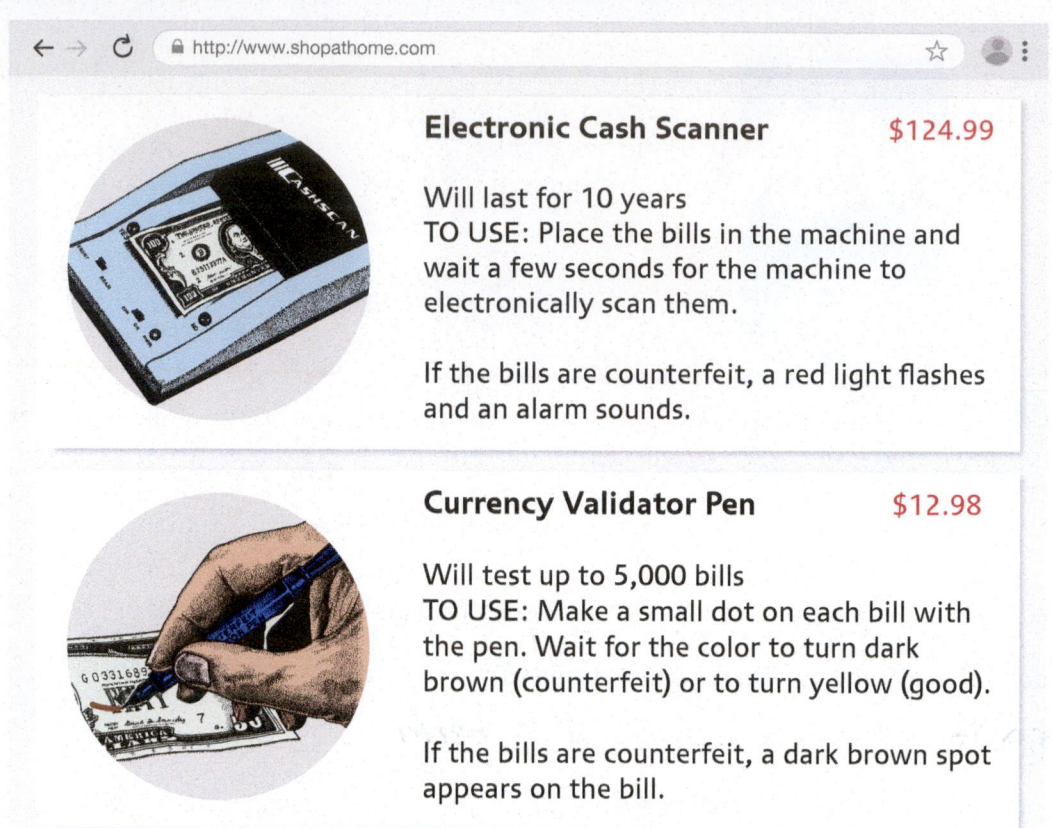

http://www.shopathome.com

Electronic Cash Scanner $124.99

Will last for 10 years
TO USE: Place the bills in the machine and wait a few seconds for the machine to electronically scan them.

If the bills are counterfeit, a red light flashes and an alarm sounds.

Currency Validator Pen $12.98

Will test up to 5,000 bills
TO USE: Make a small dot on each bill with the pen. Wait for the color to turn dark brown (counterfeit) or to turn yellow (good).

If the bills are counterfeit, a dark brown spot appears on the bill.

~~bad~~	~~difficult (to use)~~	~~expensive~~	~~good~~	~~slow~~
~~cheap~~	easy (to use)	fast	large	~~strong~~

1. *The electronic cash scanner is stronger than the currency validator pen.*
2. The currency validator Pen is worst than the E.C.S.
3. The CvP is harder then the ecs.
4. The ecs is more exPeasive than the cvP.
5. The ecs is better than the cvP.
6. The CvP is slower than the ecs.
7. The CvP is cheafer than the ecs.
8. The ecs is easier then the CvP.
9. The ecs is faster then the cvP.
10. The cvP is larger than the ecs.

➤ Go to the **Pearson Practice English App** or **MyEnglishLab** for more grammar practice. Check what you learned in **MyEnglishLab**.

In this unit, you read about counterfeit money and counterfeit products like computers, sports shoes, designer clothes, and watches.

Now you are going to *write a paragraph about a counterfeit product* of your choice. You are going to tell what the product is, where you can buy the product, and how you can tell it is fake by comparing the counterfeit to the original product. End your paragraph by saying if you think it's a good idea to buy this product. Use the vocabulary and grammar from the unit.

For an alternative writing topic, see page 77.

PREPARE TO WRITE: Clustering

One way to get ideas for your paragraph about a counterfeit product is by **clustering.** Clustering helps you see your ideas and how they are connected. In a **cluster diagram,** the topic is in a large circle in the middle. New ideas are in smaller circles and are all connected to the topic.

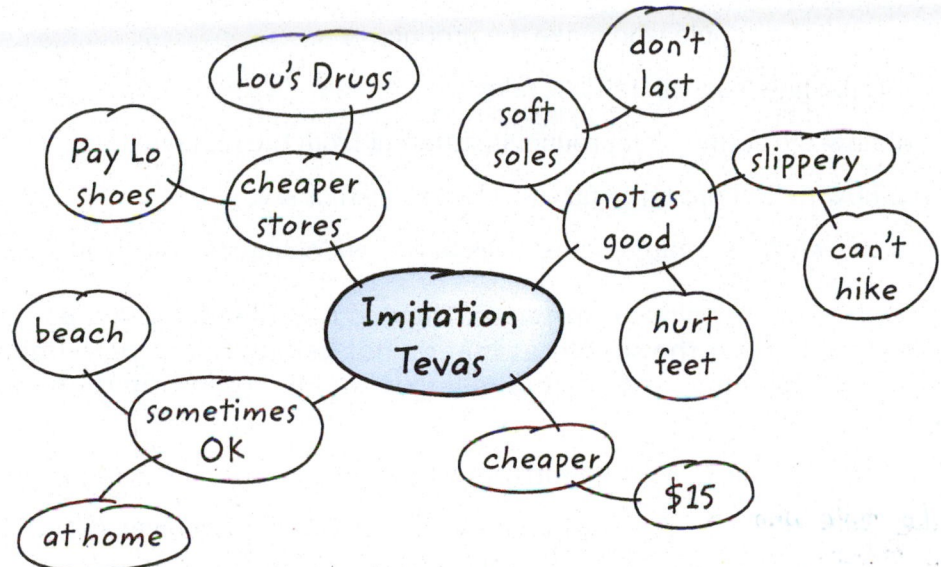

Make a cluster diagram for your product. Write the name of the product in the circle. Then link your ideas to the circle as you think of them.

WRITE: A Well-Organized Paragraph

To write a well-organized paragraph, you need to **select the right information.** Read the directions for your writing assignment carefully. They can often help you organize your ideas by telling you what information to include.

1 **Go to page 73 and reread the directions for writing your paragraph about a fake product. Then read the list and check (✓) the information you need to include. Cross out the things that you don't need to include in your paragraph.**

_____ 1. ~~Describe counterfeit money~~.

✓ 2. Tell if you think it's a good idea to buy the product.

✓ 3. Tell exactly how much the counterfeit product costs.

✓ 4. Tell what the product is.

_____ 5. Tell about a time a store checked to see if the money you used was counterfeit.

✓ 6. Tell where to buy it.

_____ 7. Describe the people who make the product.

✓ 8. Describe how you can tell it is fake.

✓ 9. Tell how the counterfeit product is different from the real one.

✓ 10. Tell how to find out if the fake product is legal or not.

_____ 11. List the ways the United States tries to prevent counterfeiting products.

2 **Read the sentences about pirated software. They do not all belong in a paragraph for this assignment. Cross out the sentences that do not belong in this paragraph. Next to each sentence that remains, write a note telling what kind of information the sentence gives.**

What the product is   1. Pirated software is one product that is counterfeit.

Describe the People who make the Product.   2. Fake designer shoes are also a big problem, especially for companies like Nike and Adidas.

Tell them where to buy it.   3. I can buy pirated software in some small computer stores I know.

How much the Counterfeit Product cost.   4. You know it is pirated if it is much cheaper than other software.

How to find out if the fake Product is legal or not.   5. You can tell the software is pirated if the label is from a copy machine.

How can you tell if it's fake.   6. Sometimes the seller changes the logo on the clothing.

How the counterfeit is different than the real one   7. Sometimes real copies of software cost more than a thousand dollars.

Tell them if you think if it's a good or bad idea   8. I think it is wrong to buy pirated software because it is like stealing from the company.

3 **Now list the information you need to include in your paragraph. Then write the first draft of your paragraph.**

1. Tell what the product is: _Pirated Jordans are counterfeit Prodct._

2. Tell where to buy it: _In Fort Lauderdale._

3. Describe how you can tell it is fake: _The quality._

4. Compare some features of the fake product with the real product: _The color is not the same._

5. Tell if you think buying the product is a good idea: _Is not a good idea but is cheap._

REVISE: Giving Explanations

Can a reader actually tell the difference between the fake product you describe and the real product? A reader often needs **more information, more detail,** and **more explanations.**

1 **Read the paragraph about Keen sandals. The reader wanted more information to really help her tell the difference. Look at the questions she wrote.**

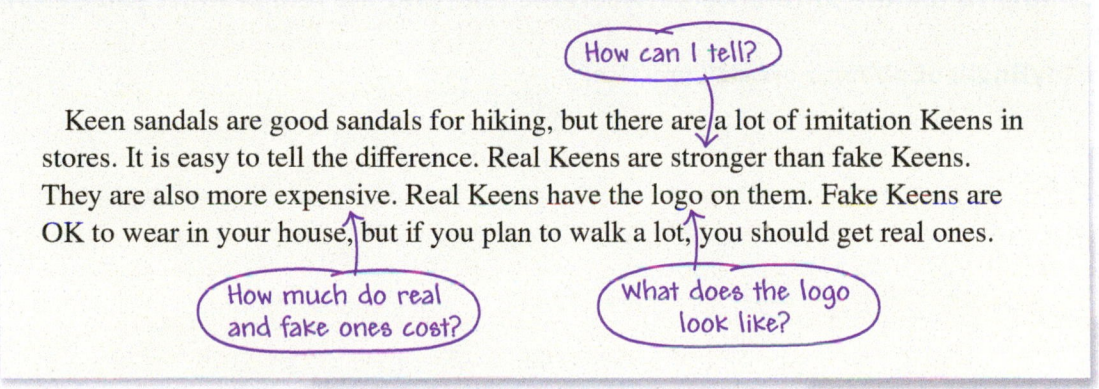

> How can I tell?
>
> Keen sandals are good sandals for hiking, but there are a lot of imitation Keens in stores. It is easy to tell the difference. Real Keens are stronger than fake Keens. They are also more expensive. Real Keens have the logo on them. Fake Keens are OK to wear in your house, but if you plan to walk a lot, you should get real ones.
>
> How much do real and fake ones cost?
>
> What does the logo look like?

Now the writer has rewritten the paragraph. See how much clearer it is.

> Keen sandals are good sandals for hiking, but there are a lot of imitation Keens in stores. It is easy to tell the difference. Real Keens are stronger than fake Keens. If you pinch the soles with your fingers, Keens feel harder, but imitations feel much softer, like a pillow. Real Keens are also more expensive. They cost about $110, but you can get them on sale for $65 sometimes. If you are paying only $30 or less, the sandals are probably not real Keens. Real Keens have the logo on them. The logo is yellow letters on a black background. Fake Keens are OK to wear in your house, but if you plan to walk a lot, you should get real ones.

2 With a partner, read the following paragraph and write questions to show where you need more detail, just as the reader of the Keen paragraph did.

> I like Obsession perfume by Calvin Klein, but I have to be careful to buy real Obsession and not fake. People sell fake Obsession perfume on the sidewalk in Los Angeles. The bottles are the same shape as real Obsession, but the label looks different. If you put the fake perfume on, it has the wrong smell. Real Obsession smells better than fake Obsession! Fake Obsession is cheaper than real Obsession. But if you buy it, you waste your money because it smells very bad.

3 Share first drafts with a partner. Write questions on your partner's draft. The questions should help your partner give more information about how to tell the difference between the fake and the real product he or she describes.

4 Now look at your first draft and at your partner's questions. Give more information about how to tell the difference between the fake and the real product you describe.

Go to **MyEnglishLab** for more skill practice.

EDIT: Writing the Final Draft

APPLY Write the final draft of your paragraph and submit it to your teacher. Carefully edit it for grammatical and mechanical errors, such as spelling, capitalization, and punctuation. Consider how to apply the vocabulary, grammar, and writing skills from the unit. Use the checklist to help you.

FINAL DRAFT CHECKLIST

☐ Is your paragraph well organized? Does it have the right information?

☐ Does your paragraph tell about a counterfeit product?

☐ Does it tell where you can buy this counterfeit product?

☐ Does it explain how you can tell that this product is fake?

☐ Does it give your opinion about why it is or isn't a good idea to buy this product?

☐ Do you use comparative adjectives correctly?

☐ Do you use new vocabulary that you learned in this unit?

ALTERNATIVE WRITING TOPIC

APPLY Write a paragraph comparing casual counterfeiters to professional counterfeiters. Use the information from the readings and the vocabulary and grammar from this unit.

CHECK WHAT YOU'VE LEARNED

Check (✔) the outcomes you've met and vocabulary you've learned. Put an X next to the skills and vocabulary you still need to practice.

Learning Outcomes	Vocabulary		Multi-word Units
☐ Infer future situations	☐ arrest	☐ illegal AWL	☐ break the law
☐ Take notes using a time line	☐ bill	☐ ink	
☐ Identify the sequence of events	☐ completely	☐ nervous	
☐ Use comparative adjectives	☐ counterfeiter	☐ prevent	
☐ Give explanations	☐ equipment AWL	☐ scanner	
☐ Write a well-organized paragraph	☐ fake	☐ technology AWL	

🔵 Go to **My**English**Lab** to watch a video about money, access the Unit Project, and take the Unit 3 Achievement Test.

LEARNING OUTCOMES

> Infer the author's attitude

> Take notes using an organizational chart

> Identify the main elements of a story

> Use imperative sentences

> Use parallel structure

> Write a blog post

🔵 Go to **MyEnglishLab** to check what you know.

Subway Etiquette

UNIT 4

1 FOCUS ON THE TOPIC

1. There are many rules that people must follow when riding the subway in New York City. What do you think are some of the rules for things people shouldn't do while riding the subway?

2. What politeness rules are important on public transportation or in other public places where you are from? Give one or two examples.

READING ONE | A Civilized Suggestion

PLEASE BE COURTEOUS AT ALL TIMES

Dude. . . Stop the Spread, Please
It's a space issue.

This Is NOT a Lunch Room
Eating in front of others is not polite.

Don't Be a Pole Hog
Leave room for others to hold on.
In other words, share the pole.

Keep the Doors Clear So Others Can Board
Bottom line: Blocking he doors blocks traffic, and slows service for everyone. You get the picture.

Subway etiquette is the set of politeness rules for the people who ride (take) the subway. Other forms of public transportation like buses or trains have similar rules. Some of these rules are written, like the ones shown by the signs above. But rules of etiquette are also often unwritten. Some examples of unwritten rules of etiquette in the New York subway are *Don't talk to people you don't know* and *Don't sit right next to passengers you don't know if there are other seats available.*

1 **What do you do in the following situations? Take the quiz to see what kind of New York subway rider (passenger) you might be. Read each situation and circle your answer. Pay attention to the boldfaced words.**

SUBWAY ETIQUETTE QUIZ

1. You are trying to enter the subway station, but your MetroCard[1] doesn't work.
   - **A** You shout **rude** words and hit the turnstile[2] with your hand until a police officer comes to see what's going on.
   - **B** You quickly try two more times, and then ask a subway employee for help.
   - **C** You try ten more times and say to the people waiting behind you. "You can never **rely on** these stupid machines! They are always broken!"

2. Your train arrives. As the doors open, you see that there are several people who want to get off the train.
   - **A** You stand to the side so that you don't **block** the way.
   - **B** You push through the doors as fast as you can to find a seat.
   - **C** You stand in front of the door and let people go around you to get off.

3. An **elderly** woman gets on the train. She looks for a seat, but there are no more seats left. You have a seat.
   - **A** You pretend to be asleep so that you don't **make eye contact with** her.
   - **B** You stay where you are and tell her to hold on to the **pole** when the train starts moving.
   - **C** You stand up and give your seat to the woman.

4. You have a cold and begin to **sneeze** on a crowded train. Someone hands you a tissue.[3]
   - **A** You take it, say thank you, and blow your nose.
   - **B** You pretend not to notice.
   - **C** You ask, "Is there a 'no sneezing' rule? Is it your job to **enforce** it?"

---

[1] **MetroCard:** name of the card you need to have to ride the subway or the bus in New York City
[2] **turnstile:** a gate that spins around and only lets one person through at a time
[3] **tissue:** a paper handkerchief for wiping noses

Add up your points using this key.

1. Your score:	2. Your score:	3. Your score:	4. Your score:	Your total score:
A—0 points	**A**—2 points	**A**—1 point	**A**—2 points	
B—2 points	**B**—0 points	**B**—0 points	**B**—1 point	_____
C—1 point	**C**—1 point	**C**—2 points	**C**—0 points	

If your score is:

8 points: New York is proud to have you riding its subway. Thank you for being an excellent example of **civilized** behavior.

6–7 points: You have a few things to learn about how to behave in New York's subway. Watch other riders more carefully to learn about subway **etiquette**. And study the NYC Transit rules of conduct.

5 points or less: Please get a car. Or move to an island in the middle of the Arctic Ocean. Learn some **manners**.

2 Match the boldfaced words and phrases on the left with the definitions on the right.

_j_ 1. **rude**

_____ 2. **rely on** (something)

_____ 3. **block**

_____ 4. **elderly**

_____ 5. **make eye contact with** (someone)

_____ 6. **pole**

_____ 7. **sneeze**

_____ 8. **enforce** (something)

_____ 9. **civilized**

_____ 10. **etiquette**

_____ 11. **manners**

a. to make sure that people do something that they are supposed to do

b. to blow air through your nose suddenly (saying "Aaaaatchoo!")

c. polite ways of behaving (*That child has no _____!*)

d. to expect something to work right

e. a long round piece of metal for holding onto

f. to stand in the way

g. old

h. to look someone in the eyes

i. a set of politeness rules

j. not polite; hurtful

k. organized so that people are nice to each other and take care of each other

↪ Go to the **Pearson Practice English App** or **MyEnglishLab** for more vocabulary practice.

PREVIEW

Editorials are articles in newspapers where writers give their opinions. The editorial on the next page is from the City section of a New York newspaper.

Read the title and the first paragraph of the editorial. What do you think the writer's suggestion might be about? Check (✓) your answer.

_____ 1. good places to visit on the subway

_____ 2. the restaurants with the best service in New York

_____ 3. how to make the subway nicer to ride

_____ 4. how to get around New York without riding the subway

READ

Read the editorial on the next page. Create a chart like the one below to take notes.

TAKE NOTES

Main Ideas	Details
Many rules—subway still unpleasant	No feet on seats
	No drinks

↪ Go to **MyEnglishLab** to view example notes.

A CIVILIZED SUGGESTION

By Dan Forman

1 There is a very long list of rules for the New York City subway. Don't put your feet on a seat, don't carry open cups of coffee or soda, don't take more than one seat, don't ride while drunk . . . Those are just a few of the rules. There are hundreds more.

2 With this many rules, why is it still so unpleasant to ride the subway?

3 Some people think that the problem is that no one **enforces** the rules. There aren't enough subway police, and the ones we have are too busy catching people who don't pay. Other passengers sometimes try to enforce rules. But you can't **rely on** them because New Yorkers have unwritten rules of **etiquette** against talking to strangers and **making eye contact with** strangers. How can you tell someone to take her shopping bags off the seat and throw away her Coke without talking to her or looking at her? It is difficult.

4 There are other New Yorkers who think that the subway is unpleasant because there are not *enough* rules. One rider wrote a letter to *The New York Times* a couple of weeks ago suggesting a few more subway rules. Here are some of the rules that she would like to see:

- Don't lean[1] on the **poles**. You prevent other people from holding on. They can fall down.

- Talk quietly. The trains are already too noisy.

- Cover your mouth and nose when you **sneeze** or cough. Other riders don't want to catch your cold.

- If your MetroCard doesn't work after three tries, ask a subway employee for help. Don't **block** the entrance.

- Give your seat to **elderly** passengers or to parents with small children.

5 Of course, anyone who knows the subway probably agrees that those are great ideas for rules. But polite people already do all of those things. If those unwritten rules of etiquette are written down, will the **rude** people be more likely to follow them? Will anyone enforce them? It doesn't make sense to make more rules that no one will enforce.

6 The real problem is that we are forgetting how to be nice to each other. It is embarrassing that we need a rule to tell us to give our seat to elderly passengers. Nobody should need to be reminded to do that.

7 I say we stop talking about the rules and try to remember our **manners**. Let's be nice to each other not because a police officer might tell us to get off the train, but because it is the right thing to do. *Then* New York City would be more **civilized**— both above ground and below.

---

[1] **lean:** to support yourself against a wall or other surface

Check (✓) the statement that best describes the main idea of the whole editorial. Use your notes to help you.

_____ a. The New York subway has plenty of rules, but police officers need to work harder to enforce them.

✓ b. People have lots of ideas about how to make the New York subway more pleasant to ride, but I think that we all need to just remember our manners.

_____ c. Elderly passengers often have to stand up on the New York subway. All passengers need to work to enforce the etiquette rules about this.

_____ d. New York has many etiquette rules, such as *Don't make eye contact* and *Don't talk to people you don't know.*

DETAILS

1 Circle the best ending for each statement. Use your notes to help you.

1. The New York subway has __a__ .

   (a.) a long list of rules

   b. only a few very important rules

   c. no rules

2. The writer thinks that riding the New York City subway is __c__ .

   a. always a good experience

   b. very difficult

   (c.) not pleasant

3. Some people think that __b__ should enforce the rules more.

   a. strangers

   (b.) police and other passengers

   c. passengers who take more than one seat

4. *Don't make eye contact* and *Don't talk to strangers* are examples of __b__ .

   a. general etiquette in New York City

   (b.) rules that one rider would like to have on the subway

   c. New York subway rules

5. *Don't lean on the poles* and *Talk quietly* are examples of __c__ .

   a. new subway rules that one rider suggested

   b. New York subway rules

   (c.) rules that the author wants to see

2 Look at your notes and at your answer in the Preview section. How did they help you understand the editorial?

MAKE INFERENCES

Inferring the Author's Attitude

Authors give clear opinions in editorials. For example, Dan Forman's opinion is at the end of the editorial, in paragraphs 6 and 7:

> "The real problem is that we are forgetting how to be nice to each other. . . . I say we stop talking about the rules and try to remember our manners."

Readers can **infer** (guess) even more about **the author's attitude** (beliefs) by **reading details** in the editorial carefully.

Look at the example and read the explanation.

Dan Forman thinks we need more enforcement of the rules.   TRUE   (FALSE)

(Answer: FALSE)

In paragraph 3, the author tells us: "Some people think that the problem is that no one enforces the rules." *(Notice he says "Some people . . . ," not "we" or "I.")*

In paragraph 7, the author tells us: "Let's be nice to each other not because a police officer might tell us to get off the train, but because it is the right thing to do." *(Police officers should not be the reason we are nice to each other.)*

After reading the text closely, we can infer that the statement is false. Dan Forman probably does not agree that we need more enforcement of the rules. We can **infer the author's attitude**.

1 **Which opinions does Dan Forman agree with? Refer to the paragraphs in parentheses, and write _T_ (true) or _F_ (false) next to each statement.**

Dan Forman agrees . . .

___F___ 1. we should tell strangers what to do. *(paragraph 3)*

___T___ 2. we need *more* rules. *(paragraph 5)*

___F___ 3. being nice to each other is part of being civilized. *(paragraph 7)*

2 **Now discuss your answers with a partner. Point out sentences, words, or phrases in the paragraphs that helped you find the answers.**

> *Enforce, Civilized, Courtesy.*

DISCUSS 🔍

Discuss the questions with a partner. Then share your answers with the class.

1. Look at the rules and etiquette descriptions for the New York subway in "A Civilized Suggestion." Compare each one to the rules and etiquette for the subway or bus in another city that you know.

2. Which of Dan Forman's opinions do you agree with? Why?

> **USE YOUR NOTES**
>
> Use your notes to support your answers with information from the reading.

▶ Go to **MyEnglishLab** to give your opinion about another question.

READING TWO | Riding the Subway in Japan

1 Look at the title and photos below. Read the first paragraph. What kind of article do you think this is? Circle your answer.

   a. a book review

   b. a story about an experience

   c. an editorial

2 Look at the boldfaced words in the reading. Which words do you know the meaning of?

READ

1 Many people write their experiences and thoughts on a blog. Read this blog post by a San Francisco woman about subway etiquette in Tokyo, Japan. As you read, guess the meanings of the words that are new to you. Remember to take notes on main ideas and details.

RIDING THE SUBWAY IN JAPAN

About Shelly

Shelly is an English teacher who has traveled and taught in many countries, including Japan.

1   I was riding the F Line streetcar today towards Fisherman's Wharf, watching a group of young American women. They got really **annoyed** at a group of international tourists who were **pushing** their way onto the streetcar. It made me think of an experience I had in Japan a few years ago when *I* was living in a culture I did not grow up in.

2   I was in my second year of living in Tokyo. I thought I was a real **expert** in Japanese etiquette and culture.

3   I knew that I had to push gently onto the subway cars. I knew that I shouldn't make eye contact with people. I knew that **blowing my nose** loudly "American style" was very rude. And I knew that I shouldn't talk to people on the subway. That wasn't a problem because my Japanese wasn't that good.

4   But one day, I was riding home from work on the subway, and I remembered that I needed to check in with a friend about meeting for dinner. She didn't

respond to my texts, so I put my earbuds in and called her. Of course, if you know the Tokyo subway, you know that there are "no phones" signs everywhere. But I also noticed that many passengers used their phones on the subway. I thought that the no cell phones rule in Japan was like the no food rule on the New York City subway. It's a rule, but no one follows it, and no one enforces it.

5 As I was talking, other passengers looked at me sideways like Japanese people do when they think you are being rude. One elderly woman shook her head and looked straight at me.

6 I finished my conversation, and I got off the train. I was very **confused**. Japanese people use their phones. Why can't I do the same? I asked myself.

7 Later that evening, I told my friend about the experience. She smiled. "The rule is *no talking* on phones," she said. "The others are all texting or playing games on their phones. Sometimes they listen to music. Occasionally they whisper[1] a very short message to someone on a phone. But they never have whole conversations on their phones in the subway. Next time, don't talk on your phone. Just text!"

8 I was embarrassed. Even though I knew a lot of Japanese habits, I was still a foreigner in their culture and had a lot to learn.

---

[1] **whisper:** speak very quietly

The subway in Tokyo gets so busy during rush hour, subway employees have to push passengers to get everyone on the train!

If you don't know the rules of etiquette in Japan, signs on the subway can help you.

If you need to make a call in Tokyo, make sure to finish it before you get on the subway.

2 Compare your notes on main ideas and details with a partner's. How can you improve your notes next time?

 Go to the **Pearson Practice English App** or **MyEnglishLab** for more vocabulary practice.

Taking Notes Using an Organizational Chart

A lot of students find it helpful to use a simple chart when taking notes on a text. There are many different kinds of organizational charts. A simple one looks like this:

Main Ideas	Details
Summary:	

On the left, write the main ideas. On the right, write the details. At the bottom, write a summary of the whole piece.

Look at the example from paragraphs 1, 2, and 3 from Reading One:

Main Ideas	Details
Lots of rules for the NYC subway	No feet on seats No open cups of coffee Take only one seat No riding drunk
Rules don't work	No one follows rules: no police—too busy Fellow passengers try to enforce—can't if want to follow rules of etiquette (no talking to strangers; no eye contact)
Summary: NYC subway has lots of rules that no one follows. Police can't help and fellow passengers can't help if they want to follow rules of etiquette.	

1 **Look at the organizational chart for paragraphs 1, 2, and 3 of Reading Two. Complete the blanks with the missing information.**

Main Ideas	Details
S reminded of living in Japan	_____
_____	Push gently
	_____
	No loud nose blowing
	_____
Summary: Shelly was reminded of her time in Japan when she saw tourists pushing onto a streetcar. In Japan she thought she was an expert. She knew a lot of the etiquette rules on subway riding.	

2 **Apply the organizational chart to your notes on paragraphs 4, 5, 6, 7, and 8 of Reading Two.**

⬤ Go to **MyEnglishLab** for more note-taking practice.

Circle the best answer to complete each statement. Use your notes from Reading Two to help you. Discuss your answers with a partner.

1. The writer _____ in Japan.
   a. went on vacation
   b. lived

2. The writer thought that she understood _____ .
   a. Japanese subway etiquette
   b. the Tokyo subway system

3. One thing that she did not understand was _____ .
   a. how to use her phone
   b. when it is OK to use a phone on the subway

4. The other passengers looked at her when she _____ .
   a. had a conversation on her phone
   b. tried to speak Japanese

5. When Japanese people use their phones on the subway, they are _____ .
   a. having long conversations with their friends
   b. texting or playing games

READING SKILL

1 Look at Reading Two again. Answer the questions.

1. What part of the story is the most exciting? _____

2. When did the people in the story feel most anxious or worried? _____

_____

3. How did the story end? _____

Identifying the Main Elements of a Story

Stories usually have these four main elements:

1. **Important background information** about the main character(s)

2. **A main conflict:** two characters or two elements that don't understand or agree with each other

3. **A climax:** a high point of the story when the elements in conflict crash together. The climax is usually the most exciting point in the story.

4. **A resolution:** something makes the conflict go away or become weaker

If you know these elements, you can understand the story quickly.

Background Information	Main Conflict	Climax	Resolution
Shelly is an American. She lived in Tokyo.	Shelly didn't understand parts of Japanese culture.	Shelly used her phone on the subway, and several passengers made her uncomfortable.	Shelly learned that Japanese people think it is rude to have a conversation on a phone in the subway.

2 Work with a partner. Read the paragraph about another experience with public transportation in a foreign country, and fill in the story chart below.

The English are famous for standing in line. But I didn't know that in 2005 when I went to England. I am from Senegal. I studied English for many years, and one summer I got a scholarship to study at an English university. I arrived at Heathrow airport and found my bus stop to go to my dormitory in London. When I started to get on the bus, an Englishwoman next to me yelled at me. "Young man! What do you think you are doing?!" She looked at me angrily. I heard her friend say, "Some people are so rude!" She was looking at me, too. I wanted to cry! I was excited to be in England, but these English people were already so angry at me, and I did not understand why. Luckily, another African man close by understood my problem. He tapped my shoulder and pointed at the line. "Brother, you need to stand in the line," he said. I looked behind me and saw 15 people in line. The man smiled and said, "It's OK. You'll learn. The English stand in line for everything." I was very embarrassed, but at least I understood.

Background Information	Main Conflict	Climax	Resolution

⬆ Go to **MyEnglishLab** for more skill practice.

CONNECT THE READINGS 🔍

ORGANIZE

Read the list of etiquette rules (written and unwritten) mentioned in Reading One (R1) and Reading Two (R2). Which rules are for the New York City subway, and which are for the Tokyo subway? Which rules are for both New York City and Tokyo? Check (✓) the correct column(s).

> **USE YOUR NOTES**
>
> Review your notes from Readings One and Two. Use the information in your notes to complete the chart.

Subway Etiquette Rules	NYC Subway (R1)	Tokyo Subway (R2)
1. Don't put your feet on a seat.		
2. Don't carry open cups of coffee or soda.		
3. Push gently when getting on crowded subway cars.		
4. Don't ride while drunk.		
5. Don't make eye contact with strangers.		
6. Talk quietly.		
7. Don't take more than one seat.		
8. Don't talk to strangers.		
9. Don't blow your nose loudly.		
10. Don't talk on your phone.		

SYNTHESIZE

Complete the conversation between Shelly, the blogger from Reading Two, and her friend Rachel. Use information from Organize.

 Rachel January 24, 2019 4:08 PM

Thanks so much for your posting about riding the Japanese subway! I just got a job in Tokyo, so I will be there soon. From your blog, I understand that there are a few subway etiquette rules that are different over there. For example,

_____

_____

Is there anything else I should know?

You don't say anything about the pushers. I have seen photos of those guys who push you onto the trains! I am worried about that! Let me know if you have any more advice!

 Shelly January 25, 2019 6:20 AM

Don't worry about the pushers. They are only at a few stations and only at the busiest times.

Most of the other subway rules are the same as here in New York.

For example, _____

_____

Send me an email when you get to Tokyo! I would love to stay in touch!

 Rachel January 25, 2019 11:20 AM

Thanks! That would be great! I will contact you. I am sure I will need more advice.

Enter your comment...

🔎 Go to **MyEnglishLab** to check what you learned.

3 FOCUS ON WRITING

REVIEW

Complete the open letter below. Choose the correct word or phrase from the appropriate list (nouns, adjectives, or verbs), and write it in the blank.

Nouns		Adjectives		Verbs	
etiquette	manners	annoyed	elderly	blocking	push
expert	pole	civilized	~~rude~~	blow his nose	rely on
eye contact		confused		enforce	sneeze

An Open Letter to New York Subway Riders

Being a New York subway rider like you, I know that in our subway it is _____*rude*_____
1.

to talk to strangers, and I also know that we should not make _____ with
2.

each other.

I am no _____ on subway rules, but I do know about being polite. And I think
3.

we, New York subway riders, are forgetting some basic rules of _____.
4.

Yesterday, I was on the A train when a very _____ man got on the train. As the
5.

train started to go, the poor man had to hold on to a _____ so that he didn't fall
6.

down. There were young people sitting in the seats around him. I was so _____
7.

with them! None of them moved. There was no one to _____ the "give your seat to
8.

elderly passengers" rule, so I stood up. I was far from the old man, so I called to him, and he

started to come my way. He certainly wanted a seat. But there was a woman who was

_____ the way. So the poor man had to stand there. He was too polite to
9.

_____ her out of the way. To make things worse, there was a kid next to him who
10.

seemed to have a terrible cold. He started to _____ on the old man. I wanted to
11.

hand that kid a tissue for him to _____, but I didn't.
12.

I thought that New York was a _____ city, but I guess I was _____.
13. **14.**

You can't _____ anyone here to have good _____ anymore.
15. **16.**

EXPAND

What is the correct response to each of the statements? Pay attention to the boldfaced words and phrases. Match each statement with a response from the list below. Each response can be used more than once.

Statements

_a_ 1. I gave my seat to a woman with three small children yesterday. It felt like the **polite** thing to do.

____ 2. My newspaper blew out of my hands when the train came. I didn't want to **litter,** but I couldn't pick the paper up off the tracks.

____ 3. I did not have a MetroCard, and I didn't have time to **wait my turn** at the MetroCard machine, so I just jumped over the turnstile.

____ 4. I know that it is **impolite** to talk on a phone on the bus. But I just found out that my father was in the hospital.

____ 5. Where I come from, it's polite to say hello to other people on a long bus ride. So I **greeted** everyone when I got on the bus to Chicago.

____ 6. I felt bad that I didn't **tip** the taxi driver. But my wallet was stolen earlier today, and I only had enough money for the taxi ride.

____ 7. I **stood in line** to wait for the train in London since that was what everyone else seemed to be doing.

Responses

a. Good, you **followed the rules.** That was the right thing to do.

b. You **broke the rules.** You shouldn't do that.

c. What you did is **against the rules** of etiquette in the United States. These are unwritten rules, but they are still rules that you should learn.

d. Well, that's an **exception to the rule.** In unusual situations it is OK not to follow the rules.

CREATE

APPLY **Read the letters to an advice column about public transportation etiquette. Write a response to each letter. Try to use the words and phrases in parentheses for each one.**

1.

> I am always annoyed when I take a taxi and I pay the driver, and he asks if I want change. Is that rude or am I crazy?
>
> —John, Chicago

Dear John: (against the rules of etiquette / tip)

Asking "Do you want change?" is not against the rules of etiquette. The driver is trying to save you time. You can simply say, "Yes, I want change," and then decide how much money you want to tip the driver.

2.

> I take the train to work every morning. I always listen to music or the radio with my earbuds. My boyfriend thinks I am rude because I can't hear what other passengers say to me when I have earbuds in. But I don't really want to talk to people early in the morning. What do you think?
>
> —Michelle, Washington, D.C.

Dear Michelle: (follow the rules / impolite / etiquette)

_____

_____

_____

_____

3.

> I just arrived here in New York from Togo, West Africa, to study for a year. I ride buses everywhere. But sometimes I get a little lost. I am afraid to ask the bus drivers for help because there are big signs on all the buses that say *Do not talk to the driver.* I am afraid to even say hello to the driver. How can I ask if I am on the right bus without breaking the rules?
>
> —Aliou, New York City

Dear Aliou: (manners / greet / exception)

_____

_____

_____

_____

⬆ Go to the **Pearson Practice English App** or **MyEnglishLab** for more vocabulary practice.

GRAMMAR FOR WRITING

1 Underline the verbs from the list of rules. Then answer the questions.

- Don't lean on the poles.
- Talk quietly.
- Don't block the entrance.
- Give your seat to elderly passengers or to parents with small children.
- Don't talk on your phone.

1. Is there a subject in any of the sentences above?
2. Who is expected to do the things listed above?

Imperative Sentences

1. Use the imperative when you want to give clear **instructions, orders, advice, warnings,** or **requests.**	**Cover** your mouth and nose. **Talk** quietly. **Don't block** the entrance.
2. To form the imperative, use the **base form** of the verb.	**Take** your feet off the seat. **Push** gently.
3. In the negative, use **don't** before the base form of the verb.	**Don't lean** on the pole.
4. The subject of an imperative sentence is always **you.** We never state the subject unless we are addressing someone in particular.	CORRECT: **Talk** quietly. INCORRECT: You talk quietly. **Mario,** talk quietly.
5. To make a polite request, use the imperative with **please** at either the beginning or end of the sentence. If **please** is at the end of the sentence, put a comma before it.	**Please** don't talk on your phone. Be quiet, **please.** Don't push, **please.**

2 Make imperative statements. Use the correct form of the verbs in parentheses.

1. _____*Don't smoke*_____ on airplanes.
   (smoke / not)
2. _____ your phone at the movies.
   (turn off)
3. _____ your phone in class, please.
   (look at / not)
4. _____ photos or video with your phone at a concert.
   (take / not)
5. _____ in a red zone.
   (park / not)
6. _____ your taxi driver at least 15 percent.
   (tip)
7. _____ your earbuds when you talk to me!
   (take out)

3 Rewrite the rules or suggestions for polite behavior using the imperative. Remember, the imperative focuses on the action that the listener should or should not do. Other information may not be included. Remember that you can use *please.*

1. People shouldn't take more than one seat on the bus—this is the rule.

   Don't take more than one seat on the bus.

2. People shouldn't play loud music on the bus.

   _____

3. There is no smoking on the bus.

   _____

4. You should always say hello to your driver. That's just the polite thing to do.

   _____

5. Shawn, you know that it's against the rules to chat with the bus driver.

   _____

6. Making eye contact with strangers is against New York's rules of etiquette.

   _____

↻ Go to the **Pearson Practice English App** or **MyEnglishLab** for more grammar practice. Check what you learned in **MyEnglishLab**.

FINAL WRITING TASK: A Blog Post to Inform 🔍 APPLY

In this unit, you read about subway etiquette in New York and Tokyo. Now think about a city you know well. What kind of etiquette does it have on its public transportation (subway, buses, trains, streetcars, etc.)? If your city does not have public transportation, you can write about etiquette in one of its public places (stores, restaurants, theaters, museums, etc.).

You are going to **write a blog post about etiquette on public transportation or in a public place** in that city. First, you will give some information about the public transportation or place you chose. Then you will give a list of important rules of etiquette for this location. Use the vocabulary and grammar from the unit.

For an alternative writing topic, see page 99.

PREPARE TO WRITE: Listing

Listing is making a list of your ideas before you begin to write. When you make a list, it is not necessary to write complete sentences.

1 Choose a public transportation system or place that you know well. Fill in the city or town and type of transportation or place you are writing about. List all of the rules that you can think of.

2 Look at your list and cross out the rules that are less important. Keep the rules that are the most important. You should list about five rules.

City or Town: _____

Type of Transportation
or Place: _____

Rules of Etiquette: _____

_____

_____

_____

_____

_____

WRITE: A Blog Post to Inform

A **blog** often gives information about a particular subject. So, writing a blog post is often writing to inform. When you write to inform people about something, you often write in the **"second person"** (using *you,* not *I*). This is not the place to tell your own stories. You should include only general information about the subject you are writing about.

1 Look at the two introductions to a blog post about the Seattle streetcars. Check (✓) the one that gives you the clearest information about streetcars in Seattle.

☐ A.

Seattle, Washington: A Civilized Way to Ride the Streetcars

Streetcars in Seattle are very easy to use. The system is very new, so the cars are nice and clean. The main streetcar line goes all the way from downtown to the airport.

☐ B.

Seattle, Washington: A Civilized Way to Ride the Streetcars

I thought the streetcars in Seattle were very easy to use. I've never been on such clean streetcars! They were much nicer than the streetcars where I live. I was able to take the streetcar right from the airport when I arrived. It was terrific!

2 Look at this introduction to a blog post about the **London Underground** (familiarly called the Tube). Rewrite each sentence so that it is not about the writer.

London, England: A Civilized Way to Ride the Tube

(1) When I was visiting my friend in London last year, I found out that the Tube is the London subway. **(2)** There are many trains in the Tube system. I couldn't believe how big it was! **(3)** At first, I tried to use it without a map, but that was a mistake. I got really lost, and I was late for my first day of school at the New English Language Institute. **(4)** The other thing I didn't realize was that the stations are really big. It took me about eight minutes of walking really fast to get from one train to another at Paddington Station the other day. I was late to meet my friend, and we almost missed our movie. **(5)** I tried taking a taxi after that experience, but I found out that a taxi takes even more time (and costs more) because traffic is usually so bad in London!

London, England: A Civilized Way to Ride the Tube

(1) The Tube is _____.

(2) It is _____.

(3) Everyone should _____.

(4) The stations _____.

(5) The Tube is generally _____.

3 Now write the first draft of your blog post about etiquette on public transportation or in a public place in the city of your choice.

1. Use the following type of title:

   Riding the _____ OR **Visiting** _____

2. Write an introduction where you give some important information about the type of public transportation or place that you are writing about.

3. List a few rules (written or unwritten) that riders or visitors should know about.

REVISE: Using Parallel Structure

When you write a list, it is a good idea to make all the items in the list **parallel.** Each item should start with the same **grammatical structure** (noun, verb form, gerund, etc.). This makes them clearer and easier to read. Lists that use different grammatical structures at the beginning of each item can be difficult to read.

1 Which list uses parallel structure? Check (✓) A or B.

☐ A. A few rules of etiquette for riding the Tube are:

- Walk quickly in the stations.
- Don't eat on the trains.
- Study your map before you begin your trip (so that you don't have to stop and block the way in the station).
- Hold large backpacks in front of you.

☐ B. There are several rules for riding the Seattle streetcars:

- Eating is against the rules.
- You should buy a ticket before you get on the train.
- You have to put your bicycle in the end of the car where it says "Bikes."
- Don't smoke.

2 Rewrite the list of rules from the list above *that does not use* parallel structure. Use parallel structure.

- _____
- _____
- _____
- _____

3 Now go back to the first draft of your blog. Look at your list of rules and underline the verb forms in each rule. If there are rules that are not parallel, correct them so that they all start with the same grammatical structure.

🔵 Go to **MyEnglishLab** for more skill practice.

EDIT: Writing the Final Draft

APPLY Write the final draft of your blog post and submit it to your teacher. Carefully edit it for grammatical and mechanical errors, such as spelling, capitalization, and punctuation. Consider how to apply the vocabulary, grammar, and writing skills from the unit. Use the checklist to help you.

FINAL DRAFT CHECKLIST

- ☐ Does the title of your blog post tell where and what kind of public transportation or public place you are writing about?
- ☐ Does it give general information about this kind of transportation or place?
- ☐ Does it avoid stories from your own personal experience?
- ☐ Does it give information that would be useful to a reader who is going to visit this city?
- ☐ Does your blog post tell about rules for riding this type of public transportation or visiting this place?
- ☐ Do the rules in the list all follow parallel structure?
- ☐ Do you use the imperative correctly?
- ☐ Do you use new vocabulary that you learned in this unit?

ALTERNATIVE WRITING TOPIC

APPLY Sometimes people from one culture think that people from another culture are rude. In reality, they are just following different rules of etiquette. Write about the differences in etiquette in two cultures that you know. Use vocabulary and grammar from the unit.

CHECK WHAT YOU'VE LEARNED

Check (✔) the outcomes you've met and vocabulary you've learned. Put an X next to the skills and vocabulary you still need to practice.

Learning Outcomes
- ☐ Infer the author's attitude
- ☐ Take notes using an organizational chart
- ☐ Identify the main elements of a story
- ☐ Use imperative sentences
- ☐ Use parallel structure
- ☐ Write a blog post

Vocabulary
- ☐ annoyed
- ☐ block
- ☐ civilized
- ☐ confused
- ☐ elderly
- ☐ enforce AWL
- ☐ etiquette
- ☐ expert AWL
- ☐ manners
- ☐ pole
- ☐ push
- ☐ rude
- ☐ sneeze

Multi-word Units
- ☐ blow your nose
- ☐ make eye contact with
- ☐ rely on AWL

🔵 Go to **MyEnglishLab** to watch a video about etiquette, access the Unit Project, and take the Unit 4 Achievement Test.

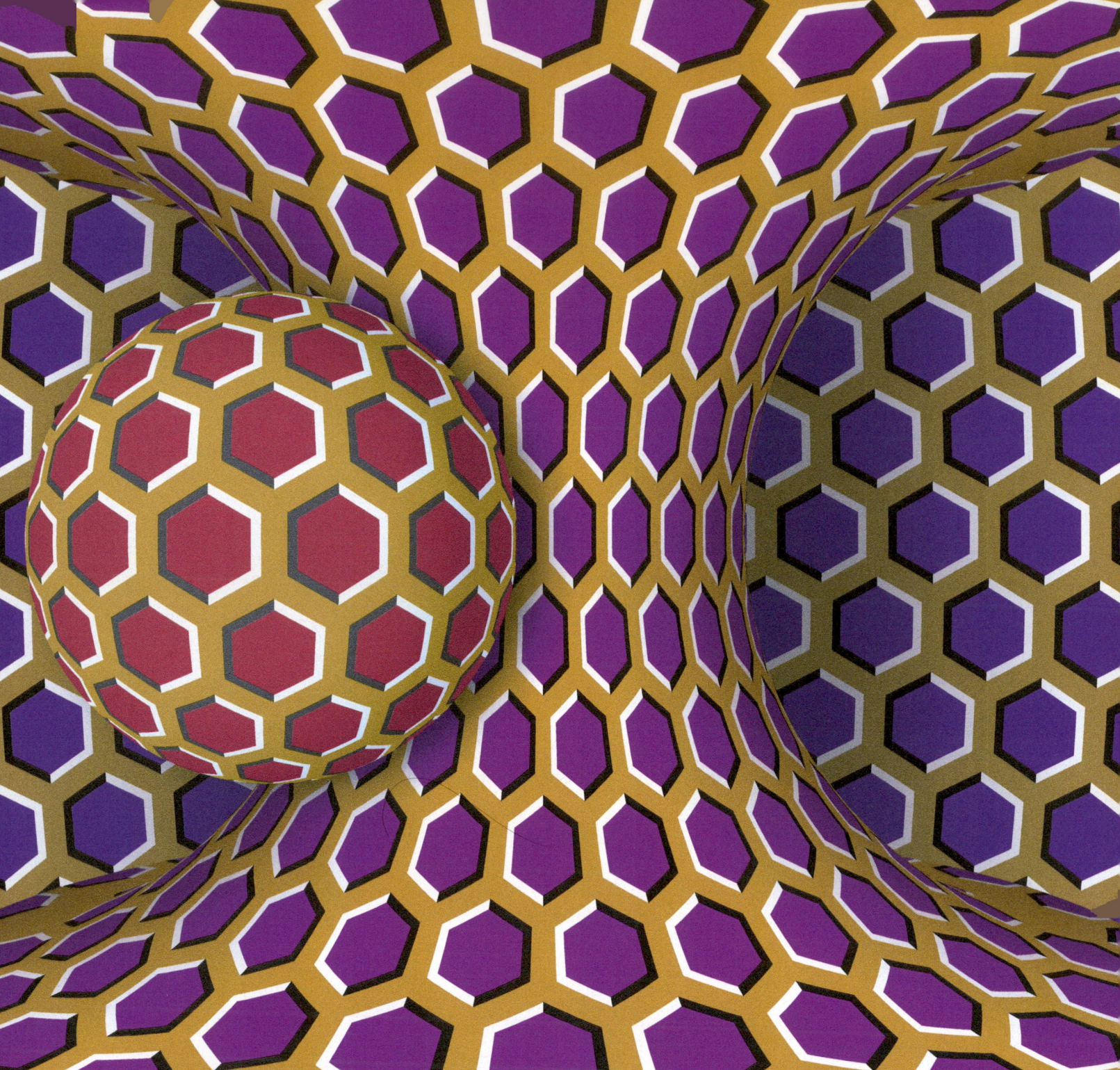

LEARNING OUTCOMES

- > Infer abstract ideas from examples
- > Take notes using abbreviations and symbols
- > Scan for information

- > Use linking verbs
- > Use descriptive adjectives
- > Write a personal experience paragraph

Go to **MyEnglishLab** to check what you know.

Perception

1 FOCUS ON THE TOPIC

1. Look at the image. Some people can see it moving. Other people see it as a still picture. What do you see?

2. Think about other senses. Can you think of things that people might taste, smell, hear, or feel differently from other people?

3. What are some reasons that people might experience the same thing in different ways?

READING ONE | Is Blue Always Blue?

VOCABULARY

1 Read this text conversation. Pay attention to the boldfaced words.

> How is that Psychology and **Perception** class that you started today?

It's great. Check this out.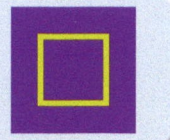

> A yellow square in a purple square?

Now look at this one.

> A green square in a yellow square?

The inside squares are the same color!!

> They are not! Are you having trouble with your **vision**?

No! I can see perfectly. Look!

> Wow. That's so weird. The whole inside square just became green.

Yes! The **context** of a color can make it look really different.

> So the **surrounding** colors make the inside square look different.

Exactly. We also learned to write secret messages with color. What does this say?

> "Crying." And there are some light blue lines.

Right. The light blue lines are actually letters. When you look through a red **lens**, you can read the blue lines! Here is the same image:

laughing

Wow. That is crazy. Is the class all about color? I thought it was a Psych[1] class?

The brain is a huge **factor** in perception. We get information with our eyes, ears, nose, etc. But our brains tell us what it all means. That's why it's a Psych[1] class.

Are you talking about any other **senses**?

Yes! We will talk about things that **affect** taste next week!

Can you find out why my orange juice tastes terrible after I brush my teeth?

You should take the class!

I'll **consider** it. I'll talk to my advisor to see if it's not too late to register. It sounds really interesting.

---

[1] **Psych:** a common casual abbreviation for Psychology class or major

2 Match the boldfaced words on the left with the definitions on the right.

_h_ 1. **perception**   a. all around

___ 2. **vision**   b. situation or information that is around something else

___ 3. **context**   c. to think about doing something

___ 4. **surrounding**   d. the ability to see

___ 5. **lenses**   e. to change

___ 6. **factor**   f. something that affects something else

___ 7. **senses**   g. thin clear parts of your eye, or pieces of glass or plastic to look through

___ 8. **affect**   h. the ability to be aware of something

___ 9. **consider**   i. seeing, hearing, smelling, tasting, and touching

🔊 Go to the **Pearson Practice English App** or **MyEnglishLab** for more vocabulary practice.

Home project websites and magazines are popular. Many readers like to read articles that help them to do projects themselves to save money. Others like to do projects because they are creative. And still others like to look at these articles to get ideas for projects that they pay other people to do for them.

The following article is from a home project website. Read the title and the first paragraph of the article. What do you think the article might mention? Check (✓) your answer.

_____ 1. reasons that the same color looks different at different times

_____ 2. the most popular paint colors for different projects this year

_____ 3. a little bit of information about the science of color

_____ 4. directions for how to build a colorful bookshelf

READ

Read the article on the next page. Create a chart like the one below to take notes.

TAKE NOTES	
Main Ideas	**Details**
Color perception affected by several factors:	
1. Light	— low light makes colors disappear — colored light can change color of objects
2.	
3.	
4.	

🔵 Go to **MyEnglishLab** to view example notes.

IS BLUE ALWAYS BLUE?

1 Choosing color is part of almost any home project. But the wrong color can ruin it. Color is not as simple as it seems. There is actually complex science behind the way we see color. You don't need to get a PhD to choose a good color for your kid's room. But here are a few basics about color that might be helpful.

2 Colors are among the first things that children learn to name. But colors do not exist in the same way that a tree or a rock exists. Our brains create our **perception** of color when light hits our eyes. There are many **factors** that **affect** how our brains see color.

Light

3 Light affects our color perception. In very low light, color disappears altogether, and everything looks black, white, and gray. Bright light affects color, too. This is because there is always a little bit of color in light, and different colored light changes how colors look. **Vision** scientist Mark Fairchild likes to tell a story about his very young daughter to illustrate this point. At dinner one night, she became very upset because her macaroni and cheese was white; she wanted yellow macaroni and cheese. Fairchild fixed the problem by blowing out the candle on the table. Like magic, the macaroni and cheese became yellow. He knew that the problem was not the dinner; it was the candlelight, which was yellow. Yellow light on yellow macaroni and cheese makes it look white, but in regular electric light, the same macaroni and cheese looks yellow.

Expectations

4 Another factor that affects our perception of color is our expectations or memory. We see what we expect to see, especially if we are not looking carefully. In the situation described above, most parents might say to their children: "Don't be silly! That macaroni and cheese IS yellow!" The parents bought and prepared the food, so they know what color it is. When they see it, even in candlelight, their brains tell them what the real color is. The little girl, on the other hand, relies on her **senses** to tell her the color. She does not know what to expect, so her brain does not correct the color for her.

5 For another example of how expectations work, ask a few people about the color of water. Most people will say it's blue. A child's drawing of water is almost always blue. But if you look at water, it is seldom really blue. Water is often more green than blue. Often, it is clear. But we have learned that water is blue, so the picture in our memory is blue. It is what we expect, so it is what we see.

Anatomy

6 Some people see color differently because of the anatomy[1] of their eyes. About 8 percent of men and 0.5 percent of women are colorblind, which means that they do not see differences between, for example, red and green. They are missing the part of the eye that helps them see those colors.

7 Eye anatomy also changes as people get older, and one common change affects color vision quite strongly. As we get older, the **lenses** in our eyes sometimes become yellow, and this makes it hard for older people to see blues and purples. It is like looking through yellow sunglasses, which makes blues and purples less bright.

Surrounding Color

8 **Surrounding** colors can affect color as well. A pale green dot might look gray on a bright green background. But that same dot will look very green on a red background. Colors are usually brightest when they are next to their opposite. So, for example, reds look brightest next to green, and blues look brightest next to orange. Colors that are directly across from each other on the color wheel are considered "opposite."

9 Understanding the science of color perception is important to many professionals. But there are many ways amateur designers can use this knowledge to make their everyday projects better as well. For example, always bring a sample of the color you are matching to the paint store so that you don't rely on your memory. **Consider** the **context** for your color. Remember that the lighting and surrounding colors affect the color you choose. Think about who needs to be able to see the color: if people with color vision problems are involved, you might need to change your choices. And finally, be sure to consider your dining room lighting when you serve dinner.

Color wheel

---

[1] **anatomy:** the structure of a body, or of a part of a body

Match each incomplete statement of a main idea from the article with the best ending. Use your notes to help you.

_h_ 1. Light, expectations, anatomy, and surrounding colors all affect our color perception, and . . .

_e_ 2. Light affects how we see color because . . .

_d_ 3. Our expectations and memory affect our perception when . . .

_a_ 4. Anatomy can affect your color perception if . . .

_c_ 5. Because surrounding colors affect our color perception, . . .

a. you are colorblind or old.

b. understanding them can help us make better color choices.

c. a color looks brighter next to its opposite color.

d. we see what we expect to see, even though it may be incorrect.

e. it always has some color in it.

DETAILS

1 Circle the best ending for each statement. Use your notes to help you.

1. Very low light _____ c _____ .
   a. makes everything more gray
   b. makes things look more yellow

2. Most people say that water is blue because _____ a _____ .
   a. they have a picture of blue water in their memory
   b. they cannot see the other colors

3. Older people might have trouble seeing _____ b _____ .
   a. reds and greens
   b. bright blues and purples

4. A color looks brightest when it is on a background of _____ a _____ .
   a. its opposite color
   b. similar colors

5. Light and surrounding color are examples of _____ a _____ .
   a. the context for a color
   b. relying on your memory

2. Look at your notes and at your answers in the Preview section. How did they help you understand the article? Did you predict the content of the article correctly?

Inferring a General Abstract Idea from a Single Concrete Example

Authors often use a **specific concrete example** to represent a more **complex or abstract idea.**

Look at the example and read the explanation.

> "Choosing color is part of almost any home project. But the wrong color can ruin it. Color is not as simple as it seems. There is actually complex science behind the way we see color. <u>You don't need to get a PhD to choose a good color for your kid's room.</u> But here are a few basics about color that might be helpful." (*paragraph 1*)

The author says: "You don't need to get a PhD to choose a good color for your kid's room."

The author isn't really worried if you have a PhD or not. She's using this concrete example of an advanced degree to represent the more general idea of expert knowledge. The author actually means: "You don't have to have a lot of color science knowledge to choose a good color."

The author also doesn't expect everyone who reads the article to have a kid. She is using the example "kid's room" to represent any room or project that a reader might want to paint.

After reading the text, especially concrete examples, closely, we can **infer** the bigger **abstract ideas** that the author wants to convey.

1 **Read paragraphs 2 and 9 again. Notice the underlined sentence in each. Then circle the general idea that each underlined sentence represents.**

Paragraph 2

2 Colors are among the first things that children learn to name. <u>But colors do not exist in the same way that a tree or a rock exists.</u> Our brains create our perception of color when light hits our eyes. There are many factors that affect how our brains see color.

a. But colors are not part of nature.

b. But colors are not "real" things that you can touch.

c. But trees and rocks are not always the same color.

Paragraph 9

9 Understanding the science of color perception is important to many professionals. But there are many ways amateur designers can use this knowledge to make their everyday projects better as well. For example, always bring a sample of the color you are matching to the paint store so that you don't rely on your memory. Consider the context of your color. Remember that the lighting and surrounding colors affect the color you choose. Think about who needs to be able to see the color: if people with color vision problems are involved, you might need to change your choices. <u>And finally, be sure to consider your dining room lighting when you serve dinner.</u>

a. Be careful about lighting your dining room because the color of food affects the taste of the food.

b. Create different lighting in different rooms to help people see color more clearly.

c. When you choose color, think about what kind of lighting it will have on it.

2 Now discuss your answers with a partner. Point out sentences, words, or phrases in the paragraphs that helped you find the answers.

DISCUSS 🔍

Discuss the questions with a partner. Then share your answers with the class.

1. Reread the section called *Surrounding Color*, and study the color wheel. Find some colored items in your immediate environment and put them next to each other. For example, put a yellow pencil on an orange notebook, then put it on a blue notebook. Where do the different colors look brightest? Do your findings match with the rule in the *Surrounding Color* paragraph?

2. Interior designers must have a strong understanding of color. What are some other jobs that require a strong understanding of color? Why? Which factors are especially important?

3. Can you think of a time when you perceived a color differently than people around you or differently from what the color truly was? Describe that experience. Based on information from the reading, can you identify the reason why your perception was different from the reality?

🔵 Go to **MyEnglishLab** to give your opinion about another question.

> **USE YOUR NOTES**
>
> Use your notes to support your answers with information from the reading.

READING TWO | The Dress that Almost Broke the Internet

PREVIEW

1 Look at the title of the reading and at the photos. Read the first paragraph. What kind of article do you think this is? Circle your answer.

a. a book review

b. a story about an experience

c. a human-interest article

2 Look at the boldfaced words in the reading. Which words do you know the meaning of?

READ

1 The following article is from the Science section of a Sunday newspaper. Read about a picture that has caused arguments because people do not agree on its color. As you read, guess the meanings of the words that are new to you. Remember to take notes on main ideas and details.

The Dress that Almost Broke the Internet

WEiRD SCIENCE

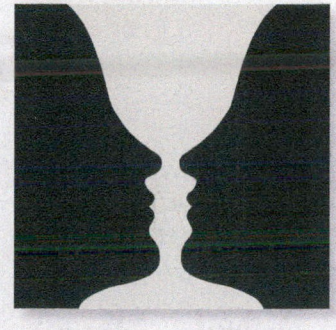

1 The day was February 26, 2015. Cate Holderness, who worked for a news website, received a message from someone at Tumblr, a social media site. Tumblr wanted the news site to answer a question about the color of a dress in a photograph: was it white and gold, or blue and black? The question didn't seem that important, so Holderness did not answer it right away. But at the end of the day, she saw that the **image** had 5,000 Tumblr notes and was getting 14,000 views per second—more than she had ever seen.

2 Holderness showed the picture to her co-workers so that they could respond to the question. Instead of answering the question, though, they began arguing about the color among themselves. Meanwhile, on Twitter, 4.4 million tweets about the dress were sent within 24 hours. The company that sold the dress had over 3.5 million visits to its website, and within a few days, 150 news channels all over the world were talking about the dress. It started as a simple message, and now the whole world seemed to be arguing about it.

3 About 57 percent of people who look at the photograph see a blue and black dress, while 30 percent see white and gold. People in both groups think that people from the other group are crazy, or that they have serious vision problems. The actual dress is blue and black. So why do so many people see white and gold when they look at it? Vision scientists explain that it depends on how our brains **interpret** the light. Is it daytime or nighttime? Is the dress in shadow or not? These answers are not clear in the photo. So our brains make decisions about all of these factors, and decide which colors we see.

4 Humans love optical illusions[1]. "What do you see?" children excitedly ask each other when they first discover the faces / vase image. They are always amazed when they can see both two faces and a vase.

Later, they may discover MC Escher, or other artists who draw pictures of impossible circles of stairs that only go up. When they look carefully, they can see that it is only lines on paper that make the illusion. Students of psychology may experience another illusion when their professor shows them a short video of people throwing balls. The video asks viewers to count the number of times the people throw the balls, but at the end of the video, the question on the screen is "Who saw the dancing gorilla?" Usually, very few people notice the gorilla the first time they see the video, but everyone sees it when they watch the video again and look for it. They can't believe they did not see it the first time. The lesson is that we often only see things that we pay attention to.

5 There can be illusions for other senses, as well. An old **joke** that children sometimes play on each other is to have a friend repeat these separate syllables: *owa ta goo siam*. Once the speaker can say them, he or she repeats them faster. The surrounding sounds blend together, and soon everyone hears, "Oh, what a goose I am!"

6 In all of the examples, our first perception changes when we get an **explanation**. The explanation helps us reorganize our perceptions and we say, "Oh! Now I get it!" We are delighted at being able to see things from many points of view.

7 But somehow, the dress illusion does not work that way. Only 10 percent of people can see both blue / black and white / gold. All of the explanations in the world do not help the other 90 percent to see the other colors in the dress, and this is deeply troubling to us. Taylor Swift, a famous American singer, even tweeted about the dress, "I'm confused and scared." The dress does seem scary to us, and that is exactly why we continue to be **fascinated** by this photo. If so many people cannot see the dress from another perspective, what else are we all seeing differently?

[1] **optical illusion:** a picture or image that tricks yours eyes and makes you see something that is not actually there

2 Compare your notes on main ideas and details with a partner's. How can you improve your notes next time?

🔵 Go to the **Pearson Practice English App** or **MyEnglishLab** for more vocabulary practice.

Taking Notes Using Abbreviations and Symbols

Common abbreviations and symbols can help you **write words and ideas in a shorter, faster way.** They can save a lot of time when you take notes.

Use abbreviations and symbols to **take notes more quickly.** Study the list below of common abbreviations and symbols.

e.g. or **ex**	for example
=	the same as
≠	not the same as
@	at
w/	with
w/o	without
s/t	something
b/c	because
∴	therefore, as a result
& or +	and
—>	becomes or leads to
♂	men
♀	women

As you read, think about using abbreviations and symbols in your notes. Do not make complete sentences. Do not worry about perfect grammar. Write short phrases or words.

Look at this example from Reading One (*paragraph 3*):

3 Light affects our color perception. In very low light, color disappears altogether, and everything looks black, white, and gray. Bright light affects color, too. This is because there is always a little bit of color in light, and different colored light changes how colors look. Vision scientist Mark Fairchild likes to tell a story about his very young daughter to illustrate this point. At dinner one night, she became very upset because her macaroni and cheese was white; she wanted yellow macaroni and cheese. Fairchild fixed the problem by blowing out the candle on the table. Like magic, the macaroni and cheese became yellow. He knew that the problem was not the dinner; it was the candlelight, which was yellow. Yellow light on yellow macaroni and cheese makes it look white, but in regular electric light, the same macaroni and cheese looks yellow.

Light
—low light —> color disappears
—bright light affects color b/c light has color e.g., candlelight + mac & cheese = white; electric light + mac & cheese = yellow

1. **Read the following paragraph about how useful yellow colored glasses can be. Notice the underlined main idea and details. Fill in the notes on the right with the correct abbreviations and symbols from the list above.**

Glasses with yellow lenses are very useful for people who work in low-light, snowy environments, for example, skiers and snowplow drivers. Snow looks very flat in low light. It is hard to see where there is a bump or a hole. And bumps and holes are important things to see for skiers and for people who are driving on the snow. Yellow lenses let 85 percent of light through, and they make the flat blueish colored snow have more shape. This leads to the wearer being able to see the snow better.

Glasses ——— yellow lenses—useful for people in low light, snow

——— skiers ——— snowplow drivers

—let 85% of light through

—flat blueish snow ——— more shape ——— easier to see

2. **Look at the following paragraph about another type of colored lenses. Notice the underlined information. Make short form notes with abbreviations and symbols for the main idea of the paragraph and each underlined supporting detail.**

Very dark green lenses are important for people who work with fire, for example, welders and glassworkers. These lenses block 90 percent of bright light. The green color of the lenses helps the workers see the orange and red color of the flames more clearly. The bright light from the fire that is used while working with metal or glass will damage a person's eyes if they don't have eye protection, so it is extremely important for people who work in these environments to protect their eyes.

Very dark green lenses important.
— People who work with fire.
— welders glassworkers - block 90% bright light. will damage a person's eye.
— It is extremely important for
— people to protect their eyes.

3. **Look at paragraphs 6 and 7 from Reading One again. First, underline the important supporting details. Then make short form notes with abbreviations and symbols for the main idea of the paragraph and each of your underlined supporting details.**

Anatomy

6 Some people see color differently because of the anatomy of their eyes. About 8 percent of men and 0.5 percent of women are colorblind, which means that they do not see differences between, for example, red and green. They are missing the part of the eye that helps them see those colors.

7 Eye anatomy also changes as people get older, and one common change affects color vision quite strongly. As we get older, the lenses in our eyes sometimes become yellow, and this makes it hard for older people to see blues and purples. It is like looking through yellow sunglasses, which makes blues and purples less bright.

People see color differently.
1. About 8% of men. and 0.5% of women.
— are colorblind. red and green.
— Missing part of the eye.
2. Changes as people get older.
— hard for older people to see blue and purples.

🔵 Go to **MyEnglishLab** for more note-taking practice.

Circle the best answer to complete each statement. Use your notes from Reading Two to help you. Discuss your answers with a partner.

1. The "dress that almost broke the Internet" is a great example of _____ *b* _____ .
   a. colorblindness in humans
   b. how our brains try to make sense of what we see

2. The real color of the dress is _____ *a* _____ .
   a. blue / black
   b. white / gold

3. In the faces / vase illusion, people can see both images when _____ *b* _____ .
   a. someone tells them that there are two possible pictures
   b. the light changes on the image

4. Only 10 percent of people can see both blue / black and white / gold versions of the dress after they _____ *b* _____ .
   a. see some background color in the photograph
   b. are given an explanation of the photograph

READING SKILL

1 Look at paragraph 4 of Reading Two again to quickly find out why the video of the gorilla is so surprising.

Scanning for Information

Sometimes a reader may look for a specific piece of information within the text. This is called **scanning.** To scan a text is to **quickly move your eyes over the words until you find the information** you are looking for.

For example:

> If you want to find information about the video with the gorilla, you do not have to read every word of paragraph 4. Instead, you can quickly move your eyes over the text until you find the words *video* and *gorilla*.

> 4 Humans love optical illusions. "What do you see?" children excitedly ask each other when they first discover the faces / vase image. They are always amazed when they can see both two faces and a vase. Later, they may discover MC Escher, or other artists who draw pictures of impossible circles of stairs that only go up. When they look carefully, they can see that it is only lines on paper that make the illusion. Students of psychology may experience another illusion when their professor shows them a short **video** of people throwing balls. The **video** asks viewers to count the number of times the people throw the balls, but at the end of the **video**, the question on the screen is "Who saw the dancing **gorilla**?" Usually, very few people notice the **gorilla** the first time they see the **video**, but everyone sees it when they watch the **video** again and look for it. They can't believe they did not see it the first time. The lesson is that we often only see things that we pay attention to.

Scanning this paragraph allowed you to quickly find the information you were looking for.

2 Work with a partner. Discuss the questions about Reading Two.

1. Scan paragraph 1 for this information: How many people viewed the dress on Tumblr by the end of the day? What did you look for when you scanned?

2. Scan paragraph 4 for this information: What is the name of the artist who draws impossible stairs? What did you look for when you scanned?

3. Scan paragraph 7 for this information: What percentage of people cannot see both the blue / black and the white / gold version of the dress? What did you look for when you scanned?

4. Scan paragraph 7 for this information: What did Taylor Swift say about the dress on Twitter? What did you look for when you scanned?

Go to **MyEnglishLab** for more skill practice.

CONNECT THE READINGS

ORGANIZE

There are several reasons or factors why two people might perceive things differently. Read each example. Check (✓) the box that shows which factor is affecting perception for that example.

USE YOUR NOTES

Review your notes from Readings One and Two. Use the information in your notes to complete the chart.

Example	FACTORS THAT AFFECT OUR PERCEPTION				
	Light (context)	Memory and expectations	Anatomy	Surrounding color (context)	Attention
1. A little girl thinks her yellow macaroni and cheese is white.	✓				
2. A person has trouble seeing differences between blues and purples.	✓				✓
3. We usually say that water is blue.	✓	✓			
4. A pale green dot looks gray on a bright green background and very green on a red background.	✓		✓		✓
5. People disagree about the color of the dress that nearly broke the Internet.	✓				
6. We see faces or a vase in the faces / vase illusion.	✓		✓		✓
7. The stairways in Escher prints seem to only go up.			✓		✓
8. People who focus on counting moving balls in a video do not notice when a gorilla walks through the scene.		✓			✓

Professor King's Teaching Assistant is holding a study session for students to help them prepare for an exam. The photos below are photos that were sent to students' phones for a class exercise.

Complete the conversation, using information from the chart in Organize. Then discuss your answers with a partner.

ASSISTANT: Check your cell phones for a picture I just sent to you. What is it?

STUDENTS: A young woman!

STUDENTS: An old woman!

ASSISTANT: The picture is the same. But some of you had the title "Young Woman," so that is what you saw first. Those of you who had the same picture with the title "Old Woman," probably saw an old woman. Why is that?

STUDENT: Because our brain takes from perception what it is.

ASSISTANT: Right! Now see if you can explain this situation: I went to a new colleague's house, to meet about a project. I just sent you a picture of what I saw when I walked in the door. Suddenly, I heard this sound: [plays a recorded sound] "Wahhhhh" from the back of the house. What was it?

STUDENTS: A cat!

STUDENTS: A baby!

ASSISTANT: Again, you have different perceptions! Some of you saw a picture of a house with a cat, and others saw a picture of a house with baby toys. Why did you perceive the sound differently?

STUDENT: We associate sound with the image we visualize.

ASSISTANT: OK, now, check your cell phones again for a photo of a kitchen. What color is the ceiling?

STUDENTS: White!

STUDENTS: Yellow!

ASSISTANT: Hmm. So, again, I sent two slightly different pictures of the same kitchen. Here they are. The paint and furniture are exactly the same in both pictures. Why do the colors look different?

STUDENT: Because light affects the color of the photos

ASSISTANT: Some people cannot tell the difference between these two photos of fruit. They think they look exactly the same. Why is that?

STUDENT: The light affects images.

ASSISTANT: Here is a similar situation, but for a different sense. There is a high-pitched alarm on my mother's fridge that tells her when the door is open for more than three minutes. Sometimes I hear it in the background when she calls me, and I have to tell her to close the door. She can't hear it.

STUDENT: It could be that she is older of for.

ASSISTANT: Here is another example from my own life. I was driving last week, and at a stop sign, I quickly glanced at the map to make sure I knew the way to my friend's house. I started to drive through the intersection because there were no cars. But suddenly, I heard shouting, and I saw three people walking across the street in front of me. I am a really careful driver. Why did this happen?

STUDENT: I think it's to stay alert.

ASSISTANT: And here is the final example. Look on the screen. You are all seeing the same image, but I bet some of you see it differently. What is it? If you see different things, why? Discuss with your neighbor for a minute.

ASSISTANT: OK, why do you think you saw different things?

STUDENT: Different Perceptions, if you focus you could see either a bunny or duck.

Go to **MyEnglishLab** to check what you learned.

3 FOCUS ON WRITING

REVIEW

Complete the paragraph with the correct words from the box.

affected	explanation	~~images~~	lenses	surrounding
consider	factor	interpret	perception	vision
context	fascinated	joke	senses	

"The arrow in the FedEx logo is an excellent example of good design," my design professor said. I didn't understand. I knew that logo well, and I knew it was just letters. I was sure that there were no _____images_____ in the logo. When my professor put the logo on the screen,
1.
I looked again. I wondered if she was making a _____ , but no one was laughing.
2.
I asked for an _____ , and she only said, "The _____ letters are *E* and *x*."
3. **4.**
Then, suddenly, I saw it. The space in between the capital *E* and the *x* of the *Ex* creates an arrow! "The space in between the letters looks empty, but it has a shape," my professor said, "You should _____ the space in between the letters when you create a logo. White
5.
space is a _____ in a logo, too. It doesn't have to be only letters and images." My
6.
_____ of that logo completely changed on that day. Now, when I see the FedEx logo,
7.
I see the arrow first! This experience _____ the way I look at letters and words. Now,
8.
I am _____ by shapes in words and letters. I notice the _____ of letters more,
9. **10.**
and that helps me _____ them. For example, in the logo for Mountain Equipment,
11.
I see two mountains in the M. But I don't see mountains when I see my friend Mark's name.
Another example is a headphones logo I saw last week. The *b* in the logo looks like an earbud.
All of these images in letters were invisible to me before. My professor says that we need to
look at everything through our "designer _____ ." My _____ is good. I don't
12. **13.**
wear glasses. All of my other _____ work well, too. But I think this is his way to say
14.
that we have to think and see like designers.

EXPAND

Read the following stories about perception. Complete the comment after each one. There are two possible answers for each item. Discuss your answers with a partner.

1. My grandma just colored her own hair. She did it herself because she doesn't like the color when the salon does it for her. But now her hair is a little purple!! She says it's not, but I can see it is a little purple.

   She can't see what you see because of _____ .

   a. her eye **anatomy**
   b. the yellow lenses in her eyes
   c. her not **paying attention**

2. I just started studying Arabic. There are three different "k" sounds in Arabic! I am having trouble hearing the difference. Why is it so hard? Will I ever be able to hear the difference?

   You will be able to **perceive** the difference. It's difficult at first because _____ .

   a. you aren't used to paying attention to these sounds in English
   b. in English, we only have one "k" sound.
   c. English speakers have a different anatomy

3. Last Monday night, I arrived at Miami Airport very late and picked up my gray rental car. I parked it at my hotel, and the next morning, I thought it was stolen. When I clicked the key to find the car, a green car in my parking space flashed its lights. I was so confused! It was my rental car. Why did I think the car was gray?

   Your perception changed because _____ .

   a. the light was low when you picked up the car at night, and light can affect how we see colors
   b. the light was different
   c. you didn't pay attention to the color at night

4. I was in Seoul, South Korea, last month, and I visited an **optical illusion** museum. My favorite part was the bridge. It was only a painting on the ground, but it looked so much like a very high bridge over the water. I got scared thinking about walking across it, even though I knew it wasn't real. Why was I so scared?

   You were scared because _____ .

   a. your brain **expects** a bridge to be high up
   b. optical illusions always trick people
   c. the surrounding space made it seem real

5. I had an awful ear infection last week, so I went to the doctor and got some strong medicine for it. I have to take the medicine for one week. I am feeling a little better now, but suddenly everything I eat tastes like metal. I can't taste my food!

   You probably have trouble tasting your food because of _____ .

   a. the medicine. It changes how your sense of taste works
   b. how the medicine affects your sense of taste
   c. the food you're eating. Try eating something with better flavor

CREATE

APPLY Complete the conversation between two students in Professor King's psychology class. The students, Rebekah and Sholi, are helping each other to prepare for presentations about incorrect or confusing perceptions in their own lives. Use the words and expressions in parentheses to complete the conversation.

REBEKAH: I might give a presentation about a purse I bought a few months ago at the mall. I loved the purse because the color was this unusual deep, rich blue. When I got home that evening, I opened the bag to take out my purse and thought: Oh no. They gave me the wrong bag. The purse was black, not blue. When I took it back to get the right color, suddenly, it was blue again! I'm not colorblind. Do you think it was the light?

SHOLI: Yes, I think so! (light / perceive it as blue and black) _____

_____

REBEKAH: Exactly. (light / factor in perception) _____

_____

SHOLI: I think that is a good example for your presentation. I want to talk about logos and how our brains connect color and design to brands. I once saw a Subway sandwich shop and went in to order a turkey sandwich. As soon as I walked in, though, I looked around and realized I was in a shoe store! The store had the same green-and-yellow-colored sign as Subway. I didn't even notice that the name of the store on the sign was Shoe Mart. Because the colors looked so much like the famous sandwich store, my brain read it as "Subway."

REBEKAH: Oh, that's a good example. (expect / factor in perception / perceived) _____

_____

SHOLI: I think that is exactly what happened. Next time, I will be sure to read the name of the store before I walk in.

REBEKAH: OK, I have one more funny experience that I might present about instead. Last year, at my parents' house, I tried to paint the bathroom walls white. I used the same white paint that my dad used for the hallway. But when the paint dried in the bathroom, it became light blue. The tile was bright white, but the paint was definitely light blue. It's strange. It looks white in the hallway, but in the bathroom, it looks light blue.

SHOLI: Wow! That's a really good story. (in different contexts / surrounding color / affected / perception) _____

_____

REBEKAH: That's exactly what I was thinking. I can't wait to tell my Dad. He was as confused as I was!

🔊 Go to the **Pearson Practice English App** or **MyEnglishLab** for more vocabulary practice.

1 **Read the email. Notice the boldfaced words. They are all linking verbs that describe how something looks, feels, tastes, etc. Some are followed by *like*.**

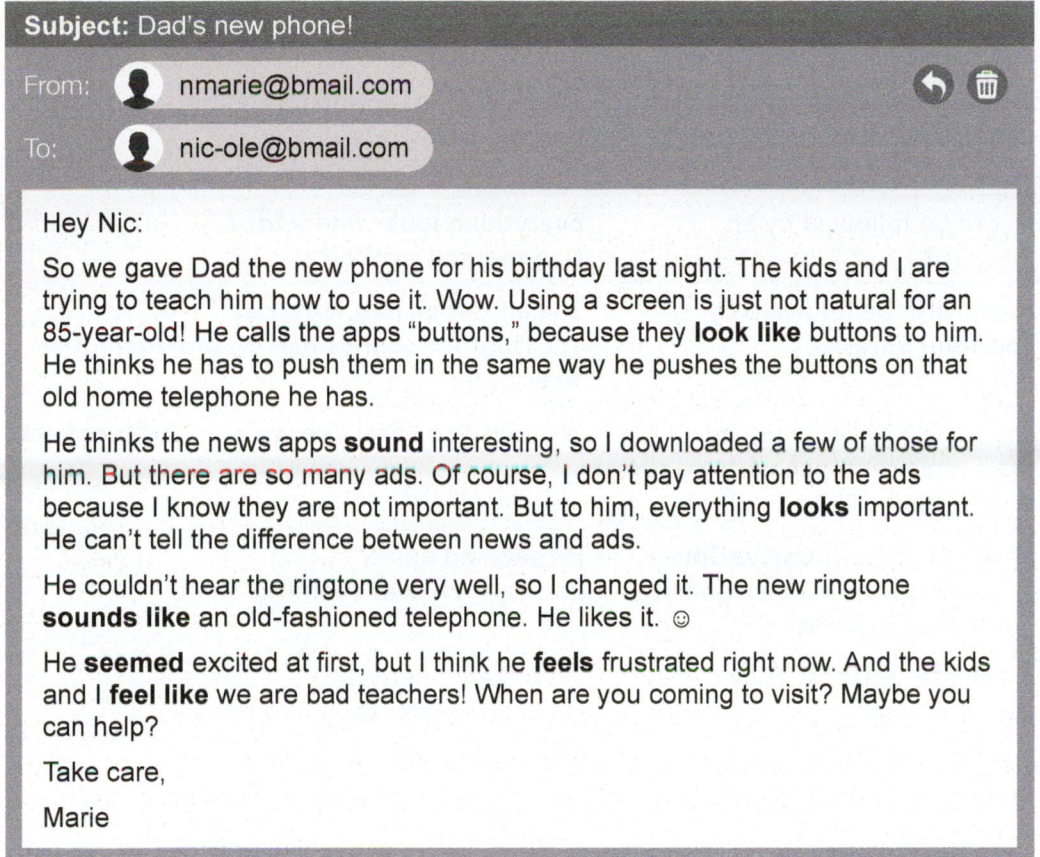

Subject: Dad's new phone!

From: nmarie@bmail.com

To: nic-ole@bmail.com

Hey Nic:

So we gave Dad the new phone for his birthday last night. The kids and I are trying to teach him how to use it. Wow. Using a screen is just not natural for an 85-year-old! He calls the apps "buttons," because they **look like** buttons to him. He thinks he has to push them in the same way he pushes the buttons on that old home telephone he has.

He thinks the news apps **sound** interesting, so I downloaded a few of those for him. But there are so many ads. Of course, I don't pay attention to the ads because I know they are not important. But to him, everything **looks** important. He can't tell the difference between news and ads.

He couldn't hear the ringtone very well, so I changed it. The new ringtone **sounds like** an old-fashioned telephone. He likes it. ☺

He **seemed** excited at first, but I think he **feels** frustrated right now. And the kids and I **feel like** we are bad teachers! When are you coming to visit? Maybe you can help?

Take care,

Marie

Write the words or phrases that come after each boldfaced word or phrase.

1. They **look like** _buttons_ .

2. The news apps **sound** _____ .

3. Everything **looks** _____ .

4. The ringtone **sounds like** _____ .

5. Dad **seemed** _____ .

6. Dad **feels** _____ .

7. We **feel like** _____ .

1. Linking verbs are verbs that introduce more **information about a subject.** Common linking verbs are *be, become, seem,* and *appear.* Verbs that **describe sense perception** like *look, smell, taste, sound,* or *feel* are also linking verbs.	Nic **is** Marie's sister. Marie **seems** kind. The news apps **sound** interesting. Dad **feels** frustrated.
2. A linking verb can be followed by an **adjective.**	Everything **looks** *important.* Dad **seemed** *excited.*
3. A linking verb can also be followed by *like* + **noun** (or noun phrase).	The apps **look** *like buttons.* The ringtone **sounds** *like an old-fashioned telephone.*
4. A linking verb can also be followed by *like* + **clause** (a simple sentence with a subject and a verb).	The kids and I **feel** *like we are bad teachers!*
5. Linking verbs usually describe **situations** (not actions), which means that we do not use them in progressive tenses. **Active verbs** describe **actions.** They can be used in progressive tenses.	He **seemed** quiet. INCORRECT: He **was seeming** quiet. He **talked** quietly. CORRECT: He **was talking** quietly.
6. *Look, taste, smell,* and *feel* each have two similar uses. They can be **linking or active verbs.** If you can replace the verb with a form of **be,** it is a linking verb. **If you can't, it is an active verb.**	The cake **tasted** good. *(Linking Verb: Similar to "The cake was good.")* I **tasted** the cake. *(Active Verb: "I was the cake" does not make sense, so this is not a linking verb.)*

2 Complete the conversation with the correct words or phrases. Choose from the words and phrases in parentheses.

SHALYA: What is that? It smells _____*strange*_____ .
 1. (strange / bad candy)

LARS: It's black licorice! Here! Have one!

SHALYA: OK. Yuck! It tastes _____ .
 2. (bitter / medicine)

LARS: Ha! I love it. I think it tastes like _____ .
 3. (sweet herbs / sweet)

SHALYA: It is completely black! It doesn't even look like _____ .
 4. (candy / delicious)

My candy is much better. Here, try a couple of pieces.

LARS: They smell _____ .
 5. (spicy / my mom's spice cupboard)

SHALYA: They are chewy. And they have a surprising flavor. Just try one.

LARS: OK. That sounds like _____ . Aaaaah! It tastes like
  6. (I might like them / interesting)

_____ !! It feels like _____ ! What is it?
  7. (joke candy / disgusting)   8. (there is fire in my mouth / very hot)

SHAYLA: It's ginger candy! They taste _____ , don't they?
  9. (a little spicy / they are spicy)

LARS: Yes. But I didn't expect spicy candy. I expected something sweet. I actually really like

ginger. Give me another one. I think I will like it, now that I know what to expect.

3 Complete the Q&A with the correct form of the verbs in parentheses. Use the simple present for the linking verbs and the present progressive for the active verbs.

Q: What are you doing?

A: I _____ these flowers. They _____ amazing!
  1. (smell)   2. (smell)

Q: How is your headache?

A: My head _____ like someone hit it with a hammer!
  3. (feel)

Q: How is your Mom today?

A: She _____ well.
  4. (feel)

Q: Where is Vincent?

A: He's in the cheese shop. He _____ all of the different kinds of cheeses!
  5. (taste)

Q: How is your dinner?

A: It _____ terrible.
  6. (taste)

4 **APPLY** Answer the questions. Write two sentences about each item: One sentence with a perception verb + adjective, the other sentence with a perception verb + *like* + noun. Try to create sentences that describe the perceptions accurately instead of sentences that just say whether or not you like something, or whether it is "good" or "bad."

1. How does your least favorite food taste?

   Blue cheese tastes strong. It tastes like very old milk.

2. How does your favorite food taste?

   _____

3. How does your favorite singer or band sound?

   _____

4. How does a restaurant you know smell?

   _____

5. How does your favorite animal feel to touch?

   _____

Go to the **Pearson Practice English App** or **MyEnglishLab** for more grammar practice.
Check what you learned in **MyEnglishLab**.

In this unit, you read about perception. You learned that what we "see" may be different from how something truly appears. You learned about different factors that affect perception and that people often have different perceptions of the same colors, objects, and experiences. What misunderstandings or confusions can happen because two people do not perceive the same thing, action, or experience in the same way?

You are going to write a ***personal experience paragraph*** about a time when your perception of something or someone was incorrect or different from the people around you. Describe three areas of this experience: your perception and what was incorrect or different, what happened as a result of this incorrect perception, and what you learned from it. Use the vocabulary and grammar from the unit.

For an alternative writing topic, see page 125.

PREPARE TO WRITE: Making an E-Chart

An **e-chart** can help you organize your ideas to start your writing. Write the topic on the single line on the left and use the three lines on the right for the three parts of the paragraph.

1 Look at the model e-chart.

	What was the incorrect or different perception?
Topic: the perception that changed	What was the result?
	What did you learn?

Perception of a Norwegian word in singing practice	I heard "flatt" (flat), but the director was saying "flott" (beautiful).
	I thought the choir director was strange.
	When something doesn't make sense in a new language, ask!

2 Create an e-chart for your perception that changed.

WRITE: Describing a Past Personal Experience

When writing about a past personal experience, you should **provide concrete details** of the story to help your reader "see" what happened. **Use verbs of perception** to describe your incorrect or different perception.

1 Read each paragraph. Then answer the questions.

Paragraph 1

> When I was 15, my family moved to Norway for a year. I only knew a few words of Norwegian at first. My mom decided I should join a choir, because that was a good way to meet people and learn more Norwegian. I also loved singing. Our director seemed nice, but her directions confused me. Often, after we finished singing a song, she said "Flatt!" and then she smiled and we moved on to the next song. This was very confusing because flat singing (a little under the correct notes) sounds terrible. I thought this director seemed like a very strange musician. Then one day, after a few weeks, I learned a new word: *flott*. It means *beautiful*. It sounds almost the same as *flatt,* which means *flat.* The *o* and the *a* vowels sounded really similar to my American ears, but to people who grew up speaking Norwegian, the two sounds are very different. Because I did not know the word *flott*, I just heard the word I knew that sounded closest to it. Suddenly, I realized that the choir director was saying, "Beautiful!"—not "Flat!"—and everything made sense. I learned that when things don't make sense in a new language, I should ask questions. I shouldn't just think that the people are saying strange things.

1. What was the author's incorrect or different perception?

2. Underline the words and phrases that give concrete details to help you understand the author's perception.

Paragraph 2

> Sometimes I forget that my husband is colorblind. He can see bright colors quite well. But if the color is a bit grayed out, like a gray-green or a gray-purple, he has a lot of trouble. So last year, we decided to paint our living room a lovely green, a gray-green. I was on a work trip, so he had to go to the store to pick up the paint. He forgot the name of the color we chose. But he remembered where it was on the paint sample chart. So he confidently pointed to a color and ordered three cans of paint. He went home and painted the living room "green." When I got back from my trip at the end of the weekend, I was surprised. I saw the living room and yelled, "Why did you paint my living room purple?" It looked like a circus tent. Now he was surprised. He honestly thought it looked green. He misremembered where the color was on the color chart and chose a gray-purple instead of the gray-green. The two of us were able to re-paint the living room the RIGHT color the next weekend. I never left color choices to my husband again!

1. What was the husband's incorrect or different perception?

2. Underline the words and phrases that give concrete details to help you understand the husband's perception.

2 Now use your e-chart to write the first draft of your paragraph.

REVISE: Using Descriptive Adjectives

In a paragraph about an incorrect or different perception, readers expect to read interesting, vivid descriptions of your perception and of how you felt when you learned that your perception was incorrect or different. **Descriptive adjectives** can help you describe your experience in an interesting and clear way.

1 Read the paragraph. Underline the adjectives in the paragraph that describe the perception or how the author felt.

> My father listened to country music when I was a little girl. My sister and I learned lots of these songs. We thought they were fun to sing, and they were often hilarious. One that was especially funny was called "Lucille," by Kenny Rogers. The chorus was, "You picked a fine time to leave me, Lucille, with four hundred children and a crop in the field." My sister and I imagined a farm with four hundred wild children and only one exhausted father to take care of them. When I got older, I played the song at a talent show, and everyone laughed when I sang that line. But they were laughing a little too much, and I felt like something wasn't right. So I went home and looked up the song on the Internet, and I was shocked when I saw the real words. It wasn't four *hundred* children; it was four *hungry* children. These words sound similar, especially in the middle of a sentence, and both of them make sense. Suddenly, the song was not so funny anymore. It was very serious. I was embarrassed. I learned that I cannot rely on my ears to understand the words of songs.

2 Read the paragraph. Look at the underlined adjectives and try to find more interesting adjectives to describe the author's perception and how the author felt.

> When I was in high school, my English teacher gave us an assignment to write a paragraph describing a lemon. I thought it was a <u>boring</u> assignment because everyone knows what a lemon is like. So I did the assignment quickly. I wrote that lemons are yellow and they are sour. They grow on trees. I got a D on this assignment and I was <u>angry</u>! My teacher told me I had to actually look at a lemon and redo the paragraph. I was <u>really angry</u>, but I did not want a D, so I bought a lemon on my way home and tried again. It was <u>very interesting</u>. When I looked at the lemon closely, I saw flecks of green and little holes in the peel. The color became more orange-yellow on one end of the lemon where the stem was. The texture of the peel was <u>smooth</u>. In the end, I wrote a very long paragraph, and I got an A on the rewrite. I was embarrassed about getting angry after the first paragraph I wrote. I understood that it was not good because I wrote from my memory, not from my perceptions.

3 Now go back to the first draft of your paragraph.

1. Add interesting descriptive adjectives that help your reader understand your perception more clearly.

2. Try to use the grammar and a few of the vocabulary items from this unit in some of your sentences.

🔵 Go to **MyEnglishLab** for more skill practice.

EDIT: Writing the Final Draft

APPLY Write the final draft of your paragraph and submit it to your teacher. Carefully edit it for grammatical and mechanical errors, such as spelling, capitalization, and punctuation. Consider how to apply the vocabulary, grammar, and writing skills from the unit. Use the checklist to help you.

FINAL DRAFT CHECKLIST

☐ Does your paragraph describe a perception?

☐ Does it describe how that perception changed?

☐ Does it describe why the perception changed?

☐ Do you use linking verbs of perception accurately?

☐ Do you use descriptive adjectives to describe your perception appropriately?

☐ Do you use new vocabulary that you learned in this unit?

ALTERNATIVE WRITING TOPIC

APPLY Write a DIY blog post explaining what someone should think about as they plan to choose a new color to paint their kitchen. Write about context, lighting, anatomy, and other factors that might affect how someone perceives the color. Use vocabulary and grammar from the unit.

CHECK WHAT YOU'VE LEARNED

Check (✔) the outcomes you've met and vocabulary you've learned. Put an X next to the skills and vocabulary you still need to practice.

Learning Outcomes

☐ Infer abstract ideas from examples

☐ Take notes using abbreviations and symbols

☐ Scan for information

☐ Use linking verbs

☐ Use descriptive adjectives

☐ Write a personal experience paragraph

Vocabulary

☐ affect AWL
☐ consider
☐ context AWL
☐ explanation
☐ factor AWL
☐ fascinated
☐ image AWL

☐ interpret AWL
☐ joke
☐ lenses
☐ perception AWL
☐ senses (*n.*)
☐ surrounding
☐ vision AWL

🔼 Go to **MyEnglishLab** to watch a video about color psychology, access the Unit Project, and take the Unit 5 Achievement Test.

LEARNING OUTCOMES

> Infer meaning from metaphors

> Create an outline to take notes

> Recognize the use of the present tense in a story about the past

> Use time clauses in the present tense

> Add explanations and examples

> Write a one-paragraph story

🔵 Go to **My**English**Lab** to check what you know.

The Heart of a Hero

1 FOCUS ON THE TOPIC

1. Hercules is a Greek hero. In the many stories describing his adventures and combats, Hercules is always extraordinarily strong and courageous. What quality do you think makes someone a hero?

2. Describe a hero from a story or folk tale[1] from your culture.

---

[1] **folk tale:** a short story that comes from the spoken word or oral tradition

READING ONE | What Is a Hero?

VOCABULARY

1 **Read short descriptions of some famous heroes. Pay attention to the boldfaced words.**

1. ODYSSEUS is a hero from Greek stories famous for his **journey** home to his family after the Trojan War.

2. MULAN is a hero from Chinese stories. She is famous for taking her father's job as a soldier. She did not have strength, but she was a good soldier because of her **intelligence.** She used her brains to help the army win.

3. KATNISS EVERDEEN is a hero from the story *The Hunger Games*. This story begins when Katniss is told she must fight to the death against other teenagers in a horrible "game." This game is entertainment for a world that has lost its way. The story follows Katniss as she **struggles** to change the rules of the game and to help her world become whole again.

4. IRON MAN is a superhero known for the power from his metal suit. In each adventure, he helps people get out of **dangerous** situations.

5. BILBO BAGGINS, the hero of the story *The Hobbit*, **succeeds** in returning the stolen gold to his friend, Thorin.

6. GOKU is a Japanese Manga hero. He is known for his strength. He uses his strength to bring people to **safety** and create peace.

7. KING ARTHUR is one of Britain's most famous heroes. He had a **mentor,** Merlin. Merlin was a wise man who taught King Arthur how to be a king and how to be a man.

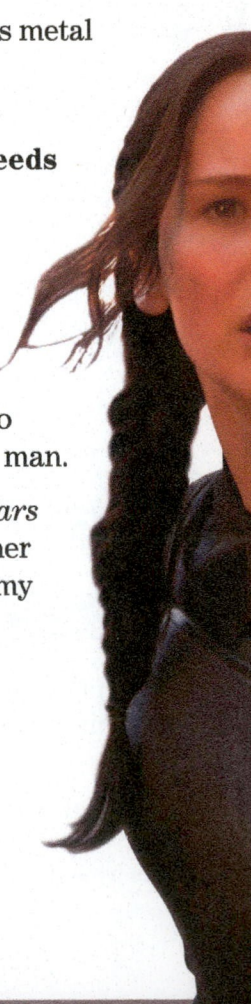

8. PRINCESS LEIA ORGANA is the female hero of the *Star Wars* movies. She was deeply **affected by** the attacks on her people by Darth Vader. She never rests until this enemy is beaten.

9. JIM HAWKINS is the young hero of the story *Treasure Island*. Jim helps the good guys find the gold hidden on an island and return it to its owners.

10. ROBIN HOOD is a British hero who helps the poor at every **opportunity.** Whenever he can, he steals money from the rich and gives it to the poor.

2 Match the boldfaced words on the left with the definitions on the right.

_e_ 1. **journey**
_h_ 2. **intelligence**
_i_ 3. **struggle**
_f_ 4. **dangerous**
_a_ 5. **succeed**
_d_ 6. **safety**
_j_ 7. **mentor**
_b_ 8. **affected by**
_c_ 9. **treasure**
_g_ 10. **opportunity**

a. to do well; to do what you tried to do
b. changed or touched by someone or something
c. a group of valuable things such as gold, silver, and jewelry
d. the state of being free from danger or harm
e. a trip, usually a long one
f. likely to harm people
g. a chance or a time to do something
h. the ability to learn and understand things
i. to try to do something that is difficult or to fight something
j. an older and wiser person who helps a younger person

🔵 Go to the **Pearson Practice English App** or **MyEnglishLab** for more vocabulary practice.

Go to **MyEnglishLab** to view example notes.

PREVIEW

You are going to read a college student's essay on the work of Joseph Campbell, a professor of literature and religion. Campbell is famous for his ideas about hero stories from around the world. Before you read, look at the list below. Check (✓) three things you think Campbell might say about heroes.

Heroes . . .

☐ are good.
☐ are handsome / beautiful.
☑ have special abilities.
☐ are strong.
☑ help others.

☐ are scared.
☐ go out into the world.
☑ fight bad people.
☑ do something difficult.

READ

Read the essay on the next page. Create a chart like the one below to take notes.

▌ TAKE NOTES

Main Ideas	Details
Hero stories all similar Key moment Hero returns home	First part: always journey Test or overcome a challenge. Get experiences, knowledge and wisdom.

🔵 Go to **MyEnglishLab** to view example notes.

Natalie Carson
English 1A

WHAT IS A HERO?

1 Joseph Campbell (1904–1987) spent his life defining what a hero is. Campbell was a professor of literature and religion at Sarah Lawrence College in New York. He studied and taught hero stories from around the world. Over the years, he noticed that a lot of myths—a kind of hero story—are very similar. In old myths or new ones, whether from Asia, Africa, the Americas, or Europe, the world's hero stories all have the same basic shape. The details of the stories may change, but every hero story has the same three parts.

2 During the first part of any hero story, the hero starts a **journey**. This can be a trip from one country to another. It can be an adventure into outer space. It can be a journey into a dream world. Often the hero does not, at first, want to go on this journey. But in the end, they[1] agree. They leave the **safety** of their home, friends, and family to go to this new place. This place is very different from the hero's home and is often dark and **dangerous**. Sometimes there is a **mentor** or a teacher who helps the hero understand this new place. The mentor gives the hero the tools or information they need. For example, a kind old lady on the road may give our hero a map for the journey. A stranger may give the young hero the key to the door of the enemy king's castle[2].

3 The second part in the hero story is the most exciting. This is when the hero must pass some kind of test or overcome a challenge. A common example of a test is fighting a monster. In these stories, the monster is much bigger and stronger than our hero. The hero does not, at first, believe they can kill the monster. Other common challenges include solving a problem or facing a fear such as the fear of snakes. In any challenge, the hero must use their strength, **intelligence**, or heart to pass the test. They must kill the dragon, answer the question, or trust their feelings. Of course, in the end, the hero always **succeeds**.

4 Finally, in the third part of the hero story, the hero returns home. They are a different person now and bring what they acquired or learned on the journey—wealth, knowledge, and wisdom—to share with family and friends. When they return home, others are also **affected by** this journey. Sometimes enemies are embarrassed. Sometimes family and friends become rich. Sometimes the hero's town becomes free.

5 Campbell believed that the adventure of the hero is the adventure of being alive. Campbell spent his life studying myths because he loved the stories and believed they were important. He believed that the hero's journey is similar to a person's life. All people live through difficult **struggles** (the test or challenge) and must use their strength, intelligence, and heart to succeed. He says that by going down into the darkness, we find the **treasures** of life. He explains that the cave[3] we are afraid to enter has the treasure we are looking for and that when we stumble[4], then we will find gold. In short, Campbell believes that **opportunities** to find deeper powers within ourselves come when life seems most difficult.

---

[1] **they:** In paragraphs 2, 3, 4 of this text, **they** (and **their**) is used as a singular generic pronoun or a person of either sex. By using **they / their** to refer to the hero, the author indicates that the hero can be male or female.

[2] **castle:** a very large stone building built in past times to protect the king from attack

[3] **cave:** a large dark hole in the side of a cliff or under the ground

[4] **stumble:** to hit something with your foot and almost fall while you are walking

Circle the word or phrase that best completes each statement about an idea discussed in the essay. Use your notes to help you.

1. Hero stories are **the same / different** all over the world.

2. Hero stories usually have **two / three** main parts.

3. Hero stories are important because they are **similar to / different from** life in general.

1 Check (✓) the words or phrases that *always* belong to the three parts of the hero story. Use your notes to help you.

Part One

☑ a journey   ☑ leaving home

☐ a castle   ☐ a mentor / teacher

☑ an adventure   ☐ coming home

☑ a dream

Part Two

☑ a test / challenge   ☑ facing a fear

☑ a monster   ☐ snakes

☑ a fight   ☐ overcoming a challenge

☑ solving a problem

Part Three

☑ returning home   ☑ wisdom

☑ bringing what they gained   ☐ others are changed, too

☑ wealth   ☐ enemies killed

☑ knowledge   ☑ friends become rich

2 Look at your notes and at your answers in Preview. How did they help you understand the essay?

Inferring Meaning from Metaphors

An **inference** is an educated guess about something that is not directly stated in the text. Sometimes a writer suggests a complex idea by using a **metaphor** (word / phrase creating an **image**) that **makes the complex idea simpler and clearer.**

Look at the example and read the explanation.

- "... the cave we are afraid to enter has the treasure we are looking for ..." (*paragraph 5*)

Cave here is used as a metaphor. From the image of a cave, the reader infers the dark, difficult things in a person's life, such as sadness, poverty, anger, poor health, or any other negative human experience. These are complex things to describe. The author simplifies these complicated ideas by using the word *cave* because this word holds all the feeling and meaning of those difficult things.

After reading the text closely, especially certain words or phrases that are used as metaphors, we can **infer the full meaning** of the complex ideas the author wants to convey.

1 Read the quotes from paragraph 5 of the reading. The underlined word in each one is used as a metaphor. What complex idea does the author want to convey here? Write the meaning of the metaphor on the line.

Metaphor	**Meaning**
1. "... the cave we are afraid to enter has the <u>treasure</u> we are looking for ..."	_____
2. "... when we <u>stumble</u>, then we will find gold."	_____
3. "... when we stumble, then we will find <u>gold</u>."	_____

2 Now discuss your answers with a partner. Point out sentences, words, or phrases in the paragraph that helped you find the answers.

DISCUSS 🔍

Discuss the questions in a small group. Then share your answers with the class.

1. The last paragraph states Campbell's idea that "by going down into the darkness, we find the treasures of life." Explain this idea.

2. Think of a hero story from your culture. Does it follow the pattern that Joseph Campbell describes for all hero stories throughout the world? Explain.

> **USE YOUR NOTES**
>
> Use your notes to support your answers with information from the reading.

🔵 Go to **My**English**Lab** to give your opinion about another question.

PREVIEW

1 Look at the title of the reading below and at the photos. Write two questions that you think will be answered in this reading.

_____

_____

2 Look at the boldfaced words and phrases in the reading. Which words or phrases do you know the meaning of?

READ

1 Now read the blog by pre-med student Alice Ogrodnik. As you read, guess the meanings of the words that are new to you. Remember to take notes on main ideas and details.

BOOK REVIEW:

HARRY POTTER AND THE SORCERER'S STONE

About Me: My name is Alice Ogrodnik. I'm a 22-year-old senior in college, studying biology. After I graduate, I am going to medical school to become a medical geneticist. I'm a big reader and use reading as a way to relax from all the hard class work.

I just finished reading *Harry Potter and the Sorcerer's Stone* by J. K. Rowling. I know I'm a little behind most of you. Most people I know read these books years ago. In fact, I think a lot of people my age who never read books for fun, started reading BECAUSE of the *Harry Potter* books. But I wasn't like those people. I read books all the time. So when everyone started reading Harry Potter, I told myself the books were bad. I told myself I read GOOD books, not silly stuff. Well, silly me. I just finished the first one and guess what? It was great. Read on to hear why . . .

First of all, I love a story where the main character is just a normal kid. No, not all kids are wizards[1]. But all kids go to school, make friends, play games, and have teachers they love and teachers they hate. Only in Harry's world all this happens at an amazing place called Hogwarts School of Witchcraft and Wizardry. Here, Harry makes two best friends, Ron and Hermione. They go to cool classes like Potions (**magic** drinks) and Magic History. They get to play a magical sport called Quidditch, which seems really fun. Harry hates his potions teacher, Snape, and he loves the headmaster, Dumbledore. Harry has no parents. When he was a baby, they died **protecting** him from the wizard Lord Voldemort. So Dumbledore acts like a father to Harry.

---

[1] **wizard:** a man who teaches and practices magic

(continued on next page)

The second reason I loved this book is because it is a great **adventure**. One day, Harry and his two friends find something strange at their school: a large three-headed dog. They learn that the dog is protecting something called the Sorcerer's Stone. This magical stone takes Hermione, Ron, and Harry on a long journey that leads them to the basement of Hogwarts. Here they must pass many tests. If they fail to pass all the tests, Lord Voldemort will get the Stone, live forever, and rule the wizard world. The challenges are really exciting! In one room they find a magical plant that tries to eat them. In another room they must play and win a life-sized game of wizard chess[2]. In the next room, they must drink dangerous potions. Because there's only enough potion for one, Harry takes it and goes on alone. When he finally arrives in the last room, Harry meets Lord Voldemort—the most dangerous wizard of all time. Will Harry be able to win? Harry does his best in a wizard battle. At last Voldemort reaches for Harry's arm. Harry thinks it is over. He falls to the ground and everything goes black.

In the last chapter, Harry wakes up in bed with his friends nearby and Dumbledore smiling down at him. Dumbledore explains that Harry didn't **fail**. When his mother saved him from Voldemort with her life, she gave Harry the most powerful magic in the world. With it, he **defeated** Voldemort. At least for now.

This brings me to the third reason I loved this book: Harry is all set to have another adventure because he must meet Voldemort again. . . . I can't wait to read *Harry Potter and the Chamber of Secrets*!

---

[2] chess: a board game requiring deep thinking

2 Compare your notes on main ideas and details with a partner's. How can you improve your notes next time?

🔵 Go to the **Pearson Practice English App** or **MyEnglishLab** for more vocabulary practice.

Creating an Outline to Take Notes

When taking notes on a reading, it can be helpful to use an **outline** to **show the basic structure** of a reading. Some readings are written in a way to make this a useful note-taking strategy.

For example, some readings are set up with a simple structure such as:

I. There are three parts in this story. OR	I. I like this story for three reasons.
II. Part One	II. Reason 1
III. Part Two	III. Reason 2
IV. Part Three	IV. Reason 3

This allows for a note-taker to focus first on the **main idea** of the whole reading, then on the **main points** (parts or reasons), and then, if needed, on the **details.**

For example, in Reading One, the main idea of the reading is that there are three parts in a hero's tale, so the main points are the parts, and each part includes details:

I. There are three parts in a hero's tale.

II. Part One: The Journey
   A. doesn't want to go
   B. dangerous
   C. usually has a mentor / helper

III. Part Two: The Challenge
   A. fight a monster
   B. face a fear
   C. use strength, intelligence, courage

IV. Part Three: The Return
   A. new person
   B. shares what they learned with family / friends

1 Look at Reading Two. Complete Reasons 2 and 3 for an outline based on the structure of the reading.

    I.   Alice Ogrodnik likes the book *Harry Potter and the Sorcerer's Stone* for three reasons.

    II. Reason 1: She loves a story with a normal kid: HP normal kid

    III. Reason 2: _____

    IV. Reason 3: _____

2 Read paragraph 2 again. Write some notes on the details for Reason 1.

    II. Reason 1: She loves a story with a normal kid: HP normal kid

        A. Detail: _____

        B. Detail: _____

        C. Detail: _____

3 Read paragraph 3 again. Write some notes on Reason 2 and the details for Reason 2.

    III. Reason 2: _____

        A. Detail: _____

        B. Detail: _____

        C. Detail: _____

➤ Go to **MyEnglishLab** for more note-taking practice.

COMPREHENSION

Number the following events in the order they happen in the story of *Harry Potter and Sorcerer's Stone.* Use your notes from Reading Two to help you. Discuss your answers with a partner.

a. __1__ Harry's parents die.

b. _____ Lord Voldemort is defeated.

c. _____ Harry makes friends with Ron and Hermione.

d. _____ Harry wakes up next to his friends and Dumbledore.

e. _____ Harry and his friends find the three-headed dog.

f. _____ Harry and his friends win at wizard chess.

g. _____ Harry goes to Hogwarts.

h. _____ Harry fights Lord Voldemort.

1 **Look at Reading Two and read the first two sentences of paragraph 3 again. What tenses are being used here? Underline the present tense once and all other tenses twice.**

Recognizing the Use of the Present Tense in a Story About the Past

As we read, we notice that **tenses** can **affect how we feel** about the text:

If a story is written in the **past tense,** we feel more **distant** from those events. Those events happened before now, so they don't matter as much.

If a story is written in the **present or present progressive tense,** we feel more **connected** to the events. Those events feel like they are happening now, and so they feel more exciting and interesting.

Look at the example and read the explanation.

- "The second reason I loved this book is because it is a great adventure. One day, Harry and his two friends find something strange at their school: a large three-headed dog." (*paragraph 3*)

The **first sentence** is part of the blog. The main verb is *loved*. This is **past tense** because the author read this book sometime in the recent past. She loved it when she read it.

The **second sentence** is the start of the Harry Potter story. The verb here is *find*. This is **present tense** because the author wants to help readers feel more connected to the story.

2 **Work with a partner. Read two versions of the same text from paragraph 3 of Reading Two. Underline the verbs in each version. What verb tense is used in Version 1? Why? What verb tense is used in Version 2? Why?**

Version 1

One day, Harry and his two friends find something strange at their school: a large three-headed dog. They learn that the dog is protecting something called the Sorcerer's Stone. This magical stone takes Hermione, Ron, and Harry on a long journey that leads them to the basement of Hogwarts.

Version 2

One day, Harry and his two friends found something strange at their school: a large three-headed dog. They learned that the dog was protecting something called the Sorcerer's Stone. This magical stone took Hermione, Ron, and Harry on a long journey that led them to the basement of Hogwarts.

3 **Agree or disagree with the statements about the two versions of the text.**

	Agree	Disagree
1. The paragraph in present tense is more exciting.	☐	☐
2. The paragraph in present tense makes me feel like I'm there in the action.	☐	☐
3. The paragraph in past tense feels like this story happened a long time ago.	☐	☐
4. The paragraph in past tense feels more natural.	☐	☐

➦ Go to **MyEnglishLab** for more skill practice.

ORGANIZE

Reading One (R1) contains lots of information about all hero stories. Reading Two (R2) describes details of one specific hero story. Read the lists of sentences describing what happens in R1 and R2, and place each sentence in the correct box in the chart below.

R1

~~The hero leaves on a journey.~~

The hero's family / friends are affected by what happened on the journey.

The hero returns home.

The hero must pass a test or overcome a challenge.

The mentor shows the hero some useful things.

The hero succeeds by using their intelligence, strength, or heart.

R2

~~Harry goes into the basement of Hogwarts.~~

Harry gets past the eating plant.

The world is saved from Lord Voldemort getting the Sorcerer's Stone.

Harry defeats Lord Voldemort.

Harry wins a magic game of chess.

Harry wakes up in bed with Dumbledore smiling down at him.

> **USE YOUR NOTES**
>
> Review your notes from Readings One and Two. Use the information in your notes to complete the chart.

	Features of Every Hero's Story (R1)	Features of Harry Potter's Story (R2)
PART ONE	The hero leaves on a journey.	Harry goes into the basement of Hogwarts.
PART TWO		
PART THREE		

SYNTHESIZE

Mugglenet is the most popular *Harry Potter* website (a *muggle* is the word in the stories for a non-magical person). Complete the website discussion with information from Organize.

Mugglenet Chat

HPBoy: I'm taking this great literature class on Joseph Campbell. Campbell describes the classic hero stories as all having the same form. Most of the stories he talks about are really, really old. But yesterday my teacher started talking about Harry Potter! I couldn't believe it. She says *Harry Potter and the Sorcerer's Stone* has the same basic form of all these really old hero stories.

RedMagic: That makes sense. I heard that J. K. Rowling studied Classics[1] at university. She probably knew a lot about these old stories and used some of the ideas.

HPBoy: Yeah, she definitely had the three main parts.

RedMagic: What are those parts?

HPBoy: Well, the first part is _____

RedMagic: And the second part?

HPBoy: _____

RedMagic: And what's the second part in *Harry Potter and the Sorcerer's Stone*?

HPBoy: _____

RedMagic: You said three parts. What's the third one, and how does it show up in *Harry Potter and the Sorcerer's Stone*?

HPBoy: _____

_____

RedMagic: That is so cool. It makes me feel like our love for these stories is important now . . . not something childish. It makes me want to go back to reread the book to see what you're talking about. Do you think it's true for all the *Harry Potter* books?

[1] **Classics:** the languages, literature, and history of ancient Greece and Rome

🔵 Go to **MyEnglishLab** to check what you learned.

VOCABULARY

REVIEW

Complete the tale of Perseus with the words from the box.

adventure	defeats	journey	opportunity	struggles
affected by	fail	magic	protect	succeeds
~~dangerous~~	intelligent	mentors	safety	treasure

Perseus is a Greek hero who lives on an island with his family. On a nearby island lives

Medusa. Medusa is a female monster with hair made of snakes. She is very ___dangerous___.

1.

When anyone looks upon her ugly face, they turn to stone. Many young men try to kill her.

But they all _____ because they do not turn their eyes away. They all lose their lives.

2.

One day, the king of the land asks Perseus to go on a _____ to bring back the head

3.

of Medusa. Perseus does not want to leave the _____ of his home and family. But he

4.

decides to say yes. For Perseus, this is a(n) _____ to show his power as a young man.

5.

On the road to find Medusa, Perseus meets two _____ who will help him. First,

6.

he meets the god Hermes. Hermes gives him _____ shoes with wings. With these

7.

shoes, Perseus can fly. Second, he meets Athena, the goddess of war. She gives him a shield[1]

to _____ himself. How can Perseus kill Medusa without looking at her? Perseus is

8.

a(n) _____ young man. He uses the shoes to fight Medusa from the air. He uses the

9.

shield as a mirror to see Medusa, so he can cut off her head without looking directly at her.

They start to fight. Medusa _____. She cannot win. In the end, Perseus _____

10. **11.**

Medusa and _____.

12.

On the trip home, Perseus meets and falls in love with Andromeda,

his true love. Together they return to the king with Medusa's

head in a bag. Perseus' _____ is over—the monster is

13.

dead and he has his _____, Andromeda. Perseus' whole

14.

community is _____ his success when he becomes king.

15.

[1] **shield:** a large piece of metal, wood, or other material used to
protect a soldier from attack

EXPAND

1 Complete the chart with the correct word forms. Some categories have more than one form. Use a dictionary if necessary. An X indicates that there is no form in the category.

	NOUN	VERB	ADJECTIVE	ADVERB
1.	defeat		*a. defeated* *b. defeating*	X
2.		X	dangerous	dangerously
3.	failure		**a.** failed **b.** failing	failingly
4.	magic	X	**a.** magical **b.** magic	magically
5.	**a.** protection **b.** protector	protect		protectively
6.	safety		safe	
7.		succeed	successful	

2 Complete each sentence using the correct form of the word in parentheses.

1. Thor, a superhero, has a _____ hammer.
   (magic)

2. Katniss Everdeen is very _____ of her younger sister, Primrose.
   (protect)

3. Perseus comes _____ close to looking at the face of Medusa and turning to stone.
   (danger)

4. Harry Potter _____ completes the challenges in the basement of Hogwarts.
   (success)

5. Robin Hood _____ rescues Maid Marion from the King's men.
   (safety)

6. The Iron Giant _____ to hide himself in the junk yard.
   (failure)

7. Lord Voldemort tries to _____ Harry Potter, but he _____ .
   (defeat) ... *(failure)*

CREATE

APPLY <u>makeyourownhero.com</u> **is a website for story writers. Use words from the box to complete the blog post and comments on a recent story that a writer posted on the site.**

adventure	defeats	journey	opportunity	struggle
affected by	fail	magic	protect	succeed
dangerous	intelligence	mentor	safety	treasure

FORUM

GS **Golemsays:** I think FictionGuys's last post was weak. I didn't like it at all. What was the story? A young mother finds a magical stone in her garden and just keeps it? . . . I don't get it. How are we supposed to see her as any kind of hero? What do you think?

COMMENT

KM **KrytoMan:** I agree. Maybe the mother uses the stone to go on a long _____ to a different land. Here she meets a _____ monster that tries to kill her and her child.

COMMENT

MM **Mythmaker:** Nice one. The mother and the monster can _____ to get the child. The mother starts to _____. We think she will lose. Then, suddenly, she finds her power and _____ the monster by killing him with his own sword.

COMMENT

NF **Norsefan:** I like that idea. What about this one: _____

_____

_____

COMMENT

SM **Supermanfan:** What if _____

_____

_____

COMMENT

➤ Go to the **Pearson Practice English App** or **MyEnglishLab** for more vocabulary practice.

1 Read the paragraph about Atalanta. Circle the word *when* every time you see it. Underline the verbs in each *when* sentence.

> Atalanta is a popular Greek hero. She is a great runner. She can run faster than any man or woman. Her father wants her to marry. But she doesn't want to belong to any man. Her father gets angry when she refuses to marry. They argue. Finally, she agrees to a deal: She will marry the first man who can beat her in a race. Many young men try to defeat her, but they all fail. She is too fast. One young man, Hippomeses, asks a god for help. The god tells him to throw down three golden apples on the race course. When he does this, Atalanta stops running to look at the beautiful golden apples. Hippomeses wins the race, and Atalanta marries him.

Time Clauses in the Present Tense

1. We can combine two sentences that tell about time by using a **time clause** and a **main clause**. ***When** Hippomeses meets Atalanta* is a time clause. The time clause and the main clause are both in the same tense. Here, that tense is the **simple present**.	Hippomeses meets Atalanta. He falls in love with her. **Time Clause** ***When** Hippomeses **meets** Atalanta,* **Main Clause** he **falls** in love with her.
2. A clause contains a subject and a verb. A **time clause** contains a *time word* + subject + verb. It cannot stand alone as a sentence. It needs to be attached to a main clause. A **main clause** can stand alone as a sentence.	[TW] [S] [V] ***When** Hippomeses **meets** Atalanta,* [S] [V] he **falls** in love with her. He falls in love with her.
3. When the time clause begins the sentence, put a **comma** before the main clause. There is **no comma** when the main clause begins the sentence.	***When** Hippomeses meets Atalanta, he falls in love with her.* Hippomeses falls in love with Atalanta ***when** he meets her.* INCORRECT: Hippomeses falls in love with Atalanta, ***when** he meets her.*
4. These are some common **time words** used for time clauses: *when, before, after.* Use the **noun in the first clause** (either the time clause or the main clause) and the **pronoun in the second clause**.	***Before** Mulan joins the army, **she** practices fighting.* **Mulan** returns to her family ***after she** becomes a successful soldier.*

2 Read each sentence. Add a comma if the sentence needs it.

1. When I choose a book to read _____ I usually choose one with exciting adventures.

2. When I read stories to my children _____ I try to decide if the hero follows Joseph Campbell's rules.

3. My son wants to be a superhero _____ when he grows up.

4. When I travel to other countries _____ I like to learn the old stories of that culture.

5. Before Harry Potter decides to fight Voldemort _____ he gets the help of his friends, Ron and Hermione.

3 Complete these sentences. Make sure you use the correct form of the verb.

1. When Harry Potter _____ , _____ .

2. Robin Hood is happy when _____ .

3. Before a hero goes on a journey, they usually _____ .

4. After they _____ , a hero _____ .

▶ Go to the **Pearson Practice English App** or **MyEnglishLab** for more grammar practice. Check what you learned in **MyEnglishLab**.

FINAL WRITING TASK: A One-Paragraph Story 🔍 APPLY

In this unit, you read about heroes and hero stories. Joseph Campbell says people tell hero stories because the stories are like life: "All people live through difficult struggles (the test or challenge) and must use their strength, intelligence, and heart to succeed."

You are going to **write a paragraph to tell the story of a hero.** You will choose a hero (from a folk tale, book, or movie) and describe the three parts of your hero's story. You will describe your hero's challenge; how this hero uses their strength, intelligence, or heart to overcome the challenge; and the effects (ways this success changes your hero and others). Use the vocabulary and grammar from this unit.

For an alternative writing topic, see page 151.

PREPARE TO WRITE: Listing

Choose a hero to write about. It can be a folk hero from your culture, a comic book superhero, a movie hero, or a real-life hero. Write a list of the main events in their adventures and important characteristics. List these events in order as in the example about the Chinese hero, Mulan.

Mulan is a hero from China from around 600 A.D.

She's the daughter of an old general.

Her father taught her how to use a knife and how to ride a horse . . . not normal for a girl.

Soldiers come to town to get men to fight in the war.

Mulan's father was too old to fight.

Mulan's father didn't have a son to send in his place.

Mulan stole her father's horse and knife.

She dressed up like a man.

She joined the army.

Mulan fought for many years.

No one knew she was a girl.

She wasn't strong.

She was smart.

She made clever plans to help the army win the war.

After the war, the emperor offered Mulan a job that would make her rich.

Mulan wanted only to return home to her family.

Her family was happy to see her.

Her father was ill, but alive.

She dressed in women's clothes again.

Friends from the army came to visit.

They learned Mulan was a woman.

She saved her father from having to fight.

She brought honor to her family.

WRITE: Outlining the Story

The writing task gives you categories to help you organize your story:

I. Background

II. Part One: The Challenge

III. Part Two: How the Hero Overcomes the Challenge

IV. Part Three: The Effects

To write your outline, you must choose only the important information from your list that matches these categories.

1 **Reread the list a student wrote about the Chinese hero, Mulan. Notice what information she crossed out and how she categorized the list.**

I.   BACKGROUND

Mulan is a hero from China from around 600 A.D.

She's the daughter of an old general.

Her father taught her how to use a knife and how to ride a horse . . . not normal for a girl.

Soldiers come to town to get men to fight in the war.

II. THE CHALLENGE

Mulan's father was too old to fight.

Mulan's father didn't have a son to send in his place.

~~Mulan stole her father's horse and knife.~~

She dressed up like a man.

She joined the army.

Mulan fought for many years.

No one knew she was a girl.

She wasn't strong.

III. HOW THE HERO OVERCOMES THE CHALLENGE

She was smart.

She made clever plans to help the army win the war.

~~After the war, the emperor offered Mulan a job that would make her rich.~~

~~Mulan wanted only to return home to her family.~~

~~Her family was happy to see her.~~

~~Her father was ill, but alive.~~

~~She dressed in women's clothes again.~~

~~Friends from the army came to visit.~~

~~They learned Mulan was a woman.~~

IV. THE EFFECTS

She saved her father from having to fight.

She brought honor to her family.

Now look at the sentences from your list about your hero. Cross out any sentences that aren't important.

2 **Write the sentences that you haven't crossed out from your list in the correct section of this outline.**

I. Background

_____

_____

_____

_____

_____

II. The Challenge

_____

_____

_____

_____

III. How the Hero Overcomes the Challenge

_____

_____

_____

_____

_____

IV. The Effects

_____

_____

_____

_____

_____

3 An outline can help a writer organize. In short texts, each section of the outline may be a few sentences. In longer texts, each section can be a paragraph. Read the paragraph below. Identify the parts of this paragraph.

- <u>Underline</u> the background information on the hero.
- Circle the information on the challenge.
- <u>Double underline</u> the information on how the hero overcomes the challenge.
- [Bracket] the effects.

> Mulan is a girl hero from China around 600 A.D. Her father is supposed to join the army to fight the Huns. He is old. She is young. She decides to join the army instead of her father. Her challenge is to pass as a boy. This is difficult because she is not very strong like the other soldiers. But she is very clever. In their first battle, when she and her men face too many enemy soldiers, her idea saves them. Mulan tells her men to make a big noise. The sound makes a wall of snow fall on the enemy soldiers. Mulan and her men win the battle. This is the first of many times when Mulan makes a plan to save her men. The leader of the soldiers is very happy with Mulan for this, and her secret is never discovered. Mulan succeeds in saving her father from fighting. Also, she brings honor to her family by being a good soldier.

4 Now write the first draft of your paragraph. Include all the information in your outline. Remember to use the simple present.

REVISE: Adding Explanations and Examples

Explanations and **examples** help the reader understand what the author is trying to say. They give the reader specific information to help explain the ideas.

1 Read the paragraph about Mulan again. Look at the underlined sentence. How do we know that Mulan is clever? What does the author show us that proves she is clever?

> Mulan is a girl hero from China around 600 A.D. Her father is supposed to join the army to fight the Huns. He is old. She is young. She decides to join the army instead of her father. Her challenge is to pass as a boy. This is difficult because she is not very strong like the other soldiers. <u>But she is very clever.</u> In their first battle, when she and her men face too many enemy soldiers, her idea saves them. <u>Mulan tells her men to make a big noise. The sound makes a wall of snow fall on the enemy soldiers.</u> Mulan and her men win the battle. This is the first of many times when Mulan makes a plan to save her men. The leader of the soldiers is very happy with Mulan for this, and her secret is never discovered. Mulan succeeds in saving her father from fighting. Also, she brings honor to her family by being a good soldier.

Read the double underlined sentence. This is an example of how Mulan is clever. It shows us she is clever.

2 **Read the paragraph about Odysseus. The author tells us that Odysseus is clever. But he doesn't <u>show</u> this idea.**

> On his journey home from fighting in the Trojan War, Odysseus faces many problems. In one story, he and his men get caught in the home of a Cyclops—a one-eyed giant. The Cyclops is very strong and very big, and he plans to eat Odysseus and his men. Odysseus must stop him. He does this by being very clever. He saves himself and his men, and they all return to their boats and sail for home.

Check (✓) the sentence that you think best shows that Odysseus is clever. Put a star in the paragraph where you think that sentence should go.

_____ a. His men want to run away from the giant with one eye, but he stays to fight him.

_____ b. He is afraid of the giant with one eye and tells his men to run away.

_____ c. Odysseus and his men dress up like sheep. The Cyclops thinks they are sheep, and they walk out and away.

_____ d. Odysseus is bigger and stronger than the Cyclops. He beats him in a fight.

3 **Now go back to the first draft of your paragraph.**

1. Add supporting sentences that give specific examples and explanations to help explain main ideas.

2. Try to use the grammar and a few of the vocabulary items from this unit in some of your sentences.

➤ Go to **MyEnglishLab** for more skill practice.

Odysseus and his men sailing for home.

EDIT: Writing the Final Draft

APPLY Write the final draft of your paragraph and submit it to your teacher. Carefully edit it for grammatical and mechanical errors, such as spelling, capitalization, and punctuation. Consider how to apply the vocabulary, grammar, and writing skills from the unit. Use the checklist to help you.

FINAL DRAFT CHECKLIST

☐ Does your paragraph describe a hero?

☐ Does it explain the hero's background, the challenge, how the hero overcomes the challenge, and the effects?

☐ Does it contain a topic sentence?

☐ Are there enough supporting sentences to explain the topic sentence?

☐ Do the supporting sentences give examples and explanations?

☐ Do you use time clauses in the present tense correctly?

☐ Do you use correct punctuation?

☐ Do you use new vocabulary that you learned in this unit?

ALTERNATIVE WRITING TOPIC

APPLY According to Joseph Campbell, every culture has hero stories. There are many websites about everyday heroes, superheroes, and comic book heroes. Write a paragraph explaining why you think people are so interested in heroes and what heroes do for our lives. Use vocabulary and grammar from the unit.

_____

_____

_____

_____

CHECK WHAT YOU'VE LEARNED

Check (✔) the outcomes you've met and vocabulary you've learned. Put an X next to the skills and vocabulary you still need to practice.

Learning Outcomes
- ☐ Infer meaning from metaphors
- ☐ Create an outline to take notes
- ☐ Recognize the use of the present tense in a story about the past
- ☐ Use time clauses in the present tense
- ☐ Add explanations and examples
- ☐ Write a one-paragraph story

Vocabulary
- ☐ adventure
- ☐ dangerous
- ☐ defeat
- ☐ fail
- ☐ intelligence **AWL**
- ☐ journey
- ☐ magic
- ☐ mentor
- ☐ opportunity
- ☐ protect
- ☐ safety
- ☐ struggle
- ☐ succeed
- ☐ treasure

Multi-word Units
- ☐ affected by

⬆ Go to **MyEnglishLab** to watch a video about heroes, access the Unit Project, and take the Unit 6 Achievement Test.

LEARNING OUTCOMES

> Infer judgements
> Take double entry notes
> Visualize while reading

> Use adverbs of manner
> Use time order words in a narrative
> Write a narrative paragraph

🔊 Go to **MyEnglishLab** to check what you know.

What's Your Medicine?

1 FOCUS ON THE TOPIC

1. Describe the objects you see in the photo.
2. What do all of these objects have in common? What are some ways that they are different?

READING ONE | Leech

Today people have a lot of choices about who can help them when they are sick. They can see modern doctors or traditional healers. But many people choose to treat themselves at home when they have a common health problem.

1 **Look at the pictures of several common health problems. Write the letter of the appropriate picture next to the name of the health problem.**

a.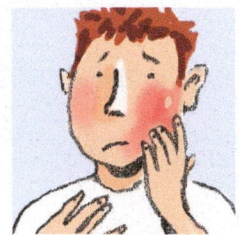
b.
c.

d.
e.
f.

g.
h.
i.

___c___ 1. headache

_____ 2. stomachache

_____ 3. earache

_____ 4. toothache

_____ 5. backache

_____ 6. sore throat

_____ 7. fever

_____ 8. sprained ankle[1]

_____ 9. a cold / the flu

---

[1] **sprained ankle:** something you get when you fall and hurt your ankle but it's not broken

2 Read the list of words and their definitions.

> **blood:** the red liquid that your heart pumps through your body
> **cure:** to make a sick person well again
> **fever:** when the body is sick and is hotter than normal
> **flow:** when a liquid (water, for example) moves steadily from one place to another
> **patients:** people who are getting medical treatment
> **popular:** liked by many people
> **saliva:** the liquid produced naturally in your mouth
> **sore throat:** when the throat is red and painful
> **swelling:** an area on your body that becomes larger than usual because of injury or sickness
> **swollen:** bigger than usual because of injury or sickness
> ~~**treat:** to do something to a sick person to try to make him or her well again~~
> **veins:** the tubes that bring blood back to the heart from the rest of the body

Now use the words from the list to complete the short descriptions of home remedies.

1. **Headache:** In China, some people _____ *treat* _____ a headache with a coin (metal money). Hold the coin in your fingers and rub it back and forth across the forehead very hard. It will leave a red mark.

2. _____: The most common remedy for this problem is cool water. Put the sick person in a cool bath or wash the person gently with a cool cloth. Don't put the person in ice water. It could be bad for him or her.

3. **Cold:** Some people believe you can _____ a cold by drinking a lot of orange juice. Orange juice has a lot of vitamin C. This helps the body heal.

4. _____: One remedy for this problem is honey. Eat one big spoonful three times a day. Most children love this remedy. The honey is sweet, and it feels nice on the throat. In fact, older _____ like it, too!

5. **Stomachache:** A _____ remedy is ginger (a spice from a light brown root). Cook 4 ounces of ginger in 1 quart of water for 1 hour. Drink a glass three times a day.

6. **Toothache:** When you have a toothache, everything that goes in your mouth hurts. Even swallowing your own _____ can hurt. For hundreds of years, the most common remedy for a toothache was to drink a glass of whiskey and have your neighbor pull out the tooth. These days, people just go to the dentist.

7. **Sprained ankle:** A sprained ankle often gets _____ . To bring down the _____, do two things. First, put a bag of ice on the ankle. The cold makes the _____ in the ankle get smaller. Put the ice on the ankle for no longer than 10 minutes every couple of hours. Second, put your foot up high. This helps the _____ _____ back to the heart and makes the ankle go back to its normal size.

Go to the **Pearson Practice English App** or **MyEnglishLab** for more vocabulary practice.

The following article is an excerpt from an encyclopedia entry. Read the title and the section headings. What kind of information do you think you will find in this article? Check (✓) the things you think you will find.

_____ 1. how many kinds of leeches are in the world

_____ 2. definition of *leech*

_____ 3. how to catch leeches

_____ 4. description of what leeches eat

_____ 5. stories about people being leeched

_____ 6. how leeches have been used in medicine in the past

_____ 7. how leeches are used in medicine today

_____ 8. how leeches will be used in medicine in the future

_____ 9. why leeches are dangerous to use

READ

Read the encyclopedia entry on the next page. Create a chart like the one below to take notes.

TAKE NOTES	
Main Ideas	**Details**
Leeches are kind of worm	Live in lakes, rivers
	1 mm–5 cm long

Go to **MyEnglishLab** to view example notes.

LEECH

1 **BIOLOGY** Leeches are a kind of worm[1] from 1 millimeter to 5 centimeters long. They live all over the world. In general, leeches live in lakes and rivers. There are 650 kinds of leeches in the world. Only one kind is used in medicine. They are called medicinal leeches.

2 Medicinal leeches live on the **blood** of other animals. They have suckers[2] at both ends—one for feeding and one for holding on. Their **saliva** has three special chemicals that help them drink the blood. One is an anesthetic[3], which allows the leech to feed without hurting the animal. The second chemical makes the **veins** open wide, and the third makes the blood **flow** from the veins for a long time.

3 A medicinal leech will drink 10 to 15 milliliters of blood at one time. This takes about 45 minutes. After the leech is full, it falls off. The bite will still bleed for another 24 hours because of the chemicals from the leech's saliva.

4 **HISTORY** Leeches have been used in medicine for over 3,000 years. Leeches were most **popular** in Europe in the early 1800s. At this time, people thought that too much blood in a person's body made the person sick. Doctors put three or four leeches (or sometimes up to fifty or sixty leeches!) on a **patient's** body. The leeches took out the extra blood. Leeches were used to **cure** many illnesses, from **fevers** to broken legs.

5 Unfortunately, leeches often hurt more than they healed. For example, the Russian writer Nikolai Gogol was leeched because he had anemia, an illness caused by too *little* blood. He died a few days later. George Washington had a **sore throat**. He was leeched four times in two days. He too died a few days later. As we know today, blood is what helps the body heal, so removing blood from a sick person usually does not help. By the mid-1850s, people began to understand some of the problems with leeching, and it became unpopular.

6 **TODAY** Today, doctors know more about leeches. They know when to use them and why. They understand that the chemicals in the leeches' saliva make leeches very useful in medicine. For this reason, the United States made it legal in 2004 to use leeches in reattachment surgeries[4].

7 Until now, reattachment surgeries often failed. Take the example of a reattached finger. After surgery, the finger often becomes **swollen** with blood and the veins can't grow back together. The finger soon dies. Leeches take away this extra blood in two ways. One, they drink some of the blood from the finger. This only removes a spoonful of blood, however. The second way leeches remove this blood is the most important. Because of the chemicals in the leech's saliva, the bite continues to bleed for hours and hours after the leech falls off. With one or two leeches put on the finger twice a day for four to five days, the **swelling** completely goes away. With the swelling gone, the veins can grow back together and the finger lives. Doctors agree that leeches work better than anything else for this problem with reattachment surgeries.

8 There might be other medical uses for leeches, too. For instance, some doctors have been able to reduce pain in patients with knee or elbow problems by **treating** them with leeches. The chemicals in the leeches' saliva reduce swelling and pain. Leeches are even being used to treat certain kinds of cancer. Doctors believe the chemicals in the saliva slow the growth of the cancer.

---

[1] **worm:** a small snake-like animal that lives in the ground

[2] **suckers:** small round parts that connect the leech to the animal it feeds on

[3] **anesthetic:** a chemical that stops you from feeling pain

[4] **reattachment surgeries:** procedures performed when someone's finger or toe is cut off and the doctor puts it back on the hand or foot

Circle the statement that best summarizes the main idea of each section of the encyclopedia entry. Use your notes to help you.

Biology

a. Leeches are worms that suck blood from other animals.

b. Leeches have suckers at both ends.

c. Leeches have both male and female parts.

History

a. People thought that too much blood caused illness. That's why leeches were popular.

b. Leeches killed George Washington and the Russian writer Nikolai Gogol.

c. Doctors treated every kind of illness with leeches. Often this caused a lot of problems.

Today

a. Many modern doctors use leeches to treat heart disease or knee and elbow pain.

b. Modern doctors are afraid that leeching will become popular again.

c. Modern medicine is finding that leeches are useful in reattachment surgeries.

DETAILS

1 **These statements are false. Cross out the incorrect word and replace it with the correct word to make each statement true. Use your notes to help you.**

1. Leeches live in ~~oceans~~ *lakes* and rivers all over the world.

2. It takes a leech 24 minutes to feed and fall off.

3. A leech bite will still bleed for 12 hours after the leech falls off.

4. Leeches were most popular in Europe in the late 1800s.

5. The United States made it legal to use leeches for reattachment surgeries in 2001.

6. Today, people think sickness comes from too much blood.

7. Leeches increase swelling after reattachment surgeries.

8. Doctors disagree that leeches are the best thing to stop swelling after reattachment surgeries.

2 **Look at your notes and at your answers in the Preview section. How did they help you understand the encyclopedia entry?**

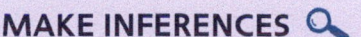

Inferring Judgments

An **inference** is an educated guess about something that is not directly stated. Readers often use inferences to **make judgments or form opinions** about what they read. They make their inferences **based on clues** or specific pieces of information in the text.

Look at the example.

Based on clues in the text, infer how effective you think leeches are for treating some ailments:

Not effective = NE, Maybe effective = ME, Effective = E. Then give the clues that helped you make your inference.

Ailment	How Effective Is Leeching?	Clues in the Text to Help You Make the Inference
anemia	NE	Paragraph 5: Anemia means very little blood. Gogol was anemic and died when they leeched him.

Fill out the chart by inferring how effective you think leeches are for treating certain ailments.

Ailment	How Effective Is Leeching?	Clues in the Text to Help You Make the Inference
1. broken leg		
2. fever		
3. finger reattachment		
4. knee pain		
5. sore throat		

Discuss the questions with a partner. Then share your answers with the class.

USE YOUR NOTES

Use your notes to support your answers with information from the reading.

1. Based on what you read, do you think people in your community would agree to be leeched if doctors recommended it as a treatment to save a finger after surgery? Explain.

2. Leeching was popular in the early 1800s. People understood that it worked sometimes. Because they didn't understand everything about leeching, they often used it when it didn't help. Do you think it's possible that today we are doing something similar? Can you think of a treatment or cure that we may use more than we should? Explain your thinking.

   Examples: medicine for children's classroom behavior problems

   medicine for depression (feeling sad all the time)

   medicine for losing weight

   Other ideas: _____

   _____

   _____

🡒 Go to **MyEnglishLab** to give your opinion about another question.

READING TWO | Gross Medicine

PREVIEW

1 **Look at the title of the reading and at the photo. Write two questions you think will be answered in this reading.**

_____

_____

2 **Look at the boldfaced words in the reading. Which words do you know the meaning of?**

READ

1 **Now read the story about one man's experience with a traditional African doctor. As you read, guess the meanings of the words that are new to you. Remember to take notes on main ideas and details.**

GROSS[1] MEDICINE

By Kai Curtis

1 I was trying to lie still and close my eyes. But I had to look.

2 They looked like green stones. Then they moved. They were sucking out the pus[2] from my ankle. They were looking for blood. They were leeches.

3 This happened to me last summer when I was in South Africa. One day, I fell while getting off a bus and got a small cut on my ankle. I forgot to wash the cut or put a **bandage** on it.

4 Three days later, I couldn't put on my shoe because my foot was so swollen. The pain in my ankle was terrible. And it was moving up my leg. I needed to find a doctor fast. But in the middle of South Africa, far from a city, a trip to the hospital looked like this: six hours by car, one day by bicycle, or three days by donkey. This is when I met Maama Siswana and the leeches.

5 Siswana was a traditional doctor from a village 4 kilometers away. She looked at the cut. She pushed on it carefully. Then she put her hand on my forehead and nodded[3] her head. Yes, I had a fever. She said she had to take the pus out of the ankle before I could travel to the city the next day to get some **antibiotics**.

6 Siswana smiled to help me **relax**. She put a wet cloth on my forehead and opened a small metal box. Inside this dirty little box were the leeches.

7 I put my head back and tried to think of other things. Then I felt something cool on my skin. Siswana put the leeches **gently** around the cut on my ankle. Suddenly, I felt them bite, and then I didn't feel anything.

8 Siswana tried to make me laugh and forget about what was happening on my ankle. She wasn't funny, but I laughed.

9 An hour later, my ankle was bandaged and Siswana was smiling. I was smiling, too. I thanked her for helping me, and we said goodbye. A day later, after traveling the 120 kilometers to the next city, I found a hospital. As the doctor was giving me a **shot** of antibiotics, I was thinking, "I sure don't like shots, but at least they aren't as gross as leeches!"

---

[1] **gross:** very unpleasant to look at or think about
[2] **pus:** yellowish liquid from a dirty cut
[3] **nodded:** moved her head up and down to say "yes"

2 Compare your notes on main ideas and details with a partner's. How can you improve your notes next time?

➤ Go to the **Pearson Practice English App** or **MyEnglishLab** for more vocabulary practice.

Taking Double Entry Notes

Good readers **interact with the text.** They read a sentence, have a thought or a question or a reaction to that sentence, and then go on to read another sentence that makes for more thoughts, questions, and reactions. This interaction is important for deep understanding. When readings are difficult, students find it hard to interact with a text. **Double entry note-taking** can help readers interact more with the text.

Look at the example and read the explanation.

Read the "double entry notes" made by a student. On the left, she wrote short descriptions of what is stated in the text. On the right, she wrote her thoughts or opinions about the text.

Fact	Text	Thought / Opinion
Difficult to lie still	I was trying to lie still and close my eyes. But I had to look.	Gross!! Not for me!
Leeches on his ankle— drinking his blood	They looked like green stones. Then they moved. They were sucking out the pus from my ankle. They were looking for blood. They were leeches.	He was scared to look at what the leeches were doing.

Double entry note-taking allows you to interact with the reading more deeply. It gives you a structured way to ask questions, have opinions, or react to a reading at the same time that you understand the details of the text.

1 Read each excerpt from Reading Two and then write a "double entry note." On the left, write a summary of what is stated in the text. On the right, write your thoughts or opinions about the text.

1.

Fact	Text	Thought / Opinion
	Three days later, I couldn't put on my shoe because my foot was so swollen. The pain in my ankle was terrible. And it was moving up my leg. I needed to find a doctor fast. But in the middle of South Africa, a trip to the hospital looked like this: six hours by car, one day by bicycle, or three days by donkey. This is when I met Maama Siswana and the leeches.	

2.

Fact	Text	Thought / Opinion
	I put my head back and tried to think of other things. Then I felt something cool on my skin. Siswana put the leeches gently around the cut on my ankle. Suddenly, I felt them bite, and then I didn't feel anything. Siswana tried to make me laugh and forget about what was happening on my ankle. She wasn't funny, but I laughed.	

2 Share your notes with a partner.

1. Compare your "fact" sections: Were your answers similar? Do you agree that what you each wrote are facts?
2. Compare your "thought / opinion" sections: Did you write the same things? Do you agree that what you each wrote are thoughts or personal opinions?

Go to **MyEnglishLab** for more note-taking practice.

COMPREHENSION

Circle the best answer to complete each statement. Use your notes from Reading Two to help you. Discuss your answers with a partner.

1. Curtis was traveling through ________________ when he fell while getting off a bus.
   a. a village
   b. South Africa
   c. the mountains
2. Curtis's ankle was swollen because ________________ .
   a. the leeches bit him
   b. he walked too far
   c. he cut his ankle and didn't wash or bandage it
3. Curtis needed a hospital. He couldn't get to one soon enough because ________________ .
   a. he didn't have a donkey
   b. it would take too long
   c. his car was too slow

(continued on next page)

4. Siswana tried to make Curtis laugh. She _____.

    a. wanted Curtis to stop thinking about the leeches on his ankle

    b. wanted Curtis to like her and think she was funny

    c. was nervous and didn't know what to do while they waited

5. The leeches helped Curtis because they _____.

    a. cured him by healing the infection in his ankle

    b. took away the swelling so he could travel to the hospital

    c. made him relax

READING SKILL

1 Look at Reading Two again. When you read the story, did you see pictures in your mind?

Visualizing While Reading

Strong readers often see images in their heads of what they are reading. This is called **visualizing.** It can help build understanding as you read. It can connect you to the story. One tool to help improve visualizing is to **create storyboards.** Storyboards are boxes of simple drawings, like comic strips, that tell the important actions or moments of a story.

Look at paragraphs 1 and 2. Which of the following storyboard drawings best describe what is happening in paragraph 1 and 2? Circle Option 1 or Option 2.

Option 1

Option 2

 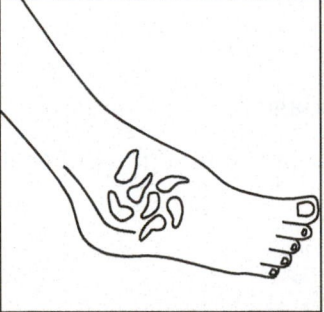

Are there any details missing? Add them to the drawings.

Don't worry about your drawing skill. This is an exercise to improve your reading skills, not your drawing skills.

2 Read paragraph 3 of Reading Two again. Complete the storyboard for paragraph 3.

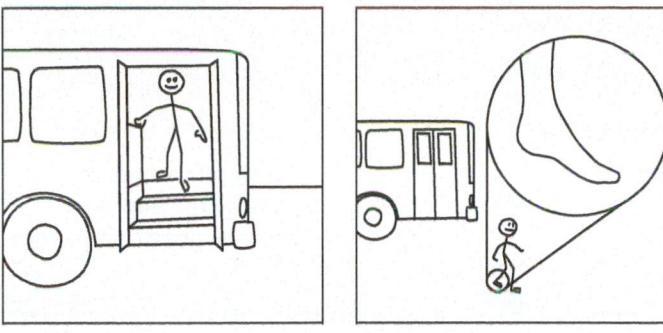

3 Read paragraph 4 of Reading Two again. Create a short storyboard for paragraph 4 (remember, drawing skills are not important).

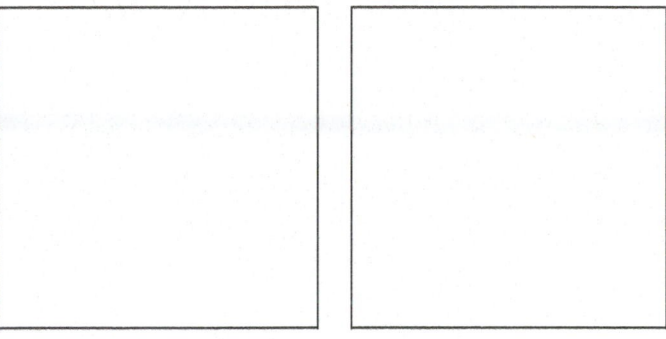

Go to **MyEnglishLab** for more skill practice.

ORGANIZE

Reading One (R1) gives lots of information about the science of leeches. Reading Two (R2) describes one patient's experience with leeches. Read the list of phrases based on Readings One and Two. Then write each phrase in the correct box in the chart.

- A few put on for about an hour

- Put on until they fall off once or twice a day for four to five days

- They suck out the pus from a dirty cut

- Make the blood flow

- Make the veins open wide

- ~~Include an anesthetic~~

USE YOUR NOTES

Review your notes from Readings One and Two. Use the information in your notes to complete the chart.

	The Encyclopedia Entry (R1)	Kai Curtis's Experience (R2)
1. How do leeches work?	Chemicals in the saliva: a. *Include an anesthetic* b. c.	
2. How are they used?		a. The doctor used them to take away the swelling from a bad cut b.

SYNTHESIZE

Kai Curtis told the doctor he saw at the hospital about his experience with the leeches. The doctor laughed and said he was lucky. Leeches are good medicine. Because this doctor spoke English, Kai Curtis could ask him some questions he had about being leeched.

Work with a partner. Complete the conversation between Kai Curtis and the doctor. Use information from Organize.

KAI CURTIS: I was nervous it would hurt when she put the leeches on. It didn't. Why not?

DOCTOR: _____

_____

KAI CURTIS: Why did the bite keep bleeding so long afterward?

DOCTOR: _____

_____

▶ Go to **MyEnglishLab** to check what you learned.

3 FOCUS ON WRITING

REVIEW

1 Match the statements or questions on the left with the responses on the right.

_d_ 1. Yoga is so **popular** these days.

_____ 2. You get headaches a lot. How do you **treat** them?

_____ 3. Do you think I have a **fever?**

_____ 4. Oh, I have a terrible **sore throat.**

_____ 5. Let's move her as **gently** as possible.

_____ 6. You need to get some **antibiotics** for that cut.

_____ 7. How can I bring down the **swelling** in my knee?

a. No, your forehead doesn't feel hot to me.

b. I drink a big glass of water and lie down in a dark room for an hour. It works most of the time.

c. Yeah, I guess you're right. It's all red and painful.

d. ~~I know. Everyone I know is taking classes. We all want to be healthy, I guess.~~

e. Would some tea with honey make it feel better?

f. Yeah, it looks like her leg is broken so we don't want to bump it or be too rough.

g. Put a bag of frozen peas on it for twenty minutes. That should help.

2 Complete the sentences with the words from the box. Use one word more than once.

~~bandage~~	cure	patients	saliva	swollen
blood	flow	relax	shots	vein

1. I need a new _____ _bandage_ _____ for this burn on my hand. My old one got wet when I washed the dishes, and I should have a dry one.

2. Some people are very afraid of getting _____ when they go to see a doctor. One friend of mine asked me to go with her to hold her hand to help her _____ !

3. Sometimes when you need a blood test, the nurse has trouble finding your _____ . This often leaves a black-and-blue mark on your arm.

4. When you are hungry, your body makes extra _____ in your mouth. It's getting ready for the food that should soon be coming!

5. The heart makes the blood _____ around the body.

6. I fell down the stairs yesterday. Today my ankle is so _____ I can't put on my shoe!

7. The doctors said they could _____ him if he took the medicine now. If he waited, they gave him six months to live.

8. Today in the United States, doctors are tired. They see twice as many _____ in a day as doctors did twenty-five years ago.

9. Most hospitals have something called a _____ bank. This is a place where they keep extra _____ for people who lose too much of their own when they have an accident or a long surgery.

EXPAND

Read each sentence. Circle the phrase that best matches the boldfaced word.

1. Last summer, I got a piece of glass in my foot. My wife washed my foot and pulled out the glass **gently.**

   a. in a way that was not hard

   b. in a way that was fast

2. If you get a bad cut, you must put a bandage on it right away. Hold the bandage to the cut **firmly.** This will stop the bleeding.

   a. in a soft way

   b. in a strong way

3. The four-year-old girl would not stop screaming. But the doctor talked to her **calmly,** and she finally sat still and listened.

   a. with a gentle, quiet voice

   b. with a loud, angry voice

4. Last summer, I broke my finger. I went to the hospital. I waited **patiently** for two hours. But after four hours, I was angry. Why did it have to take so long?

   a. becoming upset or mad

   b. without becoming upset or mad

5. The first time I met my new doctor, I was surprised. A friend had told me she was not very nice and never smiled. But, instead, she greeted me **warmly** and made me feel very welcome.

   a. in a friendly way

   b. in an unfriendly way

6. He was a new doctor, so he put the bandage on **roughly.** The patient cried "Ouch!"

   a. in a soft way

   b. in a hard way

CREATE

APPLY Complete the conversation between the first-aid teacher and a student. Use as many of the words in parentheses as you can.

TEACHER: So, to review, what do you do if someone gets a sprained ankle?

STUDENT: _____
(bandage / patient / gently / swelling / swollen)

_____

_____

TEACHER: Good. Now tell me what you do when you see someone bleeding?

STUDENT: _____
(blood / veins / flow / patient / treat / firmly)

_____

_____

TEACHER: _____
(sore throat / fever)

STUDENT: _____
(cure / popular / antibiotics)

_____

Go to the **Pearson Practice English App** or **MyEnglishLab** for more vocabulary practice.

GRAMMAR FOR WRITING

1 Read the excerpt from Reading Two. Then answer the questions.

> Siswana was a traditional doctor from a village four kilometers away. She looked at the cut. She pushed on it carefully.

1. How does the doctor push on Kai Curtis's cut?
2. How do you know?

1. **Adverbs of manner** describe action verbs. They say *how* or in what manner something happens. They are helpful when writing descriptions.	The doctor **listened** *carefully*.
2. Adverbs of manner usually come **after** the main verb. Sometimes an **object** can separate the action verb and the adverb.	The patient **talked** *slowly*. She **washed** the cut *gently*.
3. Most adverbs of manner are formed by adding *-ly* to the adjective. When adding *-ly,* some adjectives lose their last *e* or the last *y* changes to *i*.	careful care**fully** slow slow**ly** gentle gen**tly** easy eas**ily**
4. Some **adjectives** end in *-ly* and have no adverb form.	He was a **lonely** old man. She has a **friendly** neighbor.
5. Some adverbs have the **same form as the adjective**.	**hard** (*adj.*): The test was **hard**. **hard** (*adv.*): She worked **hard**. **fast** (*adj.*): He is a **fast** runner. **fast** (*adv.*): She ran **fast**.
6. The adverb for *good* is *well*. Careful! *Well* is also an adjective that means "in good health."	**Good** game! You played **well**. I don't feel **well** today. I have a sore throat.

2 Like leeches, maggots are a kind of worm-like animal; but, unlike leeches, maggots live on dead flesh[1]. Like leeches, maggots were used in the past to treat certain medical problems. Recently, doctors have started using maggots again when nothing else works. Read the paragraph and circle the adverbs.

> The patient lay quietly on her bed. She was not feeling well. As soon as the doctor arrived, the patient felt more uncomfortable. She looked nervously at what was in the doctor's hand—a small jar with hundreds of small, white, worm-like things. And they were moving. The doctor smiled warmly at the patient. The patient felt better. She remembered that the maggots in the doctor's jar were going to help her. Parts of her left leg were dead because of an infection[2]. The maggots were going to eat the dead parts and allow the rest of her leg to heal well. It wasn't very nice to think about, but it was the best choice she had to save her leg.

Now write the adjective form of the adverbs you circled.

1. _____   3. _____

2. _____   4. _____

---

[1] **flesh:** the soft part of the body of a person or animal

[2] **infection:** a disease or sickness

3 Complete each sentence with the adjective or adverb form of the word in parentheses.

1. After months of illness, the patient's health improved ___suddenly___ .
(sudden)

2. If you take an aspirin, your headache will go away _____ .
(quick)

3. Please be _____ . I don't want anyone to get hurt!
(careful)

4. My doctor is so friendly and _____ . You'll like her.
(warm)

5. Alice's husband was _____ when Alice returned from the hospital. He'd
(happy)

   missed her.

6. The nurse washed my cut _____ . It almost didn't hurt.
(gentle)

7. The baby came in the middle of a snowy night. We drove _____ to the hospital,
(careful)

   but we got there in time.

8. His cut was _____ . It hurt a lot.
(painful)

4 **APPLY** Answer each question. Use one or two adverbs from the box in each answer.

badly	easily	gently	painfully	quickly	slowly	well
carefully	fast	hard	patiently	quietly	suddenly	

1. How do you walk when you have a sprained ankle?

   _____

   _____

2. How do you want your doctor to talk to you?

   _____

   _____

3. How do you take off a bandage?

   _____

   _____

4. How do you clean a cut before you put a bandage on?

   _____

   _____

5. How do you talk to a small child who is crying?

   _____

   _____

🔵 Go to the **Pearson Practice English App** or **MyEnglishLab** for more grammar practice.
Check what you learned in **MyEnglishLab**.

In this unit, you read about people all over the world still using traditional medicine and home remedies. Do you have childhood memories of being sick or injured and being treated with a home remedy or modern medicine? What happened?

You are going to *write a narrative paragraph about an experience you had with a home remedy or a modern medical treatment*. First, you will describe when and where you had this experience, what your health problem was, and what remedy or treatment your parents or doctors chose for you. Then you will describe what happened and how it worked. Use the vocabulary and grammar from the unit.

For an alternative writing topic, see page 177.

PREPARE TO WRITE: Brainstorming

Brainstorming is a helpful way to get ideas for your writing. In brainstorming, you think of as many ideas as possible about a topic. No ideas are bad or wrong. You can brainstorm alone or in a group.

Follow the steps.

1. As a class, **brainstorm** as many home remedies as you can. Write them on the board. Ask questions about the ones that are unfamiliar to you. (For examples of some home remedies, go back to Reading One, Vocabulary, Exercise 2 on page 155.)

2. Choose one remedy that you want to write about. Make sure it is one you have experience with. If you have never used any of these home remedies, choose one medical treatment you have experienced.

3. Make a **cluster diagram**:

   a. Write the remedy or treatment in the middle of a piece of paper.

   b. In the space around it, write any words you can think of that are related to your experience of the remedy or treatment: your health problem, the place where it happened, the people who were there, how the remedy or treatment felt or tasted, etc.

Example

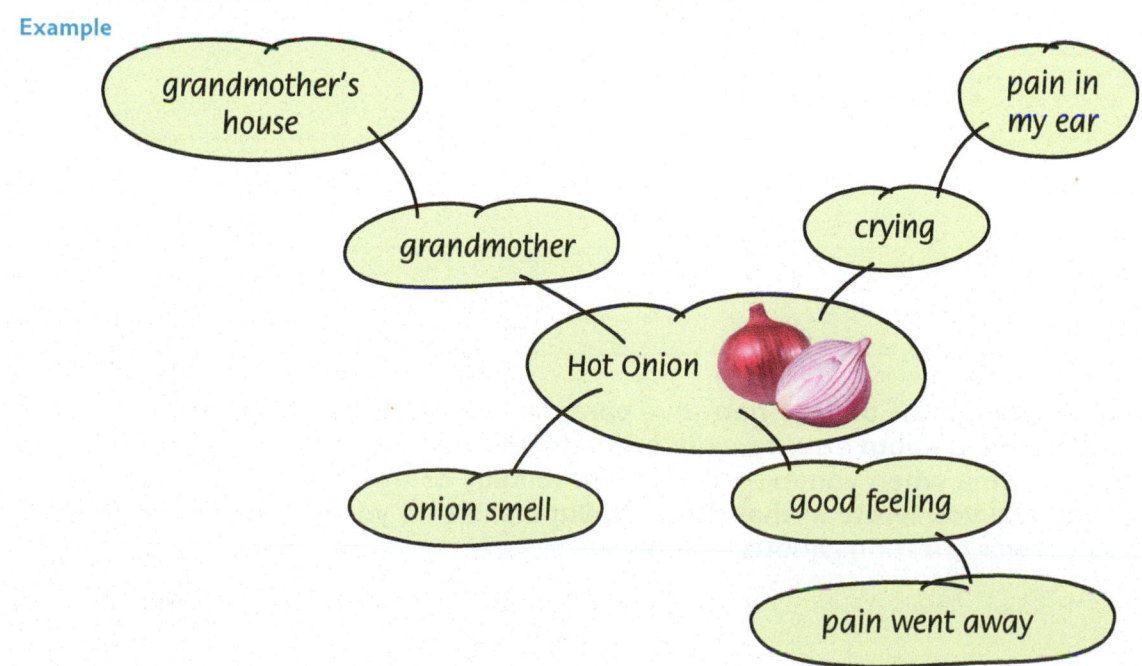

WRITE: A Narrative Paragraph

A **narrative** is a story about something that happened to you or someone else. It starts by telling *who* this story happened to, *when* it happened, and *where* it happened. Then it describes *what* happened and *how*.

1 **Read this narrative paragraph about an experience someone had with a home remedy. Then answer the questions.**

> When I was about six, I went to visit my grandmother in Canada. One day, I got a really bad earache. I was in a lot of pain, and I was crying. My grandmother said she knew what to do. First, she walked calmly to the kitchen cabinet and took out an onion. Then she cut it in half and put the two pieces in a pot of water. Next, she heated the onion in the water. Soon the smell of onion filled the kitchen. After that, she took out one half of the onion and put a small piece of cloth around it. Finally, she put the hot onion carefully against my ear. The heat from the onion felt very good on my ear. After a while, the pain went away.
>
> Sally Collingsworth
>
> Austin, Texas

1. **Who** is talking?

    _____

2. **When** did this happen?

    _____

3. **Where** did the story take place?

    _____

4. **What** was the health problem?

    _____

5. **What** was the remedy?

    _____

6. Did it work?

    _____

7. **How** did it work?

    _____

2 Now write the first draft of your narrative paragraph. Look at the diagram you made while brainstorming about your remedy or treatment. Use it to help you write a story describing one time when you experienced this remedy or treatment. You don't have to use every item you wrote in that diagram. But make sure you give the information needed to answer questions about *who, when, where, what,* and *how.*

REVISE: Using Time Order Words in a Narrative

When you tell a story in the first person, it helps the reader understand the story better if you describe what happened in **time order**—this means in the order in which things happened. We show time order by using **time order words** like these:

First, . . .   Second, . . .   Then . . .   Next, . . .   After that, . . .   Finally, . . .

1 Read the two stories. Which one is clearer (A or B)? Put a check (✓) next to it. Discuss your answer with a partner.

☐ A.

> When I grew up in Vietnam, all of us children frequently got head lice[1]. We didn't have chemicals or special shampoos to kill the lice. So my mother treated it the traditional way: with coconut[2] oil. My mother washed my hair with shampoo. I sat on a chair in front of her, and she combed out my hair slowly. This is one of my favorite memories as a kid: my mother singing to me while she combed my hair. I loved to close my eyes and listen to her rich voice. She poured some warm coconut oil carefully onto my hair. I loved this part. Usually we left the oil in for a few days. Mom shampooed and combed my hair one last time. My hair still looked oily, but the lice were gone.
>
> _____
> [1] **head lice:** very small insects that live in human hair
> [2] **coconut:** a very large brown nut; it is white inside and has liquid in the middle

☐ B.

> When I grew up in Vietnam, all of us children frequently got head lice. We didn't have chemicals or special shampoos to kill the lice. So my mother treated it the traditional way: with coconut oil. First, my mother washed my hair with shampoo. Then I sat on a chair in front of her and she combed out my hair slowly. This is one of my favorite memories as a kid: my mother singing to me while she combed my hair. I loved to close my eyes and listen to her rich voice. After that, she poured some warm coconut oil carefully onto my hair. I loved this part. Usually we left the oil in for a few days. Finally, Mom shampooed and combed my hair one last time. My hair still looked oily, but the lice were gone.

Now read Story B again, and circle the time order words.

2 The following story would be clearer with some time order words. Fill in the blanks with the appropriate time order words from the box. Make sure you use proper punctuation and capitalization.

First, . . .	Next, . . .	Then . . .	Finally, . . .

Last winter I had a bad cold. I was home from work for a week. I couldn't breathe well through my nose. I remembered an old remedy my grandmother used. _____ I put a towel over my head and put my head over the sink.

_____ I turned on the hot water all the way. The towel was like a tent over the hot steamy water.

_____ I breathed hard through my nose. I did this for about 15 minutes. _____ near the end, I could breathe more easily through one side of my nose. I did this three more times over the next 24 hours until I could breathe normally.

3 Now go back to the first draft of your narrative paragraph or story and add the time order words necessary to show in what order things happened.

🔵 Go to **MyEnglishLab** for more skill practice.

EDIT: Writing the Final Draft

APPLY Write the final draft of your paragraph and submit it to your teacher. Carefully edit it for grammatical and mechanical errors, such as spelling, capitalization, and punctuation. Consider how to apply the vocabulary, grammar, and writing skills from the unit. Use the checklist to help you.

FINAL DRAFT CHECKLIST

- ☐ Does your paragraph describe an experience you had with a home remedy or a medical treatment?
- ☐ Does it answer the questions of *who, when, where, what,* and *how?*
- ☐ Does it describe what happened in time order?
- ☐ Do you use time order words correctly?
- ☐ Do you use adverbs of manner correctly?
- ☐ Do you use new vocabulary that you learned in this unit?

ALTERNATIVE WRITING TOPIC

APPLY In this unit you've read about many methods of medicine that do not require a doctor. But modern families practice home remedies less frequently now than in the past. Do you think we should teach home remedies to college students so that these remedies and traditions can continue? Write a paragraph explaining why you think we should try to preserve these traditions. Use vocabulary and grammar from the unit.

CHECK WHAT YOU'VE LEARNED

Check (✔) the outcomes you've met and vocabulary you've learned. Put an X next to the skills and vocabulary you still need to practice.

Learning Outcomes	Vocabulary		Multi-word Units
☐ **Infer judgements**	☐ antibiotic	☐ popular	☐ **sore throat**
☐ **Take double entry notes**	☐ bandage	☐ relax AWL	
☐ **Visualize while reading**	☐ blood	☐ saliva	
☐ **Use adverbs of manner**	☐ cure	☐ shot	
☐ **Use time order words in a narrative**	☐ fever	☐ swelling (*n.*)	
	☐ flow	☐ swollen (*adj.*)	
☐ **Write a narrative paragraph**	☐ gently	☐ treat	
	☐ patient (*n.*)	☐ vein	

🔾 Go to **MyEnglishLab** to watch a video about health problems, access the Unit Project, and take the Unit 7 Achievement Test.

LEARNING OUTCOMES

> Infer the author's attitude
> Take notes with a mind map
> Identify the purpose of quoted speech

> Use *will* and *be going to* to express predictions and future plans
> Write a concluding sentence
> Write a prediction paragraph

Go to **MyEnglishLab** to check what you know.

Endangered Cultures

1 FOCUS ON THE TOPIC

1. What modern things do you see in the photo? What traditional things do you see in the photo?

2. Indigenous people are people whose families and cultures have been in one place for a very long time. What are some indigenous cultures you know about? What is happening to them today?

READING ONE | Will Indigenous Cultures Survive?

1 There are about 5,000 indigenous cultures in the world today. This map shows where a few of them live or used to live.

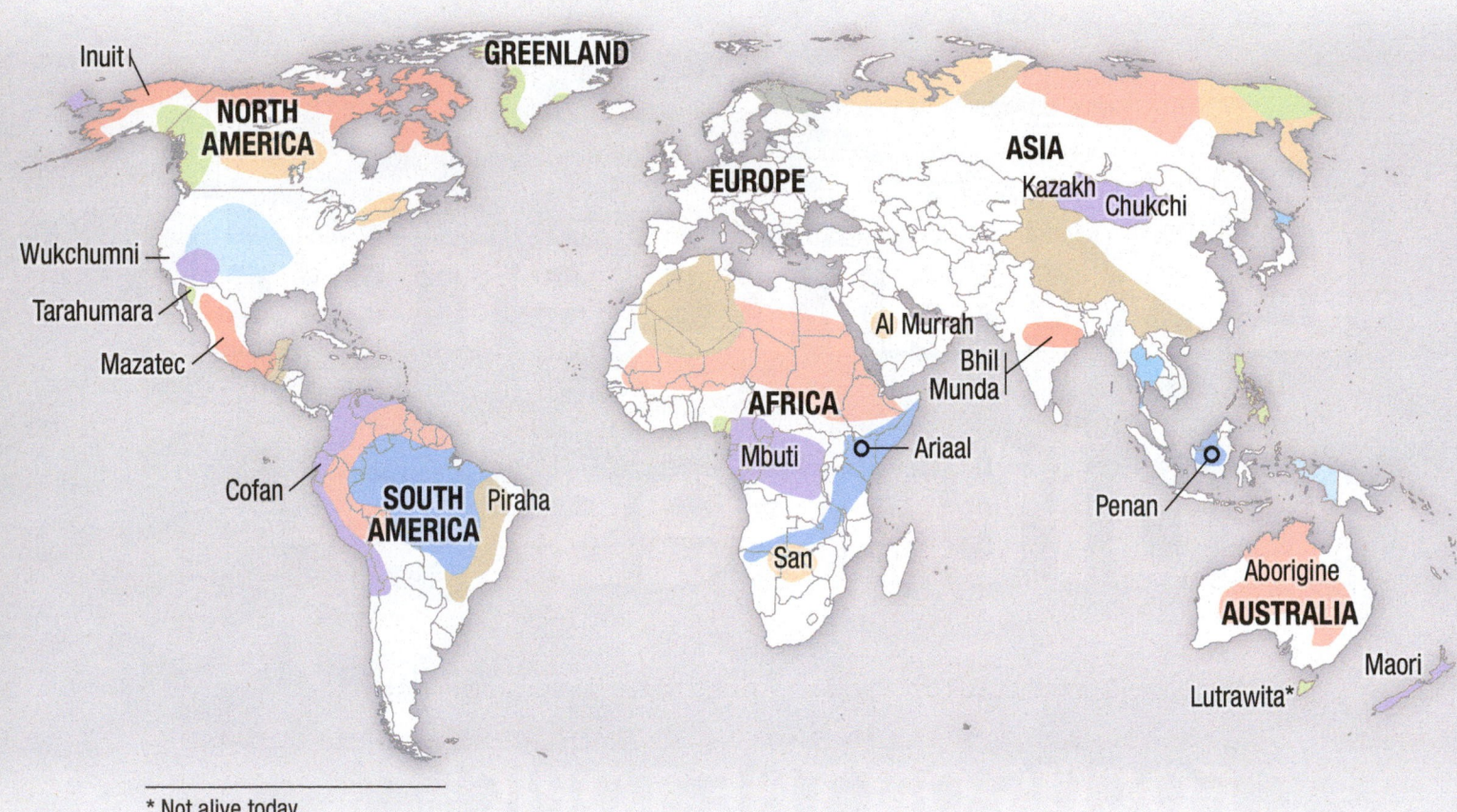

Inuit
GREENLAND
NORTH AMERICA
Wukchumni
Tarahumara
Mazatec
Cofan
SOUTH AMERICA
Piraha
EUROPE
ASIA
Kazakh
Chukchi
Al Murrah
Bhil
Munda
AFRICA
Mbuti
Ariaal
San
Penan
Aborigine
AUSTRALIA
Lutrawita*
Maori

_____

* Not alive today.

Study the map and read this list of facts about some indigenous cultures today. Pay attention to the boldfaced words.

Indigenous Cultures Today

1. Many indigenous cultures have disappeared; almost all indigenous cultures today are **endangered,** or in danger of disappearing.

2. The *Lutrawita* people of Tasmania, Australia, did not **survive** into the twentieth century. The last Lutrawita died in 1876. Most of them died between 1803 and 1833.

3. A long time ago, when the sea was lower, a land bridge connected Siberia and Alaska. The *Chukchi* people of Siberia and the *Inuit* people of Alaska were one culture. As the sea rose, it divided the land and the cultures. The Chukchi and Inuit are different today, but they share the same **roots.**

4. The *San* of southern Africa do not **adapt** well to modern life. Life in the desert is a very important part of their culture. If they move to towns and live in buildings, they become sick and sometimes die.

5. The *Al Murrah* people are from southern Arabia. Like all **nomadic** groups, they don't live in one place. The Al Murrah travel about 1,800 miles (3,000 kilometers) each year.

6. Some scientists think that the New Zealand *Maori* men and women have different ancestors. The **ancestors** of the men are from Melanesia and those of the women are from Taiwan. The scientists believe that 6,000 years ago, a group of women from Taiwan came in boats to Melanesia. At that point, some Melanesian men joined these women, and together they came to New Zealand and stayed.

7. The old ways of life for the *Mbuti* of the Democratic Republic of Congo are in danger. Large mining companies[1] are **destroying** the forest where the Mbuti live. The trees and the animals are disappearing and the water is bad.

8. The *Piraha* people of the Amazon have a **unique** language. It is unlike any other language in the world. It has no words for colors or numbers greater than two.

──────────────

[1] **mining companies:** companies that take metals, like gold, and minerals, like diamonds, from the land

2 Match the boldfaced words on the left with the definitions on the right.

<u>g</u> 1. **endangered**

____ 2. **survive**

____ 3. **roots**

____ 4. **adapt**

____ 5. **nomadic**

____ 6. **ancestors**

____ 7. **destroy**

____ 8. **unique**

a. the beginning or origin of something; the connection with a place

b. unusual, the only one of its type

c. to continue to live in spite of difficulties or illness

d. members of your family who lived a long time ago

e. to change your behavior or ideas to fit a new situation

f. traveling from place to place

g. ~~at risk of disappearing~~

h. to damage something so badly that it cannot be fixed

🔊 Go to the **Pearson Practice English App** or **MyEnglishLab** for more vocabulary practice.

Look at the title of the article on the next page. Why is it difficult for indigenous cultures to survive? Write three reasons you think the article might mention.

1. _____

2. _____

3. _____

READ

Read the article. Create a chart like the one below to take notes.

TAKE NOTES

Main Ideas	Details
Indigenous cultures are in danger	5% of the world are indigenous
	Changes of modern world are making it hard for them to survive

Go to **MyEnglishLab** to view example notes.

Will Indigenous Cultures Survive?

By James Chevalier

1 In Western Mongolia, a *Kazakh* girl offers food to a baby eagle. She wants the eagle to trust her. Trust is the first step in many years of training the eagle, so that later on the eagle will hunt with her. In Oaxaca, Mexico, a *Mazatec* child whistles[1] as he nears his cousin's house to ask if he wants to come out and play. In Australia, a young *Aborigine* boy learns to rub a rock in his armpit[2] and throw it in the water to tell the water spirits that he is there. These stories come from three different **endangered** indigenous cultures.

2 About 370 million people, or almost 5 percent of the world's population, belong to indigenous cultures. These cultures have deep **roots** in their histories, languages, and the places they live. Their ways of life go back thousands of years. Over those years, they have made many small changes to their culture in order to **survive**. For example, they find new hunting grounds when the animal populations move or they use new tools that make work a little easier. But today changes are so large and they are happening so fast that many indigenous cultures can no longer **adapt** to them. These cultures are in danger of disappearing forever.

3 The most difficult changes to adapt to are usually changes to a group's land. For example, in Ecuador, the *Cofan* homeland is full of chemicals from oil companies. The Cofan can no longer drink the water or grow food there. In India, over 250,000 indigenous people had to leave their homes in the Narmada River valley because the government built a dam[3] on the river, and now their villages are under water.

4 What happens to the people from these cultures? Where do they go? Usually they have to move away from the lands of their **ancestors**. Often they move to the poor areas outside of large cities. They have to learn a new way of living and thinking. Their children will know little of the language and culture they came from.

5 There are 5,000 indigenous cultures with their own **unique** languages alive today. Some scientists predict that by 2100, 50 percent of these will disappear. When a language disappears, the voice of a culture disappears. There are many indigenous people who are working hard to stop this from happening to their culture. They know it is important to keep their languages and their voices. They are fighting against governments who want them to become part of the modern world. They are fighting against oil and logging companies[4] who want their land.

6 The *Ariaal*, an indigenous **nomadic** group in Kenya, have been fighting for years. So far, their culture is surviving. The Ariaal understand that some changes may help them, but other changes may **destroy** their way of life. The Ariaal are trying to stop the things that will hurt their culture and accept the helpful parts of the modern world. For example, the Kenyan government wants the Ariaal to move to villages. The government wants the Ariaal and other indigenous people to become more modern. The Ariaal know that if they move to villages, their nomadic way of life will disappear. So about half of the Ariaal refuse to let go of their nomadic lives and move to villages. But many are sending their children to Kenyan schools or using health clinics. They decided that schools and clinics are modern things that can help their culture survive, but villages are not.

7 Indigenous cultures must adapt to survive. Most *want* to adapt. But in order to adapt, the world's people, governments, and businesses must respect and support them. The big questions are: Will the world let them adapt in ways that *they* decide? Or will these cultures simply have to say goodbye to their ways of life because the changes are too big and too fast?

---

1 **whistle:** to make a high or musical sound by blowing air out through your lips

2 **armpit:** the part of the body under the arm where the arm joins the body

3 **dam:** a wall built across a river to make a lake and produce electricity

4 **logging companies:** companies that cut down trees to make wood and paper

Endangered Cultures   **183**

Circle the best answer to complete each main idea from the article. Use your notes to help you.

1. Most indigenous cultures _____.

   a. are changing with modern times

   b. live the way they lived for thousands of years

2. Indigenous cultures are disappearing because _____.

   a. big changes are happening too fast

   b. their governments don't want them to adapt to the modern world

3. Changes that are especially difficult for indigenous cultures to adapt to are _____.

   a. changes to the land they live on

   b. changes to the water they drink

4. Indigenous cultures are fighting against _____ to keep their cultures.

   a. governments and big businesses

   b. other indigenous cultures

5. In order to survive, indigenous cultures must _____.

   a. listen to their governments

   b. decide how to adapt

6. For indigenous cultures to survive, the rest of the world must let them _____.

   a. have schools

   b. choose how to change

DETAILS

1 **The article gives many examples to support main ideas. List the examples below each statement. Use your notes to help you.**

   1. Three examples of the ways indigenous cultures understand the world and live their lives:

      a. _A Kazakh girl in Mongolia offers food to a baby eagle so that the eagle will trust her and hunt with her._

      b. _____

         _____

      c. _____

         _____

2. Two examples of changes to their land that indigenous cultures cannot adapt to, and their results:

   a. _____ (*result:* _____)

   b. _____ (*result:* _____)

3. One example of an indigenous group that is fighting to keep its culture:

   _____

4. One example of something that will hurt the Ariaal way of life:

   _____

5. One example of something from modern Kenyan culture that the Ariaal want:

   _____

2 **Look at your notes and at your answers in the Preview section. Were any of your ideas the same as the article's author? Put a check (✓) next to your ideas that were similar to the author's. How did they help you understand the article?**

MAKE INFERENCES 🔍

Inferring the Author's Attitude

An **inference** is an educated guess about something that is not directly stated in the text. Sometimes a text suggests the **author's attitude** (how the author feels) about the subject they are writing about. Readers can infer the author's attitude from certain words and phrases the author uses. These words and phrases make you think of particular feelings.

Look at the example and read the explanation.

- "They have to learn a new way of living and thinking. Their children will know little of the language and culture they came from." (*paragraph 4*)

Which words or phrases suggest the author's attitude?

a. have to _____

b. their children will know little _____

Have to tells us it is not the indigenous people's choice to learn new ways. Others are making them change. The author seems sad that indigenous people do not have a choice about how much they follow their history.

Their children will know little also tells us the author is sad. Everybody wants the children to know where they come from, and it is sad if they do not know their roots. He is also afraid that indigenous peoples' history will be forgotten. If the children do not learn it, no one will be able to pass it along.

After reading the text closely, especially certain words and phrases, we can **infer the author's attitude** about the situation indigenous people find themselves in: He feels bad about it; he isn't hopeful that it will get better.

1 Look at paragraphs 4 and 5 again. Answer the questions.

1. In paragraph 4, sentences 1–4, which words and phrases help you infer the author's attitude about indigenous people leaving their ancestors' land?

    a. _____

    b. _____

2. In paragraph 5, sentences 1–3, which words and phrases help you infer the author's attitude about languages?

    a. _____

    b. _____

2 Now, with a partner, discuss what the author's attitude is about each topic and how the words and phrases help you understand his attitude.

DISCUSS 🔍

Discuss the questions in a small group. Then share your answers with the class.

> **USE YOUR NOTES**
>
> Use your notes to support your answers with information from the reading.

1. The author names several things about the modern world (for example, dams and oil companies) that are hurting indigenous cultures. What are the benefits to these things? Do you think modern practices, such as dam building and oil drilling, should stop? Explain your answer.

2. Look at the section about the Ariaal again. Review which parts of modern culture they accept and which parts they reject. Why do you think they made these choices?

🔵 Go to **MyEnglishLab** to give your opinion about another question.

READING TWO | Touring Penan Country

PREVIEW

1 Look at the introduction to the reading and at its title, as well as the photo. Check (✓) the items you think will be discussed in the reading.

_____ 1. who the Penan are

_____ 2. information about good hotels in Penan country

_____ 3. a story about a trip to Penan country

_____ 4. details about Penan people

_____ 5. descriptions of food in Penan country

_____ 6. tips for finding cheap airplane tickets

2 Look at the boldfaced words in the reading. Which words do you know the meaning of?

Ecotours are tours for people who want to support and learn about the cultures and places they visit. Instead of spending a vacation in an international hotel chain and eating at McDonald's, for example, a small group of travelers on an ecotour might go to a small village to eat and stay with local people. The money the tourists spend goes to the local people, and the travelers learn about a different way of life.

The travel blog below is from a traveler named Angela who took an ecotour to Malaysia to learn more about the Penan. The Penan are an indigenous nomadic culture in Malaysia. Just about all of the Penan now live in villages, but they have kept some of their nomadic traditions. They are continuing to fight to save their forest home, and they are also trying to find ways to adapt to modern life while keeping their traditional roots.

1 **Read this travel blog about the Penan. As you read, guess the meanings of the words that are new to you. Remember to take notes on main ideas and details.**

About Angela Angela is an American woman who loves to share her tales of adventure in the world's out-of-the-way places.

TOURING PENAN COUNTRY

1 My visit to Penan country changed my life. My friend, Dianne, and I wanted to learn more about the Penan, but we had no idea how moving[1] the experience would be. Here is a short overview of our trip.

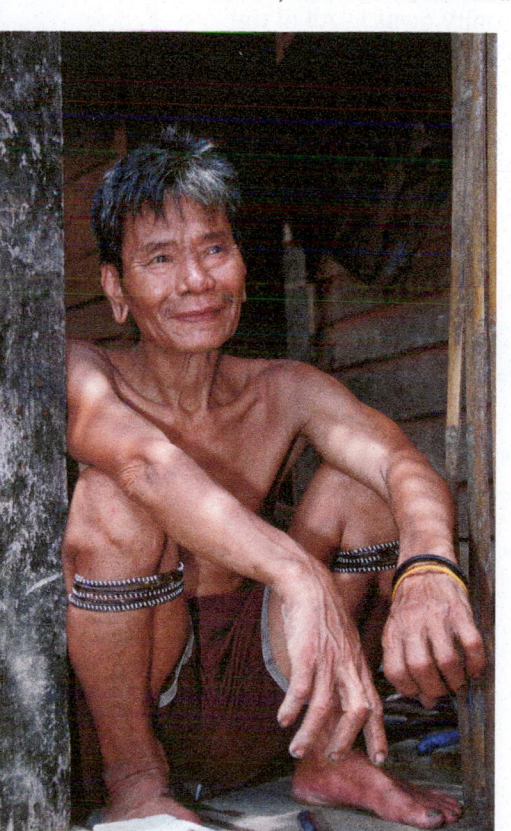

2 To arrive in the forest, we take a small airplane. Out of the airplane window, we can see the forest where the Penan live. But it looks like there are large farms in the forest. Our pilot tells us these are palm oil plantations[2]. We can also see big ships on the river below. We learn that they are carrying logs[3] from the forests where the Penan live.

3 We land in Long Lellang and meet our guide. His name is Daniel. He seems a little shy at first, but he welcomes us warmly. Daniel is Penan. Like most Penan his age, he grew up in the village and then went to school in the city for several years, so his English is very good. Now he works with an ecotour company.

4 Daniel's father was born a nomad. But forty years ago, the Malaysian government **convinced** him to move to a village. The government said that it was better for the Penan to live in villages and become part of modern Malaysia. But the government also wanted to sell the forest to the logging companies. Since that time, almost all of the Penan have **settled** in villages. The Penan fought to keep their home in the forest, but the logging companies were too **powerful**.

5 Our room in the village is clean and comfortable, but the village seems a little bit sad. The river is dirty, and there is mud[4] everywhere. In the evening, children watch television, but Daniel tells us that they don't understand the language. Daniel eats dinner with us, and he begins to seem less shy. He apologizes for the food, which is mostly from cans and packages. "My father never got used to the food in the village," Daniel says. Then he laughs a little. "My dad always said, 'Here in the village, I have a house, a bed, and a pillow, but I can't eat a pillow!'"

---

[1] **moving:** making you feel strong emotions, especially sympathy
[2] **palm oil plantations:** very large farms that produce cooking oil
[3] **logs:** trees that have been cut down to be used for wood
[4] **mud:** dirt and water mixed together

(continued on next page)

6   The next morning, we meet two more guides and we start our long walk into the forest. There are fewer than 200 Penan nomads left, and it is unlikely that we will meet any. But Daniel and our other guides know how to survive in the forest. They learned some skills to live in the forest when they were children, even though they mostly grew up in the villages. They work hard to stay **connected** to their nomadic traditions.

7   Our walk is muddy and hot, and there are leeches in the water that we walk through. It is not very comfortable, but it is beautiful. We barely notice our guides picking vegetables and fruit while we walk. At one point, we have to be very quiet while one of our guides hunts a small wild pig with a blowgun and poison dart[5]. "A few of us can still hunt with a blowgun," Daniel tells us. "But you should see my uncle hunt. He knows exactly where the pigs are at different times of day, and he never misses."

8   In the late afternoon, Dianne and I watch our guides set up our camp. They quickly build a roof, simple benches, and a table with branches and leaves from the forest. They build a fire and cook the pig, along with mushrooms and other vegetables they gathered. While Daniel is cooking, another pig comes close to our camp. Dianne asks Daniel if one of the guides is going to kill it. "We don't need to. We have enough. We only take what we need from the forest, so that it can continue to take care of us." Our guides make us leaf plates and even simple wooden spoons.

9   We eat together. The food is plentiful and delicious. We learn that sharing is such an important part of the Penan's way of life that they do not even have a word for "thank you." I think about the amount of food I throw away at home. I think about my uncle in the U.S., who hunts for sport. I think about the palm oil companies and logging companies who are destroying the forest. Suddenly, it seems **urgent** to learn as much as we can from indigenous cultures like the Penan. If we don't, this forest, this way of life, and these ways of thinking may all disappear forever.

10 Dianne and I talk much more with Daniel over the next two days about how the Penan live now. He tells us about his work with his tour company. He doesn't own it; the community owns it. All of the money is shared among the Penan. He also works hard with other Penan to **protest** new logging and palm oil projects. "We will never be able to move back to the forest," Daniel says, "but we can fight to keep our forest spirit alive."

11 Throughout our trip, Daniel and the other guides shared some ways that non-Penan can help their culture survive. Read my next blog post for information about that.

---

[5] **blowgun and poison dart:** traditional Penan hunting weapon

2 Compare your notes on main ideas and details with a partner's. How can you improve your notes next time?

▶ Go to the **Pearson Practice English App** or **MyEnglishLab** for more vocabulary practice.

Taking Notes with a Mind Map

Mind mapping is a **nonlinear way of taking notes.** It can be helpful when a **story has a lot of information** in it that you want to remember. It can help organize the information and show the relationship between ideas.

Mind Map

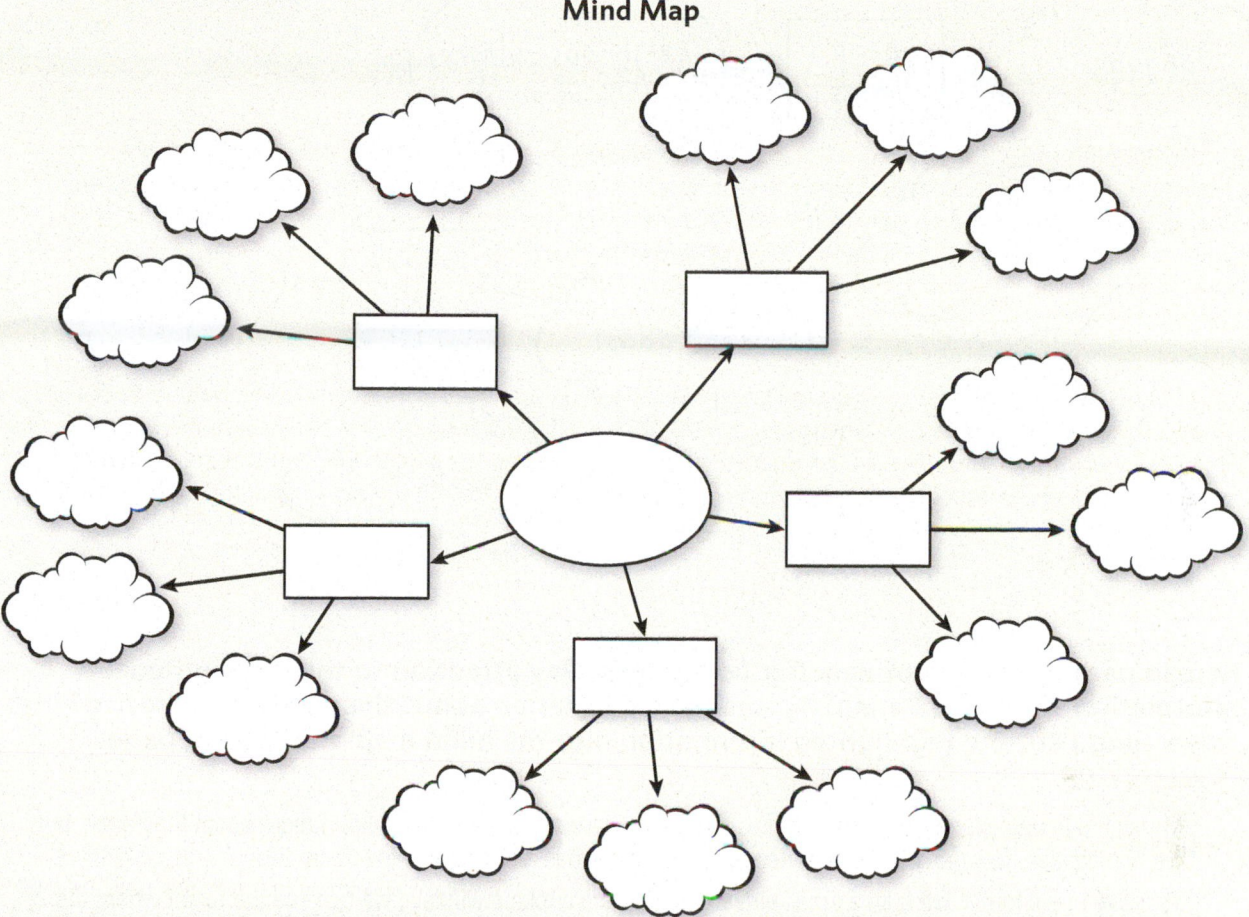

To prepare for mind mapping, highlight or underline the important information in the text.

To create a mind map, write the main topic of the content in a large bubble in the middle of the page. Then return to your highlighted text. Add the main ideas to the page in bubbles connected to the topic in the middle. Then you can add details to the main idea bubbles by drawing lines from each main idea bubble to a detail bubble.

Use **short phrases, symbols, and single keywords** you learned in earlier units in the topics of your mind map. Shortening and rephrasing sentences is difficult, but it will help you remember the information. It also helps to keep the mind map simple and easy to read later.

Look at the example of highlighted text and the mind map from paragraph 2 in Reading One:

2 About 370 million people, or almost 5 percent of the world's population, belong to indigenous cultures. These cultures have deep **roots** in their histories, languages, and the places they live. Their ways of life go back thousands of years. Over those years, they have made many small changes to their culture in order to **survive.** For example, they find new hunting grounds when the animal populations move or they use new tools that make work a little easier. But today, changes are so large and they are happening so fast that many indigenous cultures can no longer **adapt** to them. These cultures are in danger of disappearing forever.

(continued on next page)

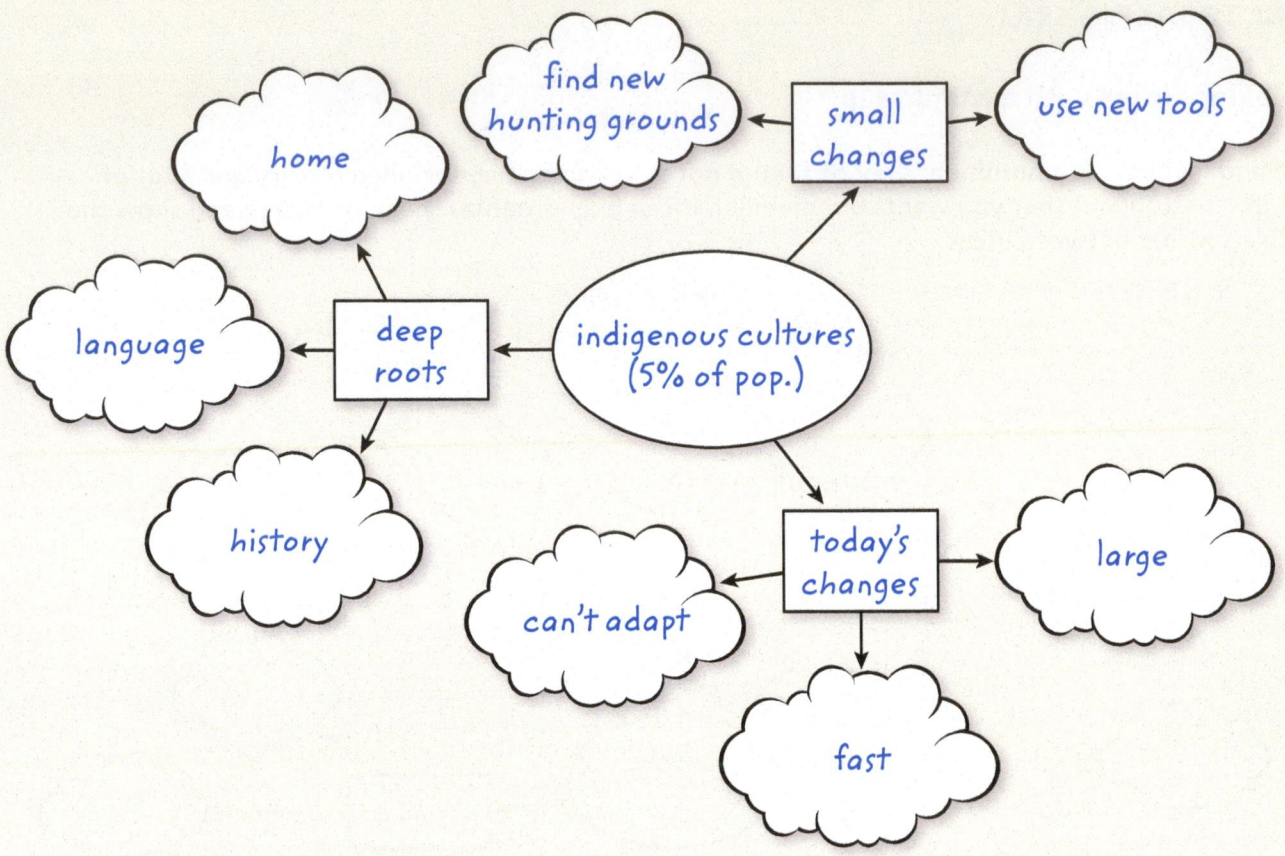

1 **Reread paragraphs 1–4 of Reading Two, below. Pay attention to the highlighted information about the Penan. (Ignore the information about the day-to-day story of the travel blog.) Put the highlighted information into the mind map on the next page.**

1 My visit to Penan country changed my life. My friend, Dianne, and I wanted to learn more about the Penan, but we had no idea how moving the experience would be. Here is a short overview of our trip.

2 To arrive in the forest, we take a small airplane. Out of the airplane window, we can see the forest where the Penan live. But it looks like there are large farms in the forest. Our pilot tells us these are palm oil plantations. We can also see big ships on the river below. We learn that they are carrying logs from the forest where the Penan live.

3 We land in Long Lellang and meet our guide. His name is Daniel. He seems a little shy at first, but he welcomes us warmly. Daniel is Penan. Like most Penan his age, he grew up in the village and then went to school in the city for several years, so his English is very good. Now he works with an ecotour company.

4 Daniel's father was born a nomad. But forty years ago, the Malaysian government convinced him to move to a village. The government said that it was better for the Penan to live in villages and become part of modern Malaysia. But the government also wanted to sell the forest to the logging companies. Since that time, almost all of the Penan have settled in villages. The Penan fought to keep their home in the forest, but the logging companies were too powerful.

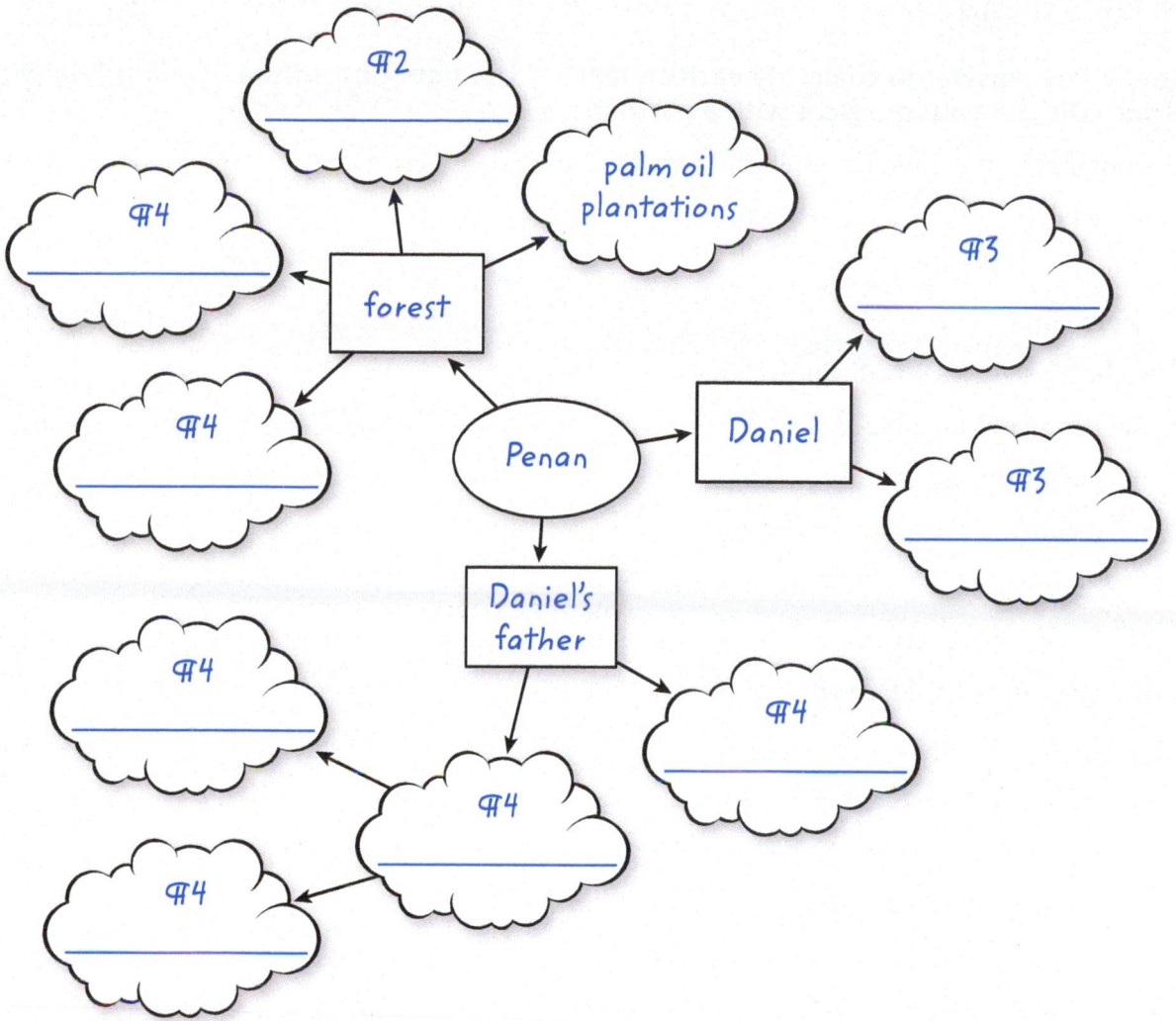

2 Reread paragraphs **5** and **6** of Reading Two, below. Use the highlighted parts of the text to make a mind map. Write *Penan* in the middle bubble. Then add bubbles for the main ideas and bubbles for the details.

5   Our room in the village is clean and comfortable, but the ==village seems a little bit sad. The river is dirty, and there is mud everywhere==. In the evening, children watch television, but Daniel tells us that they don't understand the language. Daniel eats dinner with us, and he begins to seem less shy. He apologizes for ==the food, which is mostly from cans and packages==. "My father never got used to the food in the village," Daniel says. Then he laughs a little. "My dad always said, 'Here in the village, I have a house, a bed, and a pillow, but I can't eat a pillow!'"

6   The next morning, we meet two more guides and we start our ==long walk into the forest==. There are fewer than ==200 Penan nomads left==, and it is unlikely that we will meet any. But ==Daniel and our other guides know how to survive in the forest==. They learned some skills to live in the forest when they were children, even though they mostly grew up in the villages. They ==work hard to stay **connected**== to their nomadic traditions.

↖ Go to MyEnglishLab for more note-taking practice.

Circle the best answer to complete each statement. Use your notes from Reading Two to help you. Discuss your answers with a partner.

1. The number of nomadic Penan in the forest is _____ .

   a. increasing

   b. staying the same

   c. decreasing

2. One reason the forest is disappearing is _____ .

   a. the Penan are burning it

   b. the government is building villages

   c. the logging companies are cutting it down

3. Daniel's father moved to a village because _____ .

   a. he wanted to leave the forest

   b. the government told him to

   c. he wanted a house

4. Daniel and the other guides grew up in _____ .

   a. the forest

   b. the village, but learned to survive in the forest

   c. the city so that they could go to school

5. There is no word for "thank you" in Penan because _____ .

   a. they don't need it, since they always share everything

   b. they seldom give things to each other

   c. they think it is not important to thank each other

6. The tour company that Daniel and the guides work with is owned by _____ .

   a. a community of Penan together

   b. a Malaysian company that only hires Penan

   c. Angela and Dianne

READING SKILL

1 Look at paragraphs 3 and 5 of Reading Two again. Notice the two different ways the author describes Daniel talking.

Identifying the Purpose of Quoted Speech

When telling a story, writers use **direct quotes** to **help the reader "hear" the people in the story** and understand them better.

Look at the examples and read the explanations.

- He seems a little shy at first, but he welcomes us warmly. *(paragraph 3)*

The reader cannot hear what Daniel says here. He is just a guide, and we know that he is "warm," but we don't know much more about him.

- "My father never got used to the food in the village," Daniel says. Then he laughs a little. "My dad always said, 'Here in the village, I have a house, a bed, and a pillow, but I can't eat a pillow!'" *(paragraph 5)*

The reader hears Daniel here. We hear his memory of his father. We can hear how he feels sad because his father didn't like the village food. We also hear that he remembers his father was a little bit funny. (He makes a joke about eating a pillow.)

2 Work with a partner. Look at paragraphs 7, 8, and 10 of Reading Two again. Underline the sentences that refer to Daniel speaking. Then write them on the lines. Which sentences tell you more about Daniel?

1. **Paragraph 7:** _____

   _____

   _____

2. **Paragraph 8:** _____

   _____

   _____

3. **Paragraph 10:** _____

   _____

   _____

🔾 Go to **MyEnglishLab** for more skill practice.

ORGANIZE

Reading One is about indigenous cultures in general. Reading Two is about the Penan, an example of an indigenous group.

Look at the chart. Read each general statement from Reading One (R1) and decide how the Penan (R2) are an example of that general statement. Use the information in your mind maps to help you complete the chart.

> **USE YOUR NOTES**
>
> Review your notes from Readings One and Two. Use the information in your notes to complete the chart.

General Statement (R1)	How Are the Penan an Example? (R2)
1. "These cultures have deep roots in their histories, languages, and the places they live."	The Penan only take what they need from the forest, so it can continue to take care of them. Sharing is an important part of Penan life.
2. "But today changes are so large and they are happening so fast that many indigenous cultures can no longer adapt to them. These cultures are in danger of disappearing forever."	
3. "The most difficult changes to adapt to are usually changes to a group's land."	
4. "Usually they have to move away from the lands of their ancestors."	

SYNTHESIZE

Read the web page below. Then complete the letter on the next page, using information from Organize.

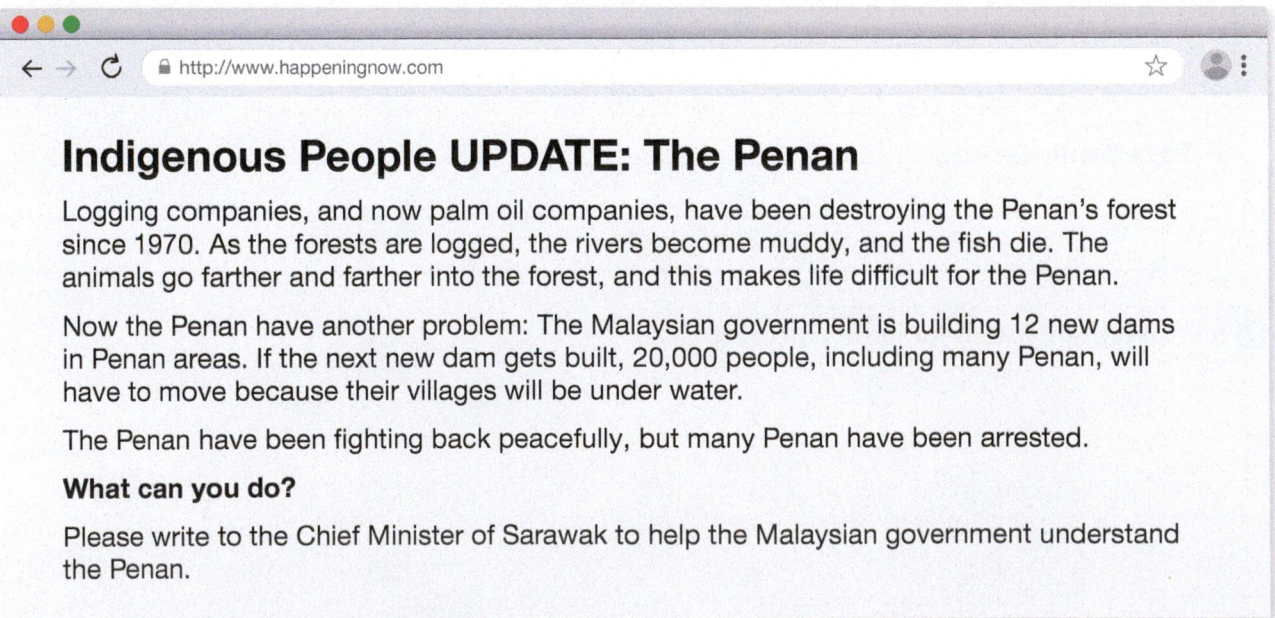

http://www.happeningnow.com

Indigenous People UPDATE: The Penan

Logging companies, and now palm oil companies, have been destroying the Penan's forest since 1970. As the forests are logged, the rivers become muddy, and the fish die. The animals go farther and farther into the forest, and this makes life difficult for the Penan.

Now the Penan have another problem: The Malaysian government is building 12 new dams in Penan areas. If the next new dam gets built, 20,000 people, including many Penan, will have to move because their villages will be under water.

The Penan have been fighting back peacefully, but many Penan have been arrested.

What can you do?

Please write to the Chief Minister of Sarawak to help the Malaysian government understand the Penan.

Dear Chief Minister,

Please. It's very important that Malaysia support the Penan.

Like all indigenous cultures around the world, the Penan have deep roots in their histories, language, and the places where they live.

_____

_____

_____

This way of life is in danger.

_____

_____

_____

Because of these changes, the Penan can no longer live as they did for thousands of years.

_____

_____

_____

Most of them have to move away from the land of their ancestors.

_____

_____

_____

Please consider these points before building a new dam.

Sincerely,

_____
(your name)

Go to MyEnglishLab to check what you learned.

VOCABULARY

REVIEW

Read each group of sentences. Pay attention to the boldfaced words. Cross out the sentence that does not make sense. Discuss with a partner why it does not make sense.

1. a. ~~The people have lived in this town for 50 years. They are **nomadic.**~~

   b. Many indigenous people were **nomadic** in the past, but now most of them live in villages.

   c. **Nomadic** people usually move after their animals eat all of the food in one area.

2. a. American blues music has its **roots** in African American culture.

   b. Our house is very old. Its **roots** are from the 1800s.

   c. Most people who live in the United States have **roots** in other countries.

3. a. These cups are all handmade, so each one is **unique.**

   b. McDonald's hamburgers in New York are **unique** because they are just like the McDonald's hamburgers in Los Angeles.

   c. Claire spent a year looking for a wedding dress that was **unique.**

4. a. The backpacking trip through Nepal was tough, but I **survived!**

   b. Today people who have AIDS can **survive** for many years because we have new medicines.

   c. From the time I was eight years old until I went to university, I **survived** in Canada. Then I moved to the United States.

5. a. Your hair is fine the way it is. Don't **adapt** anything.

   b. The most difficult thing for Noriko to **adapt** to when she moved to England was the food.

   c. Several people got headaches on the first day of the trip to the mountains. But after a couple of days, their bodies **adapted** to being in such a high place.

6. a. Indigenous cultures all over the world are **urgent** because they are losing their land.

   b. Marie Wilcox is the last fluent speaker of Wukchumni. It is **urgent** for her to create dictionaries and recordings so that the language is not lost forever.

   c. We don't have much food and water left. It is **urgent** that we get some.

7. a. This is a very old, very rare map. Please don't touch it. You'll **destroy** it.

   b. I had a small accident yesterday. I **destroyed** the car a little. I'm sure it can be fixed.

   c. In Sri Lanka in 2005, the hurricane **destroyed** thousands of homes.

8. a. Sssh! Speak quietly. You are too **powerful.**

   b. Big companies are often rich and **powerful,** so they get what they want.

   c. In 2011, a **powerful** group of people stopped a dam from being built in Peru.

9. a. We have moved three times this year. I don't feel very **settled.**

   b. In the United States, the indigenous people used to be nomadic, but now they are **settled** in places called reservations.

   c. I am tired of being **settled.** I want to go on vacation.

10. a. Assou **convinced** his father to buy a TV so that he could see programs from all over the world.

    b. Governments often **convince** new villages for indigenous people.

    c. I **convinced** my mother to visit me in the United States, but I never got her to speak any English.

11. a. My grandmother taught me Sami, so I have stayed **connected** to the Sami traditions.

    b. The logging companies are **connected** to the traditions of the places they work.

    c. I have many relatives in Nepal, but I have never met them. We are not **connected** at all.

12. a. Let's invite our **ancestors** to the wedding!

    b. My **ancestors** came to America from Germany in 1680.

    c. Most Cape Verdean people have Portuguese and African **ancestors.**

13. a. Aluo is an **endangered** language because most Yi people choose to speak Chinese now.

    b. Sumatran tigers are **endangered** because people have been killing them for years.

    c. Volkswagen Beetle cars from the 1970s must be **endangered** because I don't see them very often.

14. a. Sally and Ed don't get along very well. They always **protest** each other.

    b. Many people all over the world **protested** the Iraq war.

    c. If the schools stop teaching our indigenous language, I am going to **protest.**

EXPAND

A reporter is interviewing an indigenous people's leader. Match the questions with the responses below. Pay attention to the boldfaced words or phrases.

Questions

_b_ 1. Do you think you'll catch a lot of fish on your trip today?

_____ 2. I thought this indigenous culture was against modern culture. Why is that man using a cell phone?

_____ 3. What do you think of your young people who want to settle in the cities and leave the old ways?

_____ 4. What do you think will help your people to survive?

_____ 5. Why do all the women sit on one side and the men on the other?

_____ 6. How many children from this village do you think will attend school in the fall?

Responses

a. I'm not sure. It's been our **custom** for so long.

b. I **doubt** it. I went out yesterday and didn't get anything.

c. I **expect** we'll get a large group. Maybe fifteen to twenty.

d. We hold onto our own culture very strongly. But sometimes we **adopt** a custom or tool that we find useful.

e. I think we must learn how to **stand up to** the governments and the companies that try to take away our lands.

f. Of course, this makes us sad. But if they want to **integrate** into modern culture, we can't stop them. We hope they will bring to the modern world all that they learned in our world.

CREATE

APPLY **You are interviewing a leader of one of the indigenous groups mentioned in this unit. Complete the interview. Use at least nine words from the box. Use different types of questions.**

adapt	convinced	expect	nomadic	stand up to
adopt	custom	integrate	protest	survive
ancestors	destroy	leader	roots	unique
connected	doubt	nomad	settled	urgent

You: _What is the name of your culture?_ _____

Leader: _____

You: *What are some of the customs of your culture?* _____

Leader: _____

_____

_____

You: _____

Leader: _____

_____

_____

You: _____

Leader: _____

_____

_____

➤ Go to the **Pearson Practice English App** or **MyEnglishLab** for more vocabulary practice.

GRAMMAR FOR WRITING

1 Read about some Penan leaders' trip to the capital city. Underline the verbs that refer to the future.

> Several Penan leaders are traveling to the capital city in three days to protest the Murum Dam project. They are going to ask the government officials to stop building the Murum Dam. They will tell them how difficult it will be for whole villages of Penan to move. One elder is giving a short speech to the Parliament. The members of Parliament will listen to him politely. But the Penan wonder, "Will anyone hear us? Will anyone stop the dam?" They hope so, but they are not sure.

Write an example of each of the three different forms used to talk about the future.

1. _____

2. _____

3. _____

Will and *Be Going To* to Express Predictions and Future Plans

There are **different ways to talk about the future** in English.

1. Use *will* + **base form** of the verb for **predictions.**	They **will listen** to him politely, but they **won't do** anything.
	Will anything **change?** No, nothing **will change.**
Do not use *will* + base form of the verb for plans made before now.	Incorrect: I can't go to the capital with you because I will get married.
2. Use *be going to* + **base form** of the verb for **predictions.**	They **are going to listen** to him politely, but they **are not going to do** anything. (*prediction*)
Use it also for **plans made before now.**	They **are going to ask** the officials not to build the dam. (*plan made before now*)
	Are they **going to meet** with the president?
3. Use the **present progressive** (*be + -ing* form of the verb) for **plans made before now.**	The leader **is giving** a short speech to the Parliament *next Tuesday.*
Future time is indicated by future time words or by the context.	When **are** the leaders **coming** back?
Do not use the present progressive to make predictions.	Incorrect: The Penan are surviving in the future.

2 **Complete the speeches by three Penan leaders. Use a future form of the verb in parentheses. For each blank, two forms are possible; choose one. Use each of the three ways of expressing the future at least once.**

SPEECH 1: The government says that it is helping us. The logging companies say that

the Penan people _____ *will make* _____ lots of money. But the jobs

1. (make)

_____ with the forest. When the forest is gone, there

2. (disappear)

_____ any more jobs. Why do we need jobs anyway? My

3. (not be)

grandfather didn't have a job. My father didn't have a job. They lived off the forest.

But there _____ any more forest to live off of in a few years—

4. (not be)

for anyone.

SPEECH 2: My aunt moved to a government village twenty years ago. She

says, "This logging is like a big tree that fell on my chest. I wake

up every night and talk with my husband about the future of my

children. I always ask myself, 'When _____?'"

5. (it / end)

My elderly grandmother went to live with that aunt a year ago, but she

_____ back to the forest. "I _____ soon,"

6. (go)   7. (die)

she says. "I _____ in that government village. My spirit
  8. (not die)

_____ there."
  9. (never rest)

SPEECH 3: We _____ your trucks pass. We need some answers. Soon
           10. (not / let)

two dams _____ finished. The electricity company says they
         11. (be)

_____ more dams in the next ten years. Twenty years ago you
12. (build)

told us to move to villages. Now you tell us we must leave our villages. Where

_____ us? _____ us again in another twenty
13. (you / move)   14. (you / move)

years? If these new dams are built, our ancestors' land _____
                                                        15. (be)

under water. Our history _____ under water. How
                         16. (be)

_____ their history if they cannot see the land?
17. (our children / know)

3 **APPLY** **Write six questions about the future of the Penan and other indigenous cultures. For items 1–3, use the words given. For items 4–6, write your own questions. Make sure you use appropriate forms.**

1. Penan culture / disappear?

   _____

2. How many / Penan nomads / be alive / in fifty years?

   _____

3. anyone / speak Penan / in 100 years?

   _____

4. _____

5. _____

6. _____

4 **APPLY** **Work with a partner. Read the questions your partner wrote for Exercise 3. Then write answers to your partner's questions. Make sure you use appropriate forms for talking about the future.**

1. _____

2. _____

3. _____

4. _____

5. _____

6. _____

▶ Go to the **Pearson Practice English App** or **MyEnglishLab** for more grammar practice.
Check what you learned in **MyEnglishLab**.

In this unit, you read about endangered cultures in general and about one culture in particular, the Penan of Malaysia. Do you think the Penan will survive the next 100 years?

You are going to *write a paragraph to make a prediction about the survival of the Penan.* You will give reasons for your prediction. And you will support your reasons with facts from Reading One and Reading Two or any facts you know from your general knowledge. Use the vocabulary and grammar from the unit.

For an alternative writing topic, see page 207.

PREPARE TO WRITE: Taking Notes from a Reading

Taking notes from a reading is important when you are going to use facts from a reading to support your writing. To take useful notes, first decide what your opinion on the topic will be. Then go back to the reading and take notes on the **parts** that show that your opinion is the correct one. When you take notes, don't write in full sentences—use short phrases or one word.

1 **Read the article about the Tarahumara culture. Do you think the Tarahumara will survive? What is your opinion?**

2 **Check (✓) the notes that support the opinion that the Tarahumara will survive.**

_____ known for being strong runners

_____ have resisted modern Mexico since 1700s

_____ call themselves *Raramuri*

_____ still dress and farm like they did years ago

_____ new people get too close, they move higher

_____ live in Copper Canyon

_____ 500 years of change have not killed them

THE FEET RUNNERS

1 The *Tarahumara* people live in the mountains of Mexico. The high mountains make it difficult to know how many Tarahumara are living today. But most people agree the number is close to 70,000.

2 The Tarahumara call themselves the *Raramuri*. This means "feet runners" or "those who walk well." In fact, they are known for being very strong runners. Because their villages are far apart, the Tarahumara run long distances all the time.

3 The Tarahumara have resisted[1] the modern world since the 1700s. They refuse to adapt to the changes of modern Mexico. They run away from change. Whenever an outside group gets too close, the Tarahumara move higher into the mountains. They want to keep their people and their culture away from modern Mexican culture. Many Tarahumara still dress, farm, and live like they did long ago. They teach their children to love their customs, their language, and their way of life.

4 The Tarahumara have survived 500 years since the Spanish first came to Mexico. But what about the next 500 years?

[1] **resisted:** not allowed something to change

5 There have been many changes in the past twenty years. The Tarahumara live in the mountains called Copper Canyon. Gold and silver deep in the mountains of Copper Canyon are very interesting to mining companies. Also, logging companies are slowly destroying the forests of this area. These big companies will destroy the land and the water if they come to get the trees and the gold and silver. Tourism companies are building large hotels in the area, and that will certainly change the culture. Will the Tarahumara be able to survive? The world will have to wait and see.

3 Go back to the reading and make two notes that support the opinion that the Tarahumara will not survive. Remember: Use short phrases.

Note 1: _____

_____

Note 2: _____

_____

4 Decide if you think the Penan will survive the next 100 years or not. Then read Readings One and Two again and take notes on the facts that show why your opinion is correct.

WRITE: A Paragraph Based on an Outline

To write a well-organized paragraph, you need to select the right information. Read the directions for your writing assignment carefully. They can often help you organize your ideas by telling you what information to include.

An **outline** is another useful tool for writing. An outline helps you organize your ideas before you start writing.

1 Read the outline about the Tarahumara.

Main idea (*prediction*)

Reason 1 (*for prediction*)

Facts (*from notes*)
that support Reason 1

Reason 2 (*for prediction*)

Facts (*from notes*)
that support Reason 2

> **OUTLINE**
> **Will the Tarahumara survive?**
>
> The Tarahumara will not survive the next 100 years.
>
> A. Won't have any more land to run to
>   1. Every contact with modern world, they move higher up the mountain
>   2. If mining companies come in, they will destroy their land
> B. Refuse to adapt to change
>   1. They live today as they always have
>   2. Don't adapt, just run away

2 Read another outline on the Tarahumara. Complete the outline by choosing the best reasons for A and B from the lists on the next page.

> **OUTLINE**
> **Will the Tarahumara survive?**
>
> The Tarahumara will survive the next 100 years.
>
> A. _____
>   1. Still dress, farm, live as did 500 years ago
>   2. Teach children to love customs and language
> B. _____
>   1. 70, 000 living today

The Best Reason for A:

1. They are interested in changing their culture.

2. They work hard to stop their culture from disappearing.

3. They haven't changed anything in their culture for 500 years.

The Best Reason for B:

1. They have a small number of people.

2. They have a fairly large population.

3. We don't know exactly how many are living today.

3 Write an outline about your prediction for the Penan. Your prediction will be your main idea. Provide at least two or three reasons for your prediction. Use your notes for the facts that support your reasons.

4 Now write the first draft of your paragraph, based on your outline.

REVISE: Writing a Concluding Sentence

A **concluding sentence** can restate the main idea of a paragraph. In this case, for example, you can restate your prediction. A concluding sentence can also make a suggestion or express an opinion.

1 Read the paragraph. Then look at the three possible concluding sentences below. Decide what kind of conclusions these are. Write *R* (restates the main idea), *S* (makes a suggestion), or *O* (expresses an opinion) next to each. Write the conclusion that you prefer to complete the paragraph.

> I predict that the Tarahumara will not survive the next 100 years. One reason is they won't have any more land to run to. They won't be able to move higher into the mountains every time modern people get too close to them. Also, if mining companies come in, they will destroy the mountains where the Tarahumara live. Another reason they will not survive is that they refuse to adapt to change. They dress and farm the same way they did 500 years ago. To survive, indigenous cultures must adapt. The Tarahumara have only run away. Soon, they won't be able to even do this.
>
> _____
>
> _____
>
> _____

Concluding Sentences:

_____ 1. This is why the Tarahumara will not survive another 100 years.

_____ 2. In my opinion, if the Tarahumara can't adapt to change, they'll disappear forever.

_____ 3. To save the Tarahumara, I think the Mexican government should stop the big companies from destroying the Tarahumara's land.

2 Read the paragraph. Write a concluding sentence. Share it with a partner.

I predict that the Tarahumara will survive the next 100 years. One reason is the Tarahumara work hard to hold onto their culture. They still dress and farm the same way they did 500 years ago. Also, they teach their children to love their customs and their language. Another reason is the Tarahumara have a fairly large population. There are about 70,000 Tarahumara living today.

_____

_____

_____

3 Now go back to the first draft of your paragraph and write a concluding sentence.

Go to **MyEnglishLab** for more skill practice.

EDIT: Writing the Final Draft

APPLY Write the final draft of your paragraph and submit it to your teacher. Carefully edit it for grammatical and mechanical errors, such as spelling, capitalization, and punctuation. Consider how to apply the vocabulary, grammar, and writing skills from the unit. Use the checklist to help you.

FINAL DRAFT CHECKLIST

☐ Does your paragraph clearly predict if the Penan will or will not survive the next 100 years?

☐ Does it give clear reasons for your prediction?

☐ Does it use facts from the readings or from your general knowledge to support your prediction?

☐ Do you use the proper verb forms when making your prediction?

☐ Do you use the forms correctly?

☐ Do you use a concluding sentence?

☐ Do you use new vocabulary that you learned in this unit?

ALTERNATIVE WRITING TOPIC

APPLY Is it a good idea to try to save indigenous cultures? In a letter to an editor, explain why or why not. Give examples. Use the vocabulary and grammar from the unit.

CHECK WHAT YOU'VE LEARNED

Check (✔) the outcomes you've met and vocabulary you've learned. Put an X next to the skills and vocabulary you still need to practice.

Learning Outcomes

☐ Infer the author's attitude

☐ Take notes with a mind map

☐ Identify the purpose of quoted speech

☐ Use *will* and *be going to* to express predictions and future plans

☐ Write a concluding sentence

☐ Write a prediction paragraph

Vocabulary

☐ adapt AWL
☐ ancestor
☐ connect
☐ convince
☐ destroy
☐ endangered
☐ nomadic

☐ powerful
☐ protest
☐ roots
☐ settle
☐ survive AWL
☐ unique AWL
☐ urgent

◑ Go to **MyEnglishLab** to watch a video about endangered cultures, access the Unit Project, and take the Unit 8 Achievement Test.

EXPAND VOCABULARY

UNIT 1
Vocabulary
none

UNIT 2
Vocabulary
realize
remember

Multi-word Units
have an idea
make you think of
solve the problem

UNIT 3
Vocabulary
brand name
imitation
labels
logo

packaging
pirated
quality

UNIT 4
Vocabulary
greet
impolite
litter
polite
tip

Multi-word Units
against the rules
break the rules
exception to the rules
follow the rules
stand in line
wait your turn

UNIT 5
Vocabulary
anatomy
expects
perceive AWL

Multi-word Units
optical illusion
pay attention

UNIT 6
Vocabulary
defeat (n.)
defeat (v.)
defeated
defeating
danger
dangerous
dangerously
failure
fail
failed
failing
failingly
magic
magical

magically
protection
protector
protect
protective
protectively
safety
save
safe
safely
success
succeed
successful
successfully

UNIT 7
Vocabulary
calmly
firmly
gently

patiently
roughly
warmly

UNIT 8
Vocabulary
adopt
custom
doubt
expect
integrate AWL

Multi-word Units
stand up to

ACADEMIC WORD LIST VOCABULARY AWL

Words with an * are target vocabulary in the unit. The remainder of the words appear in context in the reading texts.

acquire
adapt*
affect* (v.)
areas
challenge*
challenge (n.)
challenges
chapter
chemical (n.)
community
complex
computer
context*
convince*
create*
culture
define
definition
designer
edit
enforce*
equipment*

expert* (n.)
factor* (n.)
finally
focus*
grade (v.)
illegal*
illustrate
image*
integrate*
intelligence
interpret*
involve
job
legal
logical*
manual (n.)
media
medical
networking
normal
perceive*
percent

perception*
perspective
predict
professional (n.)
project (n.)
psychology
relax*
relies
rely*
remove
respond
similar
specific
survive*
task (n.)
technology*
traditional
tradition
unique*
vision*

GRAMMAR BOOK REFERENCES

NorthStar: Reading and Writing Level 2, Fifth Edition	Focus on Grammar, Level 2, Fourth Edition	Azar's Basic English Grammar, Fourth Edition
Unit 1 Descriptive and Possessive Adjectives	**Unit 5** Descriptive Adjectives **Unit 12** Possessive Nouns and Adjectives	**Chapter 1** *Be* + Adjective:1-7 **Chapter 6** Adjectives with nouns: 6-3 Possessive pronouns: 178
Unit 2 Simple Past	**Part 7** Simple Past	**Chapter 8** Expressing Past Time, Part 1 **Chapter 9** Expressing Past Time, Part 2: 9-1, 9-2, 9-3, 9-4, 9-5, 9-6
Unit 3 Comparative Adjectives	**Unit 33** Comparative Adjectives	**Chapter 15** Making Comparisons: 15-1
Unit 4 Imperative Sentences	**Unit 7** Imperatives	**Chapter 13** Imperative sentences: 13-6
Unit 5 Linking Verbs	**Unit 17** Non-Action Verbs	**Chapter 4** Non-action verbs: 4-6
Unit 6 Time Clauses in the Present Tense	N/A	**Chapter 5** Talking About the Present **Chapter 9** Before and after in time clauses: 9-7 When in time clauses: 9-8 **Chapter 11** Expressing habitual present with time clauses
Unit 7 Adverbs of Manner	**Unit 34** Adverbs of Manner	**Chapter 14** Adjectives and Adverbs: 14-4
Unit 8 *Will* and *Be Going To* to Express Predictions and Future Plans	**Unit 24** *Be going to* for the Future **Unit 25** *Will* for the Future	**Chapter 10** Expressing Future Time Part 1: 10-1, 10-2, 10-6, 10-7

CREDITS

NOTES

NOTES

NOTES

NOTES

NOTES

NOTES